THE GOSPEL ACCORDING TO JESUS

What Does Jesus Mean
When He Says,
"Follow Me"?

THE GOSPEL ACCORDING TO JESUS

Revised & Expanded Edition

John F. MacArthur, Jr.

ZONDERVAN™

ZONDERVAN™

The Gospel According to Jesus
Revised and Expanded Edition
Copyright © 1988, 1994 by John F. MacArthur, Jr.

Requests for information should be addressed to:
Zondervan, *Grand Rapids, Michigan 49530*

Library of Congress Cataloging-in-Publication Data

MacArthur, John, 1939-
    The Gospel according to Jesus : what does Jesus mean
  when He says "follow me"? / John F. MacArthur, Jr. — 2nd ed.
      p.   cm.
  Includes bibliographical references (p. 285-89) and indexes.
  ISBN: 0-310-39491-0
  1. Jesus Christ — Person and offices. 2. Christian life — 1960 — I. Title.
BT202.M23   1994
230 — dc20   93-36537
                                                     CIP

All Scripture qoutations in this book, except those noted otherwise, are from the
New American Standard Bible, 1960, 1962, 1968, 1971, 1972, 1973, 1975, and 1977
by The Lockamn Foundation, and are used by permission. Quotations marked KJV
are from the Kin James Version.

Cover design and illustration by Mark Velheer

Printed in the United States of America

07 08 09 10 11 • 38 37 36 35 34 33 32 31 30 29 28

To Bob Van Kampen, Jr.
Whose leadership is wise,
Whose love of the Word is consuming,
Whose submission to the lordship of Christ
is unwavering,
And whose greatest gift to me
is a close companionship "without wax."

Contents

Foreword by J. I. Packer

That man should not separate what God has joined is a truth that applies to more than marriage. God has joined the three offices of prophet (teacher), priest, and king in the mediatorial role of Jesus Christ, and he directs us in the Bible to relate positively to them all. God has joined faith and repentance as the two facets of response to the Savior and has made it clear that turning to Christ means turning from sin and letting ungodliness go. Biblical teaching on faith joins credence, commitment, and communion; it exhibits Christian believing as not only knowing facts about Christ, but also coming to him in personal trust to worship, love, and serve him. If we fail to keep together these things that God has joined together, our Christianity will be distorted.

"Lordship salvation" is a name for the view that upholds these unities. The name sounds esoteric and slightly uncouth, and its novelty would naturally suggest that the view labeled by it is a novel product, manufactured only recently. But in fact it is no more, just as it is no less, than the mainstream Protestant consensus on the nature of justifying faith, and the real novelty is the position of those who coined this name for the view they reject and who break these unities in their own teaching. That teaching reinvents the maimed account of faith given by Scottish Sandemanianism two centuries ago, well described by D. Martyn Lloyd-Jones in his book *The Puritans*. Like Sandemanians, those who reject "lordship salvation" choose to keep works out of justification. To this end, like Sandemanians again, they represent faith as simple assent to the truth about Jesus' saving role, and thus their teaching becomes vulnerable to the criticism that it exalts faith in a way that destroys faith. Simple assent to the gospel, divorced from a transforming commitment to the living Christ, is by biblical standards less than faith, and less than saving, and to elicit only assent of this kind would be to secure only false conversions. So the gospel really is at stake in this discussion, though not in the way that the opponents of "lordship salvation" think. What is in question is the nature of faith.

Dr. MacArthur has written this book to show from the records of

ix

Christ's own ministry what saving faith in him actually amounts to. I find his demonstration conclusive, and I thank God for it. It is a fine and much-needed book—clear, cogent, and edifying—doing for us what is nowhere else done so well. I wish it a wide circulation and a thoughtful readership. It will render the Christian world great service. I commend it enthusiastically.

Foreword by
James Montgomery Boice

I have always had great admiration for John MacArthur. For a long time he has given himself to the arduous task of pastoring a large and growing congregation. Moreover, he has based his ministry on careful Bible exposition, modeling much of what is best in faithful verse-by-verse teaching of large portions of the Word of God. Since I am a pastor myself, I very much respect these qualities and achievements.

But my admiration for John MacArthur grew by quantum leaps as I read *The Gospel According to Jesus,* because the book reveals a man whose conscience is clearly taken captive by the Word of God. It reveals one who knows how to read the Bible for what it actually says (without filtering it through his or anyone else's prejudiced theological or cultural grid), and who is then fearless in proclaiming that Word to our wicked and needy generation.

Even more! In *The Gospel According to Jesus,* MacArthur is not dealing with some issue or issues external to the faith, but with the central issue of all—namely, What does it mean to be a Christian? His answers address themselves to what I consider to be the greatest weakness of contemporary evangelical Christianity in America.

Did I say weakness? It is more. It is a tragic error. It is the idea—where did it ever come from?—that one can be a Christian without being a follower of the Lord Jesus Christ. It reduces the gospel to the mere fact of Christ's having died for sinners, requires of sinners only that they acknowledge this by the barest intellectual assent, and then assures them of their eternal security when they may very well not be born again. This view bends faith beyond recognition—at least for those who know what the Bible says about faith—and promises a false peace to thousands who have given verbal assent to this reductionist Christianity but are not truly in God's family.

How did this happen? No doubt the motives of those who have fallen into this profound error have been good. They want to preserve in its purity the gospel of justification by grace through faith in Jesus Christ. They know that adding works to faith is a false gospel, and they rightly want to avoid that heresy. But preserving the gospel is precisely what they have not done. They have warped and in some cases utterly destroyed it.

These scholars, pastors, and Bible teachers need to learn:

—that there is no justification without regeneration. Jesus said, "You must be born again" (John 3:7).

—that faith without works is a dead faith and that no one will ever be saved by a dead faith. James said, "Faith without deeds is useless" (James 2:20).

—that the mark of true justification is a perseverance in righteousness—to the very end. Jesus told his disciples, "All men will hate you because of me, but he who stands firm to the end will be saved" (Matt. 10:22).

—that faith in a Jesus who is Savior but not Lord is faith in a Jesus of one's own devising. The Jesus who saves is the Lord—there is no other—and it was he who said, "Why do you call me, 'Lord, Lord,' and do not do what I say?" (Luke 6:46).

—that if one wants to serve Christ, "he must deny himself and take up his cross daily and follow [Him]" (Luke 9:23).

—that "without holiness no one will see the Lord" (Heb. 12:14).

Well, that is the problem MacArthur tackles in this book, and those are the answers he gives. He gives them very well indeed. Besides, he does this charitably. Those who distort the gospel in the way I have described are not always charitable to those of us who insist on Christ's lordship. We are accused of teaching "lordship salvation," a term we do not use ourselves. And we are often called heretics. I am not aware that John MacArthur has called any of his opponents heretics; nor have I. But they are mistaken—dreadfully mistaken in my opinion—and they need to be shown their error from Scripture, which is what this book does. They also need to be shown that their view has never been the view of any major Bible teacher or theologian in the church until our own weak times. MacArthur shows this in the book's second and very valuable appendix.

Why is today's church so weak? Why are we able to claim many conversions and enroll many church members but have less and less impact on our culture? Why are Christians indistinguishable from the world? Is it not that many are calling people Christians who are actually unregenerate? Is it not that many are settling for a "form of godliness but denying its power" (2 Tim. 3:5)?

If MacArthur's book succeeds in turning many from this weak gospel and false confidence, as I believe it will, *The Gospel According to Jesus* may be one of the most significant books of this decade.

Preface to the Revised Edition

He summoned the multitude with His disciples, and said to them, "If anyone wishes to come after Me, let him deny himself, and take up his cross, and follow Me" (Mark 8:34).

What does Jesus mean when he says, "Follow Me"? Note how frequently he links that call with terminology that speaks of self-denial, crucifixion, and daily death (cf. Luke 9:23). His "follow Me" is often prefaced by admonitions about being willing to die to self, hating one's own life in this world, and serving him (John 12:24–26). Here's how he framed his message to the multitudes:

> He turned and said to them, "If anyone comes to Me, and does not hate his own father and mother and wife and children and brothers and sisters, yes, and even his own life, he cannot be My disciple. Whoever does not carry his own cross and come after Me cannot be My disciple. For which one of you, when he wants to build a tower, does not first sit down and calculate the cost, to see if he has enough to complete it? Otherwise, when he has laid a foundation, and is not able to finish, all who observe it begin to ridicule him, saying, 'This man began to build and was not able to finish.' Or what king, when he sets out to meet another king in battle, will not first sit down and take counsel whether he is strong enough with ten thousand men to encounter the one coming against him with twenty thousand? Or else, while the other is still far away, he sends a delegation and asks terms of peace. So therefore, no one of you can be My disciple who does not give up all his own possessions" (Luke 14:25–33).

Some, however, responded eagerly to Christ while neglecting to count the cost. They received no encouragement from him:

> As they were going along the road, someone said to Him, "I will follow You wherever You go." And Jesus said to him, "The foxes have holes, and the birds of the air have nests, but the Son of Man has nowhere to lay His head." And He said to another, "Follow Me." But he said, "Permit me first to go and bury my father." But He said to him, "Allow the dead to bury their own dead; but as for you, go and proclaim everywhere the kingdom of God." And another also said, "I will follow You, Lord; but first permit me to say good-bye to those at home." But

xiii

Jesus said to him, "No one, after putting his hand to the plow and looking back, is fit for the kingdom of God" (Luke 9:57–62).

Difficult demands? Impossible in human terms. Yet those are Jesus' very words—unqualified, unadorned, untempered by any explanation or soothing rationalization.

Our Lord was sounding a note that is missing from much that passes for evangelism today. His "follow Me" was a call to surrender to his lordship.

"[We preach] Christ Jesus as Lord," the apostle Paul wrote (2 Cor. 4:5). "Jesus is Lord" was the core of the early church's confession of faith, the primary nucleus of truth affirmed by every true Christian (1 Cor. 12:3). What must we do to be saved? "Believe in the *Lord* Jesus, and you shall be saved" (Acts 16:31, emphasis added). "If you confess with your mouth *Jesus as Lord,* and believe in your heart that God raised Him from the dead, you shall be saved" (Rom. 10:9, emphasis added). The lordship of Christ is clearly at the heart of true saving faith.

Nevertheless, many influential voices in contemporary evangelicalism are preaching with great fervor that we should not tell unbelievers they must yield to Christ as Lord. His lordship has nothing to do with the gospel, they claim. They make the preposterous allegation that calling the unsaved to surrender to Christ is tantamount to preaching salvation by works.

A major controversy over Christ's lordship erupted on the evangelical scene with the publication of this book five years ago. It was not my intention to ignite such a dispute. I was aware that these had been matters of debate among some evangelicals for several decades. My aim was simply to answer several recent authors who were arguing for no-lordship evangelism. These men were charging the rest of the church with heresy, and I felt their accusations needed an answer. Of course I hoped that what I had to say would be widely read and discussed, but I admit I was unprepared for the intense and far-reaching debate that ultimately ensued. That debate continues to this day.

Recently I wrote a sequel, *Faith Works: The Gospel According to the Apostles* (Dallas: Word Books, 1993), and while working on it I began to note some revisions I wanted to make in this book. We can always learn from our critics, and as I carefully digested reviewers' comments about *The Gospel According to Jesus,* I began to note terminology that needed clarifying, details I wanted to add, and phrases I wished I had worded differently. Zondervan kindly consented to do a revised edition, and here it is.

The original edition had no treatment of the doctrine of justification by faith. My goal in writing the book, of course, was not to set forth a systematic soteriology, but simply to expound the major evangelistic messages of our Lord. I rather assumed that evangelicals on both sides of the lordship question were in basic agreement on the matter of justification. Admittedly, this omission was unfortunate. It seems to have contributed to some readers' misunderstanding of my views. A few even imagined that I was explicitly repudiating the great Reformation emphasis on justification by faith alone. Of course, that was not at all the point I was making.

I am delighted to include here a new chapter on justification, because I am convinced that a correct understanding of this crucial Reformation principle is prerequisite to doctrinal soundness on all other points of soteriology. Although the words *justification* and *justify* are rare in Jesus' recorded utterances, I regard this doctrine as the centerpiece of the gospel he proclaimed. My own understanding and appreciation of justification by faith have grown deeper as I have studied the lordship issue. I yield no ground to those who insist that "lordship salvation" is a denial of justification by faith.

I have dealt with another omission by adding a chapter dealing with Christ's work on the cross. Obviously, any account of the gospel that underestimates the significance of Christ's crucifixion would be seriously deficient. Though the earlier edition of this book made mention of the cross throughout, it had no chapter devoted exclusively to the meaning of our Lord's atoning work. At least one reviewer saw this as significant and wondered if I was purposely depreciating the work of Christ while accentuating the work of the believer. Lest a single reader gain such a wrong impression, I have sought to place even more emphasis on the meaning and importance of the cross by the addition of this new chapter.

The reasons for other revisions will probably be immediately evident to the reader. For example, I have added a chapter on John 15 because that passage seems to be a stumbling block for so many people. I have tried to anticipate and answer readers' questions throughout. That has meant softening language in some places, intensifying it in others.

I am grateful to God for the ministry this book has had so far. My prayer is that this revised edition will be even more fruitful in challenging the evangelical church to think deeply and carefully about how we present the gospel and about how we must live as believers in the One who is Lord of all (Acts 10:36; Rom. 10:12).

Preface to the First Edition

We do not preach ourselves but Christ Jesus as Lord (2 Cor. 4:5).

This book has consumed my thoughts and much of my time for nearly four years. On a few occasions I have mentioned publicly that I was working on it, and word of it apparently has spread. I have been inundated with requests from people eager to know when and where they could obtain a copy. They often refer to it as "the book on lordship salvation," "the book about the gospel," or "the book on evangelism."

The book deals with all those subjects, but from the beginning my chief goal was not merely to present my side of an argument, or to grind a favorite ax, but rather to take an honest and in-depth look at Jesus' gospel and his evangelistic methods. The study has so pricked my own heart and molded my approach to ministry that I am anxious to put it in print. Yet I do so with a certain amount of trepidation, for I know some will misunderstand my intentions.

I expect, for example, that someone will accuse me of teaching salvation by works. Let me say as clearly as possible right now that salvation is by God's sovereign grace and grace alone. Nothing a lost, degenerate, spiritually dead sinner can do will in any way contribute to salvation. Saving faith, repentance, commitment, and obedience are all divine works, wrought by the Holy Spirit in the heart of everyone who is saved. I have never taught that some presalvation works of righteousness are necessary to or part of salvation. But I do believe without apology that real salvation cannot, and will not, fail to produce works of righteousness in the life of a true believer. There are no human works in the saving act, but God's work of salvation includes a change of intent, will, desire, and attitude that inevitably produces the fruit of the Spirit. The very essence of God's saving work is the transformation of the will, resulting in a love for God. Salvation thus establishes the *root* that will surely produce the *fruit*.

Some may think I question the genuineness of anyone who is converted to Christ without a full understanding of his lordship. That is not the case. In fact, I am certain that while some understand more than others, *no one* who is saved fully understands all the implications of Jesus' lordship at the moment of conversion. I am, however, equally certain that no one can be saved who is either unwilling to obey Christ or consciously, callously rebellious against his lordship.

True salvation produces a heart that voluntarily responds to the ever-awakening reality of Christ's lordship. Because we are sinful creatures, we can never respond as obediently as we would like. In fact, we often experience pathetic failures and extended periods of spiritual dullness and sin. But if we are true believers, we can never again fall into the cold, hardhearted, determined unbelief and rebellion of our former state. Those who live like that have no reason to think they have ever been redeemed.

Moreover, the message of salvation includes a call to surrender to Jesus as Lord. Those who would come to him for salvation must be willing to acquiesce to his sovereign authority. Those who reject his right to rule cannot expect to lay claim to him as Savior.

Because of the state of the gospel in contemporary evangelicalism there is no way to teach about salvation without dealing specifically with this issue, which has come to be known as "lordship salvation." No more serious question faces the church today. It can be phrased in many ways: What is the gospel? Must a person accept Jesus as Savior *and* Lord in order to be saved? What is saving faith? How should we invite men and women to Christ? and What is salvation?

That there is so much controversy over this most foundational subject testifies to the effectiveness of the enemy's work in these latter days. Several who disagree with my views have said in print that the lordship controversy is a matter of eternal consequence. Whoever is wrong on this issue is seriously wrong about the most basic of Christian truths.

On that both sides agree. I went through a phase of thinking that the whole dispute might be a misunderstanding or semantic argument. But as I studied the issues, I came to realize that this is a fundamental difference in doctrine. After many conversations with those who disagree and hours of studying what they are saying, I am now convinced that the two sides in this argument have distinctly different views of salvation. The average person in the pew is confused, having heard two conflicting messages from the same conservative, fundamentalist, evangelical camp.

It is to those men and women in the pew that I write, for the gospel must be clearly understood by lay people, not just seminarians and pastors. Although I have included pertinent data in numerous footnotes, this is by no means a dry academic thesis.

It is also my hope that pastors who read this book will examine their own ministries. It is essential that we who proclaim God's Word from the pulpit preach it clearly and accurately. If we confuse the message of the gospel, whatever else we say cannot undo the damage.

I am not proposing any new or radical understanding of what Scripture teaches. I certainly do not advocate a works salvation. In no way would I minimize grace or seek to encourage needless doubts in the minds of those who are genuinely saved. In that regard, I believe exactly what the true church has always held to. But a different teaching has gained popularity in our generation. Christians today are in danger of losing the heart of our message—and thus the source of our very vitality—if we do not return to the gospel our Lord sent us forth to proclaim.

Many who disagree with me on this issue are faithful servants of God whose ministries have reaped abundant fruit for the kingdom. It was necessary to quote and refute many of them by name in this book—not to try to discredit them or their ministries, but because it is hardly possible to address the concept of the gospel that is spreading throughout the church without quoting some of those who are teaching it. There is no more important issue, after all, than the question of what gospel we ought to believe and proclaim. Other controversies have generated more heat and spawned more print— such as questions on prophecy, modes of baptism, styles of worship, and so on. But those are peripheral to the real issues. The gospel is not. It *is* the issue.

I have not sought to label anyone or attack any individual in a personal way. A great many of the men with whom I disagree here are my friends. I have quoted much from Zane Hodges' works. That is because he is the most vocal of the recent authors who have attacked the traditional view of salvation, and his writings appear to have considerable influence among students, pastors, and teachers. I meet hundreds of church leaders each year at pastors' conferences, and the questions they ask most frequently are related to confusion generated by Dr. Hodges' writings. It is essential to understand what he has written and respond biblically to it.

I have also quoted unfavorably from the writings of Dr. Charles C. Ryrie. I have the highest regard for Dr. Ryrie and am grateful for all he has done to train men for ministry. Many of his writings over the years have been extremely valuable to me personally, and I treasure his friendship. But in this one crucial area, what he teaches does not stand up under scrutiny in the light of Scripture.

Others I have quoted are in some cases fellow pastors, partners in ministry, personal friends, and respected colleagues. Because their views have been published or broadcast, it is right that what they teach be measured by God's Word. I am concerned, however, that readers not interpret my criticism as a condemnation of these men, their personal character, or their ministries.

I have prayed over this book and diligently sought the Lord's guidance. I know many will disagree, some will be angered, and many, I hope, will be prompted to dig in like the Bereans and search the Scriptures for themselves (Acts 17:11). I welcome their response to my teaching. My prayer is that this book will provoke discussion, arouse prayer and self-examination, and lead ultimately to a resolution of these issues within conservative evangelicalism. I am convinced that our lack of clarity on the most basic matter of all—the gospel—is the greatest detriment to the work of the church in our day.

I want to thank the many people who have given their input along the way: my fellow pastor and dear friend Chris Mueller for challenging me to begin the project; Dr. Marc Mueller, of The Master's Seminary, whose feedback from the earliest drafts has repeatedly renewed my flagging vigor for the project; Dr. James E. Rosscup, also of The Master's Seminary, whose teaching has shed much light on these issues for me; Lance Quinn, Brian Morley, Kyle Henderson, Dave Enos, Rich D'Errico, John Barnett, Allacin Morimizu, and many friends on the Grace Community Church and Grace to You staffs for encouragement and editorial input.

Most of all I am deeply grateful for the loving, skillful labor of my loyal friend and colleague Phil Johnson, who has applied his excellent insights and editorial assistance to every page of this book.

May God use this book greatly to his glory.

Introduction

What is the gospel?

That question fuels the passion that has driven me all the years of my ministry. It is not merely an academic quest. I want to know what God's Word teaches so that I can proclaim it with accuracy and clarity. Above all, I want the doctrine I teach to be purely biblical— growing out of Scripture itself rather than just conforming to some popular system of theology. A particular theologian's view of this or that doctrine is only of incidental interest to me. All that really matters is what God's Word says.

And nothing matters more than what Scripture says about the good news of salvation.

Several years ago I began to study and preach through the gospel of Matthew. As I worked through the life and ministry of our Lord, a clear understanding of the message he proclaimed and the evangelistic method he used crystallized in my thinking. I came to see Jesus' gospel as the foundation upon which all New Testament doctrine stands. Many difficult passages in the Epistles became clearer when I understood them in that light.

This book grew out of seven years of study in the Gospels. As I immersed myself in the gospel Jesus taught, I became acutely aware that most of modern evangelism—both witnessing and preaching— falls far short of presenting the biblical evangel in a balanced and biblical way. The more I examined Jesus' public ministry and his dealings with inquirers, the more apprehensive I became about the methods and content of contemporary evangelism. On a disturbing number of fronts, the message being proclaimed today is not the gospel according to Jesus.

The gospel in vogue today holds forth a false hope to sinners. It promises them they can have eternal life yet continue to live in rebellion against God. Indeed, it *encourages* people to claim Jesus as Savior yet defer until later the commitment to obey him as Lord.[1] It

[1]Lewis Sperry Chafer, whose teachings helped generate the popularized gospel of today, held that "to impose a need to surrender the life to God as an added condition of salvation is most unreasonable. God's call to the unsaved is

promises salvation from hell but not necessarily freedom from iniquity. It offers false security to people who revel in the sins of the flesh and spurn the way of holiness. By separating faith from faithfulness,[2] it teaches that intellectual assent is as valid as wholehearted obedience to the truth.

Thus the good news of Christ has given way to the bad news of an insidious easy-believism that makes no moral demands on the lives of sinners. It is not the same message Jesus proclaimed.

This new gospel has spawned a generation of professing Christians whose behavior is indistinguishable from the rebellion of the unregenerate. Statistics reveal that 1.6 billion people worldwide are considered Christians. A well-publicized opinion poll indicated that nearly a third of all Americans claim to be born again.[3] Those figures surely represent millions who are tragically deceived. Theirs is a damning false assurance.

The church's witness to the world has been sacrificed on the altar of cheap grace. Shocking forms of open immorality have become commonplace among professing Christians. And why not? The promise of eternal life without surrender to divine authority feeds the wretchedness of the unregenerate heart. Enthusiastic converts to this new gospel believe their behavior has no relationship to their spiritual status—even if they continue wantonly in the grossest kinds of sin and expressions of human depravity.[4]

It now appears that the church of our generation will be remembered chiefly for a series of hideous scandals that have uncovered the rankest exhibitions of depravity in the lives of some highly visible media evangelists. Most troubling of all is the painful reality that most Christians continue to view these people as insiders, not as wolves and false shepherds who have crept in among the flock (cf.

---

never said to be unto the Lordship of Christ" (*Systematic Theology* [Dallas: Dallas Seminary, 1948], 3:385). Cf. also Rich Wager, "This So-Called 'Lordship Salvation,'" *Confident Living* (July–August 1987), 54–55. Wager comes to the astonishing conclusion that it is a perversion of the gospel to invite an unsaved person to receive Jesus Christ as Savior and Lord. To present Christ as Lord to a non-Christian is "to add to scriptural teachings concerning salvation," he declares.

[2]Chafer, *Systematic Theology*, 3:385.

[3]George Gallup, Jr., and David Poling, *The Search for America's Faith* (Nashville: Abingdon, 1980), 92.

[4]According to at least one writer, Paul's lists of gross sinners and their vices in 1 Corinthians 6:9–10 and Galatians 5:19–21 actually describe true believers, but they are Christians who will forfeit the reward of "inheriting" the kingdom of God because of their sin (Zane C. Hodges, *The Gospel Under Siege* [Dallas: Redención Viva, 1981], 114–15).

Matt. 7:15). Why should we assume that people who live in an unbroken pattern of adultery, fornication, homosexuality, deceit, and every conceivable kind of flagrant excess are truly born again?

Yet that is exactly the assumption Christians of this age have been taught to make. They have been told that the only criterion for salvation is knowing and believing some basic facts about Christ. They hear from the beginning that obedience is optional. It follows logically, then, that someone's one-time profession of faith is more valid than the evidence of that person's ongoing lifestyle in determining whether to embrace him or her as a true believer. The character of the visible church reveals the detestable consequence of this theology.

As a pastor I regularly rebaptize people who once "made a decision," were baptized, yet experienced no change. They come later to true conversion and seek baptism again as an expression of genuine salvation. We hear such testimonies nearly every week from the baptistery of Grace Community Church.

What is needed is a complete reexamination of the gospel. We must go back to the basis for all New Testament teaching about salvation—the gospel proclaimed by Jesus. I think you will be surprised to find how radically different the message of Christ is from what you might have learned in a personal evangelism seminar.

My purpose in writing this book is to deal with the biblical accounts of Jesus' major evangelistic encounters and his teaching on the way of salvation. We will explore a series of questions: Who is Jesus? How is he to be identified in the gospel proclamation and received by sinners? What is saving faith? What occurs in the saving act? Those are basic questions, affecting all we affirm and proclaim as believers in Christ; they are not theological trivia. After all, the message we proclaim has eternal consequences. We dare not preach a message that sows confusion or false hope.

Galatians 1:6–9 is a curse on anyone who distorts the gospel of Christ:

> I am amazed that you are so quickly deserting Him who called you by the grace of Christ, for a different gospel; which is really not another; only there are some who are disturbing you, and want to distort the gospel of Christ. But even though we, or an angel from heaven, should preach to you a gospel contrary to that which we have preached to you, let him be accursed. As we have said before, so I say again now, if any man is preaching to you a gospel contrary to that which you received, let him be accursed.

That is a sober warning of eternal damnation to those who would tamper with the message of salvation and corrupt it to make "a different gospel." Paul applied it to the Judaizers, who had exchanged a system of works for the gospel of grace. His warning underscores the importance of getting the gospel right. The difference between the gospel of Christ and "another gospel" is the difference between the blessed and the cursed, the sheep and the goats, the saved and the lost, the true church and cults, the truth and a lie.

Am I suggesting that the popular gospel of our day is so seriously adulterated that it has become "another gospel," a message so corrupt that its purveyors doom themselves to perdition? No. I have not written this book to label anyone a heretic. But I do believe that the danger of "another gospel" is a very real threat. As the message is further weakened and cheapened, the church must be on guard lest we embrace a message so profoundly altered that it bears no resemblance to the biblical message.

And I am aware that "lordship salvation" has already been labeled by some of its opponents as "another gospel."[5] With that in mind, I have not undertaken this study lightly.

But after years of grappling with the issues and seeing the confusion that surrounds the gospel, I cannot keep silent. The doctrine of salvation is basic to all we teach. We cannot confidently point people to the way of life unless we get the gospel right.

My prayer is that this study will not be just another voice in an already confused dialogue. I want it to be a genuine step for all of us toward a clear and precise understanding of the eternal gospel (cf. Rev. 14:6). I for one want to understand in its fullness the gospel Jesus taught, so that I might be a more faithful and effective communicator of the way of life (cf. Acts 5:20).

[5]Charles C. Ryrie, *Balancing the Christian Life* (Chicago: Moody Press, 1969), 170.

PART ONE

TODAY'S GOSPEL:
GOOD NEWS OR BAD?

1

A Look at the Issues

Listen to today's typical gospel presentation. You will hear sinners entreated with such phrases as "accept Jesus Christ as personal Savior"; "ask Jesus into your heart"; "invite Christ into your life"; or "make a decision for Christ." You may be so accustomed to hearing those phrases that it will surprise you to learn that none of them is based on biblical terminology. They are the products of a diluted gospel. It is not the gospel according to Jesus.

The gospel Jesus proclaimed was a call to discipleship, a call to follow him in submissive obedience, not just a plea to make a decision or pray a prayer. Jesus' message liberated people from the bondage of their sin while it confronted and condemned hypocrisy. It was an offer of eternal life and forgiveness for repentant sinners, but at the same time it was a rebuke to outwardly religious people whose lives were devoid of true righteousness. It put sinners on notice that they must turn from sin and embrace God's righteousness. It was in every sense good news, yet it was anything but easy-believism.

Our Lord's words about eternal life were invariably accompanied by warnings to those who might be tempted to take salvation lightly. He taught that the cost of following him is high, that the way is narrow and few find it. He said many who call him Lord will be forbidden from entering the kingdom of heaven (cf. Matt. 7:13–23).

Present-day evangelicalism, by and large, ignores those warnings. The prevailing view of what constitutes saving faith continues to grow broader and more shallow, while the portrayal of Christ in preaching and witnessing becomes fuzzy. Anyone who claims to be a Christian can find evangelicals willing to accept a profession of faith, whether or not the person's behavior shows any evidence of commitment to Christ. A few years ago the national media reported on the spectacle of a notorious pornographer who claimed to be "born again" yet continued to publish the worst kinds of smut. A well-known sports figure professed faith in Christ and was baptized in a highly publicized ceremony, then weeks later was accused and later convicted of rape. Another celebrity who claims to be a Christian is renowned for the profligacy of his lifestyle. What troubles me about all these is that many Christians insist such people really are born again and should be embraced by the rest of the church as true believers.

The Abandonment of Jesus' Gospel

One segment of evangelicalism even propounds the doctrine that conversion to Christ involves "no spiritual commitment whatsoever."[1] Those who hold this view of the gospel teach that Scripture promises salvation to anyone who simply believes the facts about Christ and claims eternal life. There need be no turning from sin, no resulting change in lifestyle, no commitment—not even a *willingness* to yield to Christ's lordship.[2] Those things, they say, amount to human works, which corrupt grace and have nothing to do with faith.

The fallout of such thinking is a deficient doctrine of salvation. It is justification without sanctification, and its impact on the church has been catastrophic. The community of professing believers is populated with people who have bought into a system that encourages shallow and ineffectual faith. Many sincerely believe they are saved, but their lives are utterly barren of any verifying fruit.

Jesus gave this sobering warning: "Not everyone who says to Me, 'Lord, Lord,' will enter the kingdom of heaven; *but he who does the will of My Father who is in heaven.* Many will say to Me on that day, 'Lord, Lord, did we not prophesy in Your name, and in Your name cast out demons, and in Your name perform many miracles?' And then I will declare to them, 'I never knew you; depart from Me, *you who practice lawlessness*'" (Matt. 7:21–22, emphasis added). Clearly no past experience—not even prophesying, casting out demons, or doing signs and wonders—can be viewed as evidence of salvation apart from a life of obedience.

Our Lord was not speaking about an isolated group of fringe followers. There will be *"many"* on that day who will stand before him, stunned to learn they are not included in the kingdom. I fear

---

[1]Zane C. Hodges, *The Gospel Under Siege* (Dallas: Redención Viva, 1981), 14.
[2]Charles C. Ryrie, *Balancing the Christian Life* (Chicago: Moody Press, 1969), 169–70.

that multitudes who now fill church pews in the mainstream of the evangelical movement will be among those turned away because they did not do the will of the Father.

Contemporary Christians have been conditioned to believe that because they recited a prayer, signed on a dotted line, walked an aisle, or had some other experience, they are saved and should never question their salvation. I have attended evangelism training seminars where counselors were taught to tell "converts" that any doubt about their salvation is satanic and should be dismissed. It is a widely held misconception that anyone who questions whether he or she is saved is challenging the integrity of God's Word.

What misguided thinking that is! Scripture encourages us to examine ourselves to determine if we are in the faith (2 Cor. 13:5). Peter wrote, "Be all the more diligent to make certain about his calling and choosing you" (2 Peter 1:10). It is right to examine our lives and evaluate the fruit we bear, for "each tree is known by its own fruit" (Luke 6:44).

The Bible teaches clearly that the evidence of God's work in a life is the inevitable fruit of transformed behavior (1 John 3:10). Faith that does not result in righteous living is dead and cannot save (James 2:14–17).[3] Professing Christians utterly lacking the fruit of true righteousness will find no biblical basis for assurance of salvation (1 John 2:4).

Real salvation is not only justification. It cannot be isolated from regeneration, sanctification, and ultimately glorification. Salvation is the work of God through which we are "conformed to the image of His Son" (Rom. 8:29; cf. 13:11). Genuine assurance comes from seeing the Holy Spirit's transforming work in one's life, not from clinging to the memory of some experience.

Some Historical Background

In a study of Jesus' gospel, we cannot be concerned primarily with academic systems of theology or the views of specific theologians on

---

[3]James asks the rhetorical question, "What use is it, my brethren, if a man says he has faith, but he has no works? Can that faith save him?" (James 2:14). One branch of contemporary theology seems to be saying yes. Cf. Hodges, *The Gospel Under Siege*, 19–33. Nevertheless, James's message seems clear. Even the demons have faith enough to grasp the basic facts (v. 19), but that is not redeeming faith. "Faith without works is useless" (v. 20) and "faith without works is dead" (v. 26). Putting those three verses together, we must conclude that this is a description of ineffectual faith, not faith that was once alive but now has died. (See further discussion on p. 187, n. 5.)

a given doctrine. Nevertheless, in seeking to understand the issues, we must look at how the contemporary perspective of the gospel has evolved.

Prior to this century, no serious theologian would have entertained the notion that it is possible to be saved yet see nothing of the outworking of regeneration in one's lifestyle or behavior.[4] In 1918 Lewis Sperry Chafer published *He That Is Spiritual,* articulating the concept that 1 Corinthians 2:15—3:3 speaks of two classes of Christians: carnal and spiritual. Chafer wrote, "The 'carnal' Christian is . . . characterized by a 'walk' that is on the same plane as that of the 'natural' [unsaved] man."[5] That was a foreign concept to most Christians in Dr. Chafer's generation,[6] but it has become a central premise for a large segment of the church today. Dr. Chafer's doctrine of spirituality, along with some of his other teachings, have become the basis of a whole new way of looking at the gospel. It is therefore essential to confront what he taught.

Chafer's dichotomy between carnal and spiritual Christians was seen by Dr. B. B. Warfield as an echo of "the jargon of the Higher

[4]See appendix 2 for an overview of the historic church's understanding of the relationship between faith and works.

[5]Lewis Sperry Chafer, *He That Is Spiritual,* rev. ed. (Grand Rapids: Zondervan, 1967), 21.

[6]Those schooled in dispensationalist theology may be surprised to learn that Chafer's book was extremely controversial when first released. In a scathing review, B. B. Warfield took issue with Chafer's basic premise. While not denying the obvious truth that Christians can behave in carnal ways, Warfield objected vigorously to the classification of carnality as a separate state of the spiritual life. Warfield makes some excellent points:

> This teaching is indistinguishable from what is ordinarily understood by the doctrine of a "second blessing," "a second work of grace," "the higher life."
>
> . . . .
>
> The remainders of the flesh in the Christian do not constitute his characteristic. He is in the Spirit and is walking, with however halting steps, by the Spirit; and it is to all Christians, not to some, that the great promise is given, "Sin shall not have dominion over you," and the great assurance is added, "Because ye are not under the law but under grace." He who believes in Jesus Christ is under grace, and his whole course, in its process and in its issue alike, is determined by grace, and therefore, having been predestined to be conformed to the image of God's Son, he is surely being conformed to that image, God himself seeing to it that he is not only called and justified but also glorified. You may find Christians at every stage of this process, for it is a process through which all must pass; but you will find none who will not in God's own good time and way pass through every stage of it. There are not two kinds of Christians, although there are Christians at every conceivable stage of advancement towards the one goal to which all are bound and at which all shall arrive (Benjamin B. Warfield, review in *The Princeton Theological Review* [April 1919], 322–27).

Life teachers,"[7] who taught that a higher plane of victorious living was available to Christians who would lay hold of it by faith. This idea of two classes of believers was undoubtedly an unfortunate result of Chafer's predilection for dispensationalist distinctions. It is a classic example of how dispensationalism's methodology can be carried too far.

Dispensationalism is a fundamentally correct system of understanding God's program through the ages. Its chief element is a recognition that God's plan for Israel is not superseded by or swallowed up in his program for the church. Israel and the church are separate entities, and God will restore national Israel under the earthly rule of Jesus as Messiah. I accept and affirm that tenet, because it emerges from a consistently literal interpretation of Scripture (while still recognizing the presence of legitimate metaphor in the Bible). And in that regard, I consider myself a traditional premillennial dispensationalist.[8]

Dr. Chafer was an early and articulate spokesman for dispensationalism, and his teachings helped chart the course for much of the movement. He was a brilliant man, gifted with both a keen analytical mind and the ability to communicate clearly. The systematic methodology of traditional dispensationalism is in part his legacy.

There is a tendency, however, for dispensationalists to get carried away with compartmentalizing truth to the point that they make unbiblical differentiations. An almost obsessive desire to categorize and contrast related truths has carried various dispensationalist interpreters far beyond the legitimate distinction between Israel and the church. Many would also draw hard lines between salvation and discipleship, the church and the kingdom, Christ's preaching and the apostolic message, faith and repentance, and the age of law and the age of grace.

The age-of-law/age-of-grace division in particular has wreaked havoc on dispensationalist theology and contributed to confusion about the doctrine of salvation. Of course, there is an important distinction to be made between law and grace. But it is wrong to conclude, as Chafer apparently did, that law and grace are mutually exclusive in the program of God for any age.[9] Actually, elements of

---

[7]Ibid., 322.

[8]A definition of biblical dispensationalism is given in Charles C. Ryrie, *Dispensationalism Today* (Chicago: Moody Press, 1965), 43–44.

[9]Chafer wrote:

In respect to the character of divine government, both the age before the cross and the age following the return of Christ represent the exercise of pure law; while the period between the two ages represents the exercise of

both law and grace are part of the program of God in every dispensation. Most critical is this truth: Salvation has *always* been by grace through faith, not by the works of the law (Gal. 2:16). Clearly, even Old Testament saints who preceded or were under the Mosaic Law were saved by grace through faith (Rom. 4:3, 6–8, 16). Just as clearly, New Testament saints have a law to fulfill (Gal. 6:2; 1 Cor. 7:19; 9:21). That is not "careless co-mingling"[10] of law and grace, as Chafer implied. It is basic biblical truth.

Chafer's view of all Scripture was colored by his desire to maintain a stark distinction between the age of "pure grace" (the church age) and the two ages of "pure law" (the Mosaic era and the millennial kingdom) he saw sandwiching it.[11] He wrote, for example, that the Sermon on the Mount was part of "the Gospel of the kingdom," the "Manifesto of the King."[12] He believed its purpose was to declare "the essential character of the [millennial] kingdom." He judged it to be law, not grace, and concluded it made no reference to either salvation or grace. "Such a complete omission of any reference to any feature of the present age of grace, is a fact which should be carefully weighed," he wrote.[13]

Other dispensationalist writers did weigh those ideas and went on to state in more explicit terms what Chafer only hinted at: that the teachings of the Sermon on the Mount "have no application to the Christian, but only to those who are under the Law, and therefore must apply to another Dispensation than this."[14] This lamentable

pure grace. It is imperative, therefore, that there shall be no careless co-mingling of these great age-characterizing elements, else the preservation of the most important distinctions in the various relationships between God and man are lost, and the recognition of the true force of the death of Christ and his coming again is obscured. (Lewis Sperry Chafer, *Grace* (Grand Rapids: Zondervan, 1922), 124.

[10]Ibid. It is noteworthy that *The New Scofield Reference Bible* places far more weight than Chafer did on the importance of the law and its ministry in the age of grace (New York: Oxford, 1967), 3, 1254.

[11]Chafer, *Grace*, 124.

[12]Ibid., 138.

[13]Ibid., 139. Contrast this with Luther's statement that "the Sermon on the Mount is not Law, but Gospel." Cited in John R. W. Stott, *Christian Counter-Culture* (Downers Grove, Ill.: InterVarsity, 1978), 37.

[14]Clarence Larkin, *Dispensational Truth* (Philadelphia: Larkin, 1918), 87. Larkin, whose books and charts are still in print and used by many dispensationalists, also pointed to the phrase "Thy kingdom come" in the Lord's Prayer as proof the prayer is meant only "for those who shall be living in the 'Tribulation Period.'" His conclusion is unwarranted. The kingdom is also yet to come for those living today, before the Tribulation.

hermeneutic is widely applied in varying degrees to much of our Lord's earthly teaching, emasculating the message of the Gospels.[15]

It is no wonder that the evangelistic message growing out of such a system differs sharply from the gospel according to Jesus. If we begin with the presupposition that much of Christ's message was intended for another age, why should our gospel be the same as the one he preached?

But that is a dangerous and untenable presupposition. Jesus did not come to proclaim a message that would be invalid until the Tribulation or the Millennium. He came to seek and to save the lost (Luke 19:10). He came to call sinners to repentance (Matt. 9:13). He came so the world through him might be saved (John 3:17). He proclaimed the saving gospel, not merely a manifesto for some future age. His gospel is the only message we are to preach.

Wrongly Dividing the Word

Let's look a little more closely at the dispensationalist tendency to make unwarranted contrasts between related or parallel truths. It is important that we delineate carefully between essentially different biblical axioms (2 Tim. 2:15). But it is also possible to go overboard. The unbridled zeal of some dispensationalists for making dichotomies has led to a number of unfortunate impositions on the gospel.

For example, Jesus is both Savior and Lord (Luke 2:11), and no true believer would ever dispute that. "Savior" and "Lord" are separate offices, but we must be careful not to partition them in such a way that we divide Christ (cf. 1 Cor. 1:13). Nevertheless, loud voices from the dispensationalist camp are putting forth the teaching that it is possible to reject Christ as Lord yet receive him as Savior.

Indeed, there are those who would have us believe that the norm for salvation is to accept Jesus as Savior without submitting to him as Lord. They make the incredible claim that any other teaching amounts to a false gospel "because it subtly adds works to the clear

---

[15]It should be pointed out that many dispensationalists resent the criticism that they relegate the Sermon on the Mount and other teachings of Jesus to a future age. Most dispensationalists will say that they see application of the sermon to the church age but still stop short of saying that its primary message is for Christians. Even Ryrie, who wrote a passionate counterattack to this charge, falls short of embracing the Sermon on the Mount as truth for today. After a lengthy defense of the traditional dispensationalist view of the Sermon on the Mount, Ryrie concludes that it cannot be applied "primarily and fully . . . to the believer in this age" (Ryrie, *Dispensationalism Today*, 109). Yet virtually every detail in the Sermon is repeated in the Epistles.

and simple condition set forth in the Word of God."[16] They have tagged the view they oppose "lordship salvation."

Lordship salvation, defined by one who labels it heresy, is "the view that for salvation a person must trust Jesus Christ as his Savior from sin and must also commit himself to Christ as Lord of his life, submitting to his sovereign authority."[17]

It is astonishing that anyone would characterize that truth as unbiblical or heretical, but a growing chorus of voices is echoing the charge. The implication is that acknowledging Christ's lordship is a human work. That mistaken notion is backed by volumes of literature that speaks of people "making Jesus Christ Lord of their lives."[18]

We do not "make" Christ Lord; he *is* Lord! Those who will not receive him as Lord are guilty of rejecting him. "Faith" that rejects his sovereign authority is really unbelief. Conversely, acknowledging his lordship is no more a human work than repentance (cf. 2 Tim. 2:25) or faith itself (cf. Eph. 2:8–9). In fact, surrender to Christ is an important aspect of divinely produced saving faith, not something added to faith.

The two clearest statements on the way of salvation in all of Scripture both emphasize Jesus' lordship: "Believe in the Lord Jesus, and you shall be saved" (Acts 16:31); and "If you confess with your mouth Jesus as Lord, and believe in your heart that God raised Him from the dead, you shall be saved" (Rom. 10:9).[19] Peter's sermon at Pentecost concluded with this declaration: "Let all the house of Israel know for certain that God has made Him *both Lord and Christ*—this Jesus whom you crucified" (Acts 2:36, emphasis added). No promise of salvation is ever extended to those who refuse to accede to Christ's lordship. Thus there is no salvation except "lordship" salvation.[20]

[16]Livingston Blauvelt, Jr., "Does the Bible Teach Lordship Salvation?" *Bibliotheca Sacra* (January–March 1986), 37.

[17]Ibid.

[18]Ibid., 38.

[19]Some dispensationalists would confine the application of Romans 10:9–10 to unbelieving Jews. It is true that Romans 9–11 deals with the question of Israel's rejection of the Messiah and the nation's place in God's eternal plan. But the soteriological significance of those verses cannot be limited to Israel alone, because of verses 12–13: "There is no distinction between Jew and Greek; for the same Lord is Lord of all, abounding in riches for all who call upon Him; for whoever will call upon the name of the Lord will be saved."

[20]I do not like the term "lordship salvation." It was coined by those who want to eliminate the idea of submission to Christ from the call to saving faith, and it implies that Jesus' lordship is a false addition to the gospel. As we shall see, however, "lordship salvation" is simply biblical and historic evangelical soteriology. I use the term in this volume only for the sake of argument.

Opponents of lordship salvation have gone to great lengths to make the claim that "Lord" in those verses does not mean "Master" but is a reference to his deity.[21] Even if that contention is granted, it simply affirms that those who come to Christ for salvation must acknowledge that he is God. The implications of that are even more demanding than if "Lord" only meant "Master"!

The fact is, "Lord" *does* mean "God" in all those verses. More precisely, it means "God who rules,"[22] and that only bolsters the arguments for lordship salvation. No one who comes for salvation with genuine faith, sincerely believing that Jesus is the eternal, almighty, sovereign God, will willfully reject his authority. True faith is not lip service. Our Lord himself pronounced condemnation on those who worshiped him with their lips but not with their lives (Matt. 15:7–9). He does not become anyone's Savior until that person receives him for who he is—Lord of all (Acts 10:36).

A. W. Tozer said:

> The Lord will not save those whom He cannot command. He will not divide His offices. You cannot believe on a half-Christ. We take Him for what He is—the anointed Saviour and Lord who is King of kings and Lord of all lords! He would not be Who He is if He saved us and called us and chose us without the understanding that He can also guide and control our lives.[23]

Faith and True Discipleship

Those who teach that obedience and submission are extraneous to saving faith are forced to make a firm but unbiblical distinction

---

[21]Ibid., 38–41. See also G. Michael Cocoris, *Lordship Salvation—Is It Biblical?* (Dallas: Redención Viva, 1983), 13–15.

[22]Proper understanding of any biblical term depends on etymology, context, and history. Etymologically, *kurios* comes from a Greek root that means "rule, dominion, or power." Contextually, taking Peter's use of *kurios* in Acts 2:36, it is important to note that verses 34–35 quote from Psalm 110, a messianic Psalm of rule and dominion ("Rule in the midst of Thine enemies," Ps. 110:2). Peter was not saying merely that "God has made Him . . . God"; he was affirming Jesus' right to rule. Historically, Peter's sermon addressed the Jews' role in crucifying their Messiah (v. 23). At the trial of Jesus before Pilate and the Jewish mob, the issue was clearly his kingship, mentioned at least a dozen times in John 18:33—19:22. Clearly, careful historical-grammatical exegesis of Acts 2:36 can lead to only one conclusion: Jesus is the divine King who rules in the midst of both friends and foes. Having thus identified Christ as Lord of all, Peter makes his gospel appeal. Note carefully that Paul preached Jesus in exactly the same way (2 Cor. 4:3–5): Jesus is our sovereign Lord, and we are his servants.

[23]A. W. Tozer, *I Call It Heresy!* (Harrisburg, Pa.: Christian Publications, 1974), 18–19.

between salvation and discipleship. This dichotomy, like that of the carnal/spiritual Christian, sets up two classes of Christians: believers only and true disciples. Most who hold this position discard the evangelistic intent of virtually every recorded invitation of Jesus, saying those apply to discipleship, not to salvation.[24] One writer says of this view, "No distinction is more vital to theology, more basic to a correct understanding of the New Testament, or more relevant to every believer's life and witness."[25]

On the contrary, no distinction has done so much to undermine the authority of Jesus' message. Are we to believe that when Jesus told the multitudes to deny themselves (Luke 14:26), to take up a cross (v. 27), and to forsake all and follow him (v. 33), his words had no meaning whatsoever for the unsaved people in the crowd? How could that be true of One who said he came not to call the righteous but sinners? (Matt. 9:13).

James M. Boice, in his book, *Christ's Call to Discipleship*, writes with insight about the salvation/discipleship dichotomy, which he frankly describes as "defective theology":

> This theology separates faith from discipleship and grace from obedience. It teaches that Jesus can be received as one's Savior without being received as one's Lord.
>
> This is a common defect in times of prosperity. In days of hardship, particularly persecution, those who are in the process of becoming Christians count the cost of discipleship carefully before taking up the cross of the Nazarene. Preachers do not beguile them with false promises of an easy life or indulgence of sins. But in good times, the cost does not seem so high, and people take the name of Christ without undergoing the radical transformation of life that true conversion implies.[26]

The call to Calvary must be recognized for what it is: a call to discipleship under the lordship of Jesus Christ. To respond to that call is to become a believer. Anything less is simply unbelief.[27]

---

[24]Hodges, *Gospel Under Siege*, 35–45; Cocoris, *Lordship Salvation—Is It Biblical?* 15–16; Blauvelt, "Does the Bible Teach Lordship Salvation?" 41.

[25]Charles C. Ryrie in the foreword to Zane C. Hodges, *The Hungry Inherit* (Portland: Multnomah, 1980), 7.

[26]James M. Boice, *Christ's Call to Discipleship* (Chicago: Moody Press, 1986), 14.

[27]Jesus' Great Commission in Matthew 28:18–20 does not talk about making believers in distinction to disciples. "Make disciples . . . baptizing them" implies that every new believer is a disciple, for all Christians are to be baptized (Acts 2:38), not just those who go on to some deeper level of commitment. (See further discussion of this issue in chapter 21.)

The gospel according to Jesus explicitly and unequivocally rules out easy-believism. To make all of our Lord's difficult demands apply only to a higher class of Christians blunts the force of his entire message. It makes room for a cheap and meaningless faith—a faith that has absolutely no effect on the fleshly life of sin. That is not saving faith.

This means, no believer can ever sin or sin for a time??

By Grace Through Faith

Salvation is solely by grace through faith (Eph. 2:8). That truth is the biblical watershed for all we teach. But it means nothing if we begin with a misunderstanding of grace or a faulty definition of faith.

God's grace is not a static attribute whereby he passively accepts hardened, unrepentant sinners. Grace does not change a person's standing before God yet leave his character untouched. Real grace does not include, as Chafer claimed, "the Christian's liberty to do precisely as he chooses."[28] True grace, according to Scripture, teaches us "to deny ungodliness and worldly desires and to live sensibly, righteously and godly in the present age" (Titus 2:12). Grace is the power of God to fulfill our New Covenant duties (cf. 1 Cor. 7:19), however inconsistently we obey at times. Clearly, grace does not grant permission to live in the flesh; it supplies power to live in the Spirit.

a process

Contradict

Faith, like grace, is not static. Saving faith is more than just understanding the facts and mentally acquiescing. It is inseparable from repentance, surrender, and a supernatural longing to obey. None of those responses can be classified exclusively as a human work, any more than believing itself is solely a human effort.

Misunderstanding on that key point is at the heart of the error of those who reject lordship salvation. They assume that because Scripture contrasts faith and works, faith must be incompatible with works. They set faith in opposition to submission, yieldedness, or turning from sin, and they categorize all the practical fruits of salvation as human works. They stumble over the twin truths that salvation is a gift, yet it costs everything.

Who is they? This is not taught

Those ideas are paradoxical, but they are not mutually exclusive. The same dissonance is seen in Jesus' own words, "I will give you rest," followed by "take My yoke upon you" (Matt. 11:28–29). The rest we enter into by faith is not a rest of inactivity.

Who thinks it is?! He reads minds?!

[28]Chafer, *Grace*, 345. Chafer would be the last person to countenance lawless Christian living. Yet because of his extreme emphasis on "pure grace," he often made statements with a strange antinomian flavor that may have conveyed impressions he did not want to convey.

and so is MacArthur!

Salvation is a gift, but it is appropriated through a faith that goes beyond merely understanding and assenting to the truth. Demons have that kind of "faith" (James 2:19). True believers are characterized by faith that is as repulsed by the life of sin as it is attracted to the mercy of the Savior. Drawn to Christ, they are drawn away from everything else. Jesus described genuine believers as "poor in spirit" (Matt. 5:3). They are like the repentant tax-gatherer, so broken he could not even look heavenward. He could only beat his breast and plead, "God, be merciful to me, the sinner!" (Luke 18:13).

That man's desperate prayer is one of the clearest pictures of genuine, God-wrought repentance in all of Scripture. His plea was not in any sense a human work or an attempt at earning righteousness. On the contrary, it represented his total abandonment of confidence in religious works. As if to prove it he stood "some distance away" from the praying Pharisee. He understood that the only way he could ever be saved was by God's merciful grace. On that basis, having first come to the end of himself, he received salvation as a gift. Jesus said that man "went down to his house justified" (v. 14).

Our Lord's point in relating that account was to demonstrate that repentance is at the core of saving faith. The Greek word for repentance, *metanoia*, literally means "to think after." It implies a change of mind, and some who oppose lordship salvation have tried to limit its meaning to that.[29] But a definition of repentance cannot be drawn solely from the etymology of the Greek word.

Repentance as Jesus characterized it in this incident involves a recognition of one's utter sinfulness and a turning from self and sin to God (cf. 1 Thess. 1:9). Far from being a human work, it is the inevitable result of *God's* work in a human heart. And it always represents the end of any human attempt to earn God's favor. It is much more than a mere change of mind—it involves a complete change of heart, attitude, interest, and direction. It is a conversion in every sense of the word.

The Bible does not recognize "conversion" that lacks this radical change of direction (Luke 3:7–8). A true believer cannot remain rebellious—or even indifferent. Genuine faith will inevitably provoke some degree of obedience. In fact, Scripture often equates faith

[29]Cocoris, *Lordship Salvation—Is It Biblical?* 11. Also, Ryrie claims that repentance is "a change of mind about Jesus Christ so that He is believed and received as personal Saviour from sin." Repentance, by this definition, has nothing to do with one's attitude toward sin and does not necessarily result in any change in lifestyle. It is merely a Christological focus. Ryrie, *Balancing the Christian Life*, 175–76.

with obedience (John 3:36; Rom. 1:5; 16:26; 2 Thess. 1:8).[30] "By faith Abraham [the father of true faith] . . . obeyed" (Heb. 11:8). That is the heart of the message of Hebrews 11, the great treatise on faith.

Faith and works are not incompatible. Jesus even calls the act of believing a work (John 6:29)—not merely a human work, but a gracious work of God in us. He brings us to faith, then enables and empowers us to believe unto obedience (cf. Rom. 16:26).

It is precisely here that the key distinction must be made. Salvation by faith does not eliminate works per se. It does away with works that are the result of human effort alone (Eph. 2:8). It abolishes any attempt to merit God's favor by our works (v. 9). But it does not deter God's foreordained purpose that our walk should be characterized by good works (v. 10).

We must remember above all that salvation is a sovereign work of God. Biblically it is defined by what it produces, not by what one does to get it. Works are *not* necessary to earn salvation. But true salvation wrought by God will not fail to produce the good works that are its fruit (cf. Matt. 7:17). No aspect of salvation is merited by human works, but it is all the work of God (Titus 3:5–7). Thus salvation cannot be defective in any dimension. "We are His workmanship, created in Christ Jesus for good works, which God prepared beforehand, that we should walk in them" (Eph. 2:10). As a part of his saving work, God will produce repentance, faith, sanctification, yieldedness, obedience, and ultimately glorification. Since he is not dependent on human effort in producing these elements, an experience that lacks any of them cannot be the saving work of God.

If we are truly born of God, we have a faith that cannot fail to overcome the world (1 John 5:4). We may sin (1 John 2:1)—we will sin—but the process of sanctification can never stall completely. God is at work in us (Phil. 2:13), and he will continue to perfect us until the day of Christ (Phil. 1:6; 1 Thess. 5:23–24).

---

[30]Those who reject the lordship position often claim that texts such as Romans 1:5 ("the obedience of faith") indicate that believing itself is the only obedience called for in salvation. By believing in the Son, we obey the Father's will (John 6:29). This is "the obedience of faith," they say; it is one-time obedience to the Father, not lasting obedience to the commandments of Christ. But obedience to Christ's authority is clearly enjoined by texts such as John 3:36 ("He who does not obey the Son shall not see life, but the wrath of God abides on him") and Hebrews 5:9 ("[Christ] became to all those who obey Him the source of eternal salvation").

PART TWO

JESUS HERALDS
HIS GOSPEL

2

He Calls for a New Birth

Not everyone who claims to be a Christian really is. Unbelievers *do* make false professions of faith in Christ, and people who are not truly Christians can be deceived into thinking they are.

That might have been taken for granted a couple of decades ago, but no more. The cheap grace and pseudo faith of a distorted gospel are ruining the purity of the church. The softening of the New Testament message has brought with it a putrefying inclusivism that in effect sees almost any kind of positive response to Jesus as tantamount to saving faith. Christians today are likely to accept anything other than utter rejection as authentic faith in Christ. Modern-day evangelicalism has developed a large and conspicuous fringe, embracing even those whose doctrine is suspect or whose behavior indicates a heart in rebellion against the things of God.

The gospel Jesus proclaimed did not foster that kind of gullibility. From the time he first began to minister publicly, our Lord eschewed the quick, easy, or shallow response. He turned away far more prospects than he won, refusing to proclaim a message that would give anyone a false hope. His words, always tailored to the individual's needs, never failed to puncture an inquirer's self-righteousness, unveil wrong motives, or warn of false faith or shallow commitment.

Jesus' meeting with Nicodemus in John 3 is an example of this. It is the earliest of his one-on-one evangelistic encounters recorded in the Gospels. It is ironic that Jesus, who so often confronted the Pharisees' unbelief and outright antagonism, began his evangelistic ministry by answering a leading Pharisee who approached him with an enthusiastic word of affirmation. We might expect Jesus to welcome Nicodemus warmly and interpret his positive response as a profession of faith, but that was not the case. Far from encouraging

43

Nicodemus, Jesus, who knew the unbelief and self-righteousness of Nicodemus's heart, dealt with him as an unbeliever.

Some view this passage of Scripture as a statement about how easy it is to believe in Jesus Christ.[1] That is not the point of this episode at all. It is true that here we see the simplicity of the gospel outlined clearly, but Jesus was not bringing this self-righteous Pharisee a message of easy-believism. On the contrary, our Lord challenged everything the man stood for. In the course of their dialogue, Jesus confronted Nicodemus's spurious faith, his works-based religion, his Pharisaical righteousness, and his biblical illiteracy. The Savior called for nothing short of complete regeneration. Without such a spiritual rebirth, he told Nicodemus, *no one* has any hope of eternal life. Nicodemus was clearly jolted by Jesus' words, and there is no evidence in this passage that his immediate response was positive.

John included this account in the process of making the argument that Jesus is God. The gospel of John begins and ends with declarations of Jesus' deity (1:1; 20:30–31), and nearly everything else John says expands on that theme. The encounter between Jesus and Nicodemus is no exception. The narrative flows out of John 2:23–25, which says Jesus "knew all men, and . . . knew what was in man." The story of Nicodemus goes on to prove Christ's omniscience by demonstrating his ability to read Nicodemus's heart. It further confirms Jesus' deity by revealing that he is the way of salvation (3:14–17).

Nicodemus was one of those John described at the end of chapter 2 who believed just because they saw Jesus' miracles. Their kind of belief had nothing to do with saving faith, as we see from John's testimony that "Jesus, on his part, was not entrusting Himself to them, for He knew all men" (2:24). That is a clear statement about the inefficacy of artificial faith.[2] Nicodemus, then, stands as an illustration of inadequate faith. His mind accepted to some extent the truth of Christ, but his heart was unregenerate.

Nicodemus begins the conversation with this confession of faith:

---

[1] Cocoris cites John 3:14–15 as support for a definition of faith that explicitly eliminates the idea of commitment. G. Michael Cocoris, *Lordship Salvation—Is It Biblical?* (Dallas: Redención Viva, 1983), 13.

[2] Cf. Zane Hodges, "Untrustworthy Believers—John 2:23–25" *Bibliotheca Sacra* (April–June 1978), 139–52. Hodges makes the startling claim that the people described here are true, albeit secret, believers. Still, he acknowledges the obvious link between John 2:23–25 and the account of Nicodemus (ibid., 150). Clearly, Jesus dealt with Nicodemus as an unbeliever. If he was one of those described in John 2:23–25, he could not have been a genuine believer at the time. As Hodges himself concedes, commentators are nearly unanimous in the view that John 2:23–25 describes something less than saving faith.

"Rabbi, we know that you have come from God as a teacher; for no one can do these signs that You do unless God is with him" (3:2). He was intrigued with Christ. Being a religious leader, Nicodemus obviously would have had a keen interest in anyone he felt was sent from above. He had seen Jesus' miracles, and he knew he was from God. There had not been a prophet for four hundred years, and Nicodemus was probably thinking that he had found one. Perhaps he even was wondering whether Jesus was the Messiah, but he had not yet come to see Christ as God incarnate.

Jesus, who "knew all men" (2:24), understood what was really on Nicodemus's heart. He ignored Nicodemus's profession of faith, and instead answered a question Nicodemus did not even ask.

Without confirming, denying, refuting, or even acknowledging Nicodemus's statement that he was from God, Jesus gave an answer that demonstrated his omniscience. Thus our Lord confronted Nicodemus with the fact that he had fallen short of realizing the full truth. Nicodemus was not dealing with a mere teacher sent from God—he was standing before God in the flesh. John 3:3 says, "Jesus answered and said to him, 'Truly, truly, I say to you, unless one is born again, he cannot see the kingdom of God.'"

The Savior's words were shocking to Nicodemus (John 3:9). Do not miss that point or minimize Jesus' challenge to this man. Our Lord's strategy in witnessing was always frank, direct, and to the point. He took a confrontive approach in this first encounter. Nicodemus was drawn up short by Jesus' answer. It included four critical truths that must have astonished him.

The Futility of Religion

Nicodemus was "a ruler of the Jews" (3:1), a member of the Sanhedrin, the powerful ruling body of the Jewish nation. Perhaps he came by night because he did not want the whole world to see him and think he was representing all the Sanhedrin. Or maybe he was afraid of what the other Pharisees would think. They were known to put people out of the synagogue for believing in Jesus (John 9:22). Nevertheless, he came—unlike his colleagues—with a sincere desire to learn.

The Pharisees were hyperlegalists who externalized religion. They were the very epitome of all who pursue a form of godliness with no reality (2 Tim. 3:5). Although they were fanatically religious, they were no nearer the kingdom of God than a prostitute. Their credo included fastidious adherence to more than six hundred laws, many of which were simply their own inventions. They believed, for example, that it was all right to swallow vinegar on the Sabbath but not to gargle it—gargling constituted labor. One Pharisaical teaching held that it was permissible to eat an egg that had been laid on the Sabbath only if the chicken was killed the next day for having violated the Sabbath! The Pharisees were so enamored with the law and religion that when Christ came offering grace and salvation to even the grossest of sinners, they would not receive him.

When Nicodemus heard Christ talking about a new birth, his mind must have been a bog. He had always believed that salvation was to be earned by good works. He probably even expected Christ to commend him for his strict legalism! Instead, Jesus confronted him with the futility of his religion. What a letdown! Unlike religious works, being born again was something Nicodemus could not do himself!

Nicodemus's reply has often been misunderstood: "How can a man be born when he is old? He cannot enter a second time into his mother's womb and be born, can he?" (v. 4). Nicodemus was not speaking in literal terms. We must give him credit for a little common sense. Surely he was not so feebleminded as to think Jesus was really talking about reentering the womb and literally being born again. A teacher himself, Nicodemus understood the rabbinical method of using figurative language to teach spiritual truth, and he was merely picking up Jesus' symbolism. He was really saying, "I *can't* start all over. It's too late. I've gone too far in my religious system to start over. There's no hope for me if I must begin from the beginning."

Jesus was demanding that Nicodemus forsake everything he stood for, and Nicodemus knew it. Far from offering this man an easy conversion, Christ was challenging him with the most difficult demand he could make. Nicodemus would gladly have given money, fasted, or performed any ritual Jesus could have prescribed. But to call him to a spiritual rebirth was asking him to acknowledge his own insufficiency and turn away from everything he was committed to.

Jesus merely reiterated, "Truly, truly, I say to you, unless one is born of water and the Spirit, he cannot enter into the kingdom of God" (v. 5). Some people say that means literal water—H_2O. It doesn't. This has nothing to do with water or baptism. Salvation cannot be accomplished by a bath. John 4:2 says Jesus baptized no one. If baptism were a condition of salvation, he would have been baptizing people; after all, he came to seek and to save the lost (Luke 19:10). The water Jesus is speaking of is merely symbolic—as it was in the Old Testament—of purification.

Nicodemus would have understood this reference to the Old Testament water of purification, which was sprinkled on the altar and on sacrifices in most of the rituals. Being a scholar, Nicodemus no doubt remembered Ezekiel 36:25 and the promise of the new covenant: "Then I will sprinkle clean water on you." Two verses later is the promise, "I will put My Spirit within you" (v. 27). Those statements, bringing the ideas of water and the Spirit together, sandwich another promise: "I will give you a new heart, and put a new spirit within you; and I will remove the heart of stone from your flesh and give you a heart of flesh" (v. 26). That is the Old Testament promise of regeneration by water and the Spirit.

The only baptism implied here is the baptism in the Holy Spirit. John the Baptist said, "He who sent me to baptize in water said to me, 'He upon whom you see the Spirit descending and remaining upon Him, this is the one who baptizes in the Holy Spirit'" (John 1:33). Spirit baptism takes place at salvation, when the Lord places the believer into the body of Christ by means of the Holy Spirit (1 Cor. 12:13) and purifies the believer by the water of the Word (Eph. 5:26; cf. John 15:3). Paul refers to this as "the washing of regeneration, and renewing by the Holy Spirit" (Titus 3:5), almost perfectly echoing Jesus' words in John 3:5: "Unless one is born of water [the washing of regeneration] and the Spirit [and renewing by the Holy Spirit], he cannot enter into the kingdom of God."

Thus Jesus was saying to Nicodemus, "You need to be spiritually purified and spiritually reborn." The whole point was that law and religious rituals—including baptism—cannot give eternal life. We can assume Nicodemus got the message, because it apparently jarred him fiercely.

The Unity of Revelation

Jesus then gently chided the shocked teacher, saying, "Do not marvel that I said to you, 'You must be born again'" (John 3:7).

Nicodemus's next question revealed the turmoil in his heart: "How can these things be?" (v. 9). He simply could not believe what he was hearing.

"Jesus answered and said to him, 'Are you the teacher of Israel, and do not understand these things?'" (v. 10). That rebuke from the Lord completely silenced Nicodemus. He made no further response. Perhaps he stood and listened as Jesus graciously explained the new birth. Perhaps he turned and left in anger. John does not tell us. Nicodemus seems to have ultimately become a believer—if not here, at some later date. After the crucifixion he, along with Joseph of Arimathea, claimed the body of Christ and prepared it for burial (John 19:38–39).

Yet if Nicodemus said any more in this conversation with the Lord, John does not record it. The silence is understandable. Jesus' challenge of his aptitude as a spiritual teacher was a devastating putdown. The Lord's use of the definite article ("the teacher of Israel") indicates that Nicodemus had a reputation as the preeminent teacher in all of Israel. Christ's rebuke, however, insinuated that he really understood very little of the truth of the Scriptures. This must have been a painful jab at his ego.

Jesus' challenge also made an important doctrinal point. The clear implication is that the Old Testament plainly taught the way of salvation (cf. 2 Tim. 3:15). Jesus was not announcing a new way of salvation distinct from Old Testament redemption (cf. Matt. 5:17). This is to say that salvation under the dispensation of grace is no different from salvation under the law. There is perfect unity in God's Word, and the way of salvation revealed in the Old Testament was the same as salvation after Christ's work on the cross. Salvation was never a reward for human works; it has always been a gift of grace for repentant sinners, made possible by the work of Christ.

The experience of conversion—a new birth, involving the washing of regeneration and renewing of the Holy Spirit—has been the plan of God from the beginning. Even in the Old Testament, salvation was not a payoff for those who observed the law; it was a gift to those who humbly and by faith sought redemption from their sin. Yet it always meant a new start, a rebirth, a turning from sin to God. Nicodemus, as a teacher of the law, should have understood that. He should have been familiar with the words of the Lord recorded by Isaiah:

> "Wash yourselves, make yourselves clean;
> Remove the evil of your deeds from My sight.
> Cease to do evil,
> Learn to do good. . . .
> Come now, and let us reason together,"
> Says the LORD,
> "Though your sins are as scarlet,
> They will be as white as snow;
> Though they are red like crimson,
> They will be like wool." (Isa. 1:16–18)

The central theme of the Old Testament is redemption by grace. But incredibly, the Pharisees entirely missed it. In their rigid emphasis on religious works, they deemphasized the truth of God's grace and forgiveness to sinners, evident throughout the Old Testament. They stressed obedience to law, not conversion to the Lord, as the way to gain eternal life. They were so busy trying to earn righteousness that they neglected the marvelous truth of Habakkuk

2:4: "The righteous will live by his faith." They looked to Abraham as their father, but overlooked the key lesson of his life: "He believed in the Lord; and [the Lord] reckoned it to him as righteousness" (Gen. 15:6). They scoured the psalms for laws they could add to their list, but they ignored the most sublime truth of all—that God forgives sins, covers transgressions, and refuses to impute iniquity to sinners who turn to him (Ps. 32:1–2). They anticipated the coming of their Messiah but closed their eyes to the fact that he would come to die as a sacrifice for sin (Isa. 53:4–9). They were confident that they were guides to the blind, lights to those in darkness, correctors of the foolish, and teachers of the immature (cf. Rom. 2:19–20), but they missed the most basic lesson of God's law: that they themselves were sinners in need of redemption.

People have always stumbled over the simplicity of salvation. That is why there are so many cults. Each one has a unique slant on the doctrine of salvation—and each one corrupts the simplicity of the gospel revealed in God's Word (cf. 2 Cor. 11:3) by espousing salvation by human works. Each one of the major cults claims to have a key that unlocks the secret of salvation, yet they are all alike in propagating self-righteous achievement as the way to God.

From start to finish, God's Word disproves them all, and in a wonderfully consistent way. Its message, woven through sixty-six books, written over a span of fifteen hundred years by more than forty different authors, is marvelously unified and congruous. The message is simply that God graciously saves repentant sinners who come to him in faith. There is no secret there, no mystery, no obscurity, and no complexity. If Nicodemus had truly understood God's Word, he would have known that much. And if he had sincerely embraced and believed the written Word, he would not have resisted or rejected the incarnate Word, who was standing before him, the embodiment of God's eternal way of truth (cf. John 5:39).

The Necessity of Regeneration

Despite his great ability as a teacher and his obsession with the details of the law, Nicodemus had fallen short. Jesus did not mask the truth or try to make it palatable. Nicodemus was nurturing a great sin he was not even aware of—the sin of unbelief. When Nicodemus said, "I don't understand," what he really meant was, "I don't believe." Unbelief always begets ignorance.

Verses 11–12 confirm that unbelief was the real issue. There Jesus says, "Truly, truly, I say to you, we speak that which we know, and bear witness of that which we have seen; and you do not receive our witness. If I told you earthly things and you do not believe, how shall you believe if I tell you heavenly things?" "You do not receive" and "you do not believe" mean the same thing. Nicodemus claimed that he did not understand. Jesus wanted him to know that faith comes before full understanding. As Paul wrote in 1 Corinthians 2:14, "A natural man does not accept the things of the Spirit of God; for they are foolishness to him, and he cannot understand them, because they are spiritually appraised." Spiritual truth does not register in the mind of one who does not believe; unbelief understands nothing.

What a blow this was to Nicodemus's self-righteousness! He had come to Jesus with a smug profession of faith: "We know that you have come from God as a teacher" (v. 2). In essence, Jesus responded, "No you don't. You don't understand Scripture. You don't know the basics about salvation. You don't even understand earthly things. What good would it do for Me to expound heavenly truth to you?"

Like most religious unbelievers, Nicodemus did not want to confess that he was a helpless sinner. Jesus knew the truth. Nicodemus thought of himself as a great spiritual leader. Jesus had reduced him to nothing.

"No one has ascended into heaven, but he who descended from heaven, even the Son of Man" (v. 13). With that statement of his divine origin, Jesus rebuked Nicodemus's shallow faith and destroyed his system of religion by works. No one can ascend to heaven; that is, no one can earn his or her way there. God has come down from heaven and spoken to us by his Son (Heb. 1:1–2). We could never climb to heaven and find the answers for ourselves. The only Person who has that kind of access to God is the One who descended from heaven. He is not just a teacher sent by God; he is in fact God in human flesh. We either accept what he says, or we are left with our sin.

This, then, is his message: "You must be born again" (v. 7). Regeneration is no option, but rather an absolute necessity. No one—not even the most religious Pharisee—is exempt from the divine call to a new birth. And thus we have the starting point of Jesus' gospel: that salvation is impossible apart from divinely wrought regeneration.

The Reality of Redemption

When Nicodemus offered no further response, Jesus lovingly and graciously explained to him the new birth in all its simplicity. Beginning in verse 14, Jesus introduced the details of the way of salvation. He chose an Old Testament illustration of salvation, as if to underscore his rebuke to Nicodemus for not understanding the truth of Scripture: "As Moses lifted up the serpent in the wilderness, even so must the Son of Man be lifted up; that whoever believes may in Him have eternal life" (vv. 14–15). Surely Nicodemus knew that story. Why hadn't he ever understood its truth?

Numbers 21 gives the full account of the serpent in the wilderness. The Israelites were wandering around, having left Egypt but having not yet entered the Promised Land. They had been complaining incessantly—grumbling about the food, muttering about Moses, and whining about how bad their condition was. Finally, when God had had enough, he sent a plague, in the form of hundreds of poisonous snakes. The snakes overran the camp, and the rebellious people were bitten. When they realized they were dying, they repented. They came to Moses, asking him to intercede on their behalf. God in his mercy forgave them and told Moses to construct a pole with a bronze serpent at the top. He was to erect it in the center of the camp. The Lord gave this promise: "Everyone who is bitten, when he looks at it, he shall live" (Num. 21:8). He did not prescribe a ritual or a chant. Just so, salvation does not happen by religious ceremony. That was true when the Israelites were in the wilderness; it was true for Nicodemus; it is true today.

Those who reject obedience to Christ as an element of saving faith claim that Jesus selected this illustration to show that faith is simply embracing the facts of the gospel. "In 'looking,'" one author writes, "there is no idea of committal of life, no thought of healing being deserved, no question concerning the subsequent life of the looker, no possibility of surrender to the object of vision."[3] Zane Hodges adds, "Could anything be more profoundly simple than that! Eternal life for one look of faith! Clearly here too we meet the unconditional gift which may be acquired by any who desires it. . . . The issue is simply faith in the divine offer."[4]

Is that the case? Certainly not. The issue is not faith in the offer, but faith in the One who was lifted up. A more careful study of Numbers 21 reveals that Jesus was not painting a picture of "simple" faith. He was showing Nicodemus the necessity of repentance. In fact, Jesus used this particular illustration precisely because it challenged Nicodemus's Pharisaism. Nicodemus knew the story of

[3]William LeGrange Hogan, "The Relationship of the Lordship of Christ to Salvation" (Th.M. thesis, Dallas Theological Seminary). Hogan has since rejected no-lordship doctrine, but this statement was cited with approval by Cocoris, *Lordship Salvation—Is It Biblical?* 13.

[4]Zane C. Hodges, *The Gospel Under Siege* (Dallas: Redención Viva, 1981), 17–18.

the bronze serpent well. As a leader of the Jewish nation, no doubt he identified with Moses. Jesus was showing him instead that he must identify with the sinning, rebellious Israelites.

Nicodemus knew well the helpless state of the Israelites for whom the bronze serpent was erected. They were sinful, defiant rebels against God. They had been judged, and they were dying. They came to Moses in absolute shame and utter repentance, saying, "We have sinned, because we have spoken against the Lord and you" (Num. 21:7). Undoubtedly many were already sick and dying, fast losing their strength. They were in no position to glance flippantly at the pole and then proceed with lives of rebellion. It is noteworthy that Moses records no further occurrence of the kind of rebellion that had brought about their judgment. They turned to God in desperation and with genuine repentance. Jesus was demanding that Nicodemus do the same.

The issue was sin. Jesus was challenging this great teacher of the law to acknowledge that he had been bitten by the great serpent, Satan, and to come to the Lord for salvation. The very concept would have been repugnant to a Pharisee. It cut at the core of his self-righteousness. Far from giving Nicodemus an illustration of the ease of belief, our Lord established a painful condition for Nicodemus's salvation: he must acknowledge his sinfulness and repent. He must be willing to include himself among the sinful, snake-bitten, repentant Israelites.

The illustration of the bronze serpent also pictured Jesus' death as the price for salvation. Just as Moses lifted up that serpent, so the Son of Man would be lifted up on a pole—the cross of crucifixion. The word "must" in verse 14 is significant; Christ had to die. "Without shedding of blood, there is no forgiveness" (Heb. 9:22). God's sacrificial system demanded a blood atonement, for "the wages of sin is death" (Rom. 6:23). Someone must die to pay the price of sin.

That truth leads into what is undoubtedly the most familiar and magnificent statement in all of Scripture: "For God so loved the world, that He gave His only begotten Son, that whoever believes in Him should not perish, but have eternal life" (John 3:16). What does it mean to believe in Christ? It means more than accepting and affirming the truth of who he is—God in human flesh—and believing what he says. Real faith has at its heart a willingness to obey. There is no way to eliminate that truth from this passage. Jesus does not allow for "faith" that gives lip service to the truth and then goes ahead in sin. Look at verses 20–21: "Everyone who does evil hates the light, and does not come to the light, lest his deeds should be exposed. But he who practices the truth comes to the light, that his deeds may be manifested as having been wrought in God."

Verse 36 goes even further, equating disobedience with unbelief: "He who believes in the Son has eternal life; but he who does not obey the Son shall not see life, but the wrath of God abides on him." Thus the test of true faith is this: Does it produce obedience? If not, it is not saving faith. Disobedience is unbelief. Real faith obeys.

John 3:17 is another rebuke to the religious system Nicodemus represented. The Pharisees were looking for a Messiah who would come to destroy the Gentiles and set up a utopia for the Jews. But Jesus said, "God did not send His Son into the world to judge the world, but that the world should be saved through Him." Those who thought the coming of the Messiah meant glory for Israel and destruction for everybody else were going to be disappointed. He came to bring salvation not just to Israel but to the whole world. That is the reality of redemption. It is offered not just to Pharisees, not just to the Jews, but to "whoever believes in Him" (v. 16).

Jesus made this wonderful promise to sinners: "He who believes in Him is not judged" (v. 18). He balanced it with a chilling warning to the Pharisees and all others who reject Christ: "He who does not believe has been judged already, because he has not believed in the name of the only begotten Son of God." Condemnation for unbelievers is not relegated to the future. What will be consummated in the final judgment has already begun. "And this is the judgment, that the light is come into the world, and men loved the darkness rather than the light; for their deeds were evil" (v. 19). Having hated and rejected the light, those whose deeds are evil consign themselves to eternal darkness.

Thus our Lord introduced his gospel. Note how exclusive it is; Jesus is the only source of salvation. Those who do not believe in his name are condemned, excluded from eternal life. No matter how sincere, how religious, how immersed in good works, everyone must be born again. There is no promise of life—only a guarantee of condemnation—for those who will not identify with the sinful, dying Israelites and turn from sin in obedient faith to the One who was lifted up so that they would not have to perish.

II Cor 12:20+21 Paul fears returning to the church & finding 'believers' still living as pagans. Untaught, rebellious or not receiving the teaching. It is possible!

3

He Demands True Worship

The message of Christ rebukes both the self-righteousness of a Pharisee and the sultry lifestyle of a wanton adulterer. Christ's ministry in John 3 and 4 covered both ends of the moral spectrum.

John 4 contains one of the most familiar and beautiful conversations in all Scripture. Here our Lord offers salvation to an outcast woman as if he were handing her a drink of water. But do not mistake his straightforward offer for a shallow message.

Those who oppose lordship salvation often point to this account as proof that salvation is a gift apart from any demand for commitment of the sinner's life.[1] But we dare not base our theology of salvation only on information gleaned from this account—or worse, label crucial elements of the gospel as nonessential because they are omitted in John 4. Remember first of all that Jesus, knowing the woman's heart, understood exactly what message she needed to hear to be brought to faith. He made no mention of sin's wages, repentance, faith, atonement, his death for sin, or his resurrection. Are we to conclude

[1]Cf. Zane C. Hodges, *The Hungry Inherit* (Portland: Multnomah, 1980). Hodges sees great significance in the fact that "Jesus . . . said nothing to [the Samaritan woman] about the repair of her life which, plainly, was so urgently needed" (p. 25). That dismisses the obvious truths that Jesus' words to her did confront her with the reality of her sin (John 4:7–19), that he challenged her to worship God in Spirit and in truth (vv. 23–24), and that the apparent response of her heart was repentance (v. 29). Hodges concludes rather that "He had said nothing to her of her obligations to God's will for a very simple reason: He was there to offer her a gift" (ibid.). "She could not have comprehended the dazzling splendor of that gift, its sublime and total freeness, had He encumbered His offer with a call to reform her life (p. 26). Hodges views this passage as the key to understanding the gospel, and thus refers to it frequently to support his view that the gospel makes no moral demands on the life of a sinner.

54

that those are not indispensable elements of the gospel message? Certainly not.

The woman was uniquely prepared by the Holy Spirit for this moment. There is no use speculating about how much spiritual truth she had acquired prior to this exchange. Unlike Nicodemus, she was no theologian, but her heart was ready to acknowledge her sin and embrace Christ. His message to her was meant to draw her to himself, not to provide a comprehensive gospel outline intended to be normative for every episode of personal evangelism. We must learn from our Lord's methods, but we cannot isolate this passage and try to draft a model for a universal gospel presentation from it.

All we know about the woman's background is that her life was a tangle of adulteries and broken marriages. In her society, that would have made her a spurned outcast with no more social status than a common prostitute. She seemed anything but a prime target for conversion. To call her to himself, Jesus had to force her to face her indifference, lust, self-centeredness, immorality, and religious prejudice.

The woman makes a vivid contrast to Nicodemus. They were virtual opposites. Nicodemus was a Jew; she was a Samaritan. He was a man; she was a woman. He was a religious leader; she was an adulteress. He was learned; she was ignorant. He was a member of the highest class; she was of the lowest—lower even than an outcast of Israel, for she was a Samaritan outcast. He was wealthy; she was poor. He recognized Jesus as a teacher from God; she did not have a clue who he was. The two of them could hardly have been more dissimilar.

But it was the same powerful and omniscient Christ who revealed himself to her. Take note; this is not primarily the tale of a Samaritan woman. Rather this is the account of Jesus' self-revelation as Messiah. Of all occasions for Jesus to disclose who he was, he chose to tell this unknown woman of Samaria first. We might wonder why he did not go to downtown Jerusalem, walk into the temple, and there announce to the assembled leaders that he was the Messiah. Why would he reveal it first to an obscure, adulterous woman?

Certainly he intended to demonstrate that the gospel was for the whole world, not just the Hebrew race, and that his ministry was to poor outcasts as well as the religious elite. It was a rebuke to the Jewish leaders that their Messiah ignored them and disclosed himself to a Samaritan adulteress. When he finally did unveil the truth to Israel's leaders, they did not believe it anyway.

We are told only the barest essentials of the Lord's conversation with the woman. Scripture reveals nothing specific about her thoughts or emotions. We are given no insight into how much she understood—or if she understood at all—about the Lord's offer to give her living water. It is not clear when she realized he was actually speaking about spiritual life. The only insight we have into the response of her heart is what we infer from her words and actions.

In fact, although we assume she embraced Christ as Messiah and became a believer, even that is not explicitly stated in the text. We make that judgment on the basis of her behavior—specifically the fact that she ran to tell others about him, and they believed.

So we must be careful to realize that this passage in and of itself is not an appropriate foundation upon which to base an understanding of what constitutes the gospel. Unlike us, Jesus knew the woman's heart. As he spoke to her, he could judge her response and know exactly how much she understood and believed. He was able to bear down on precisely the truth she needed to hear; he used no canned presentation or four-point outline of gospel facts.

Nevertheless, Jesus' discourse with the Samaritan woman establishes some clear guidelines for personal evangelism. As the master evangelist seeks to win her, he expertly directs the conversation, taking her from a simple comment about drinking water to a revelation that he was the Messiah. Along the way, he skillfully avoids her attempts to control the conversation, change the subject, and ask irrelevant questions. Five lessons in particular stand out as critical truths to be emphasized in presenting the way of salvation.

The Lesson of the Well:
Christ Came to Seek and Save the Lost

Notice the events that led to this encounter. Jesus had left Judea and was on his way to Galilee (John 4:3). Verse 1 tells us that the word was out about his success. Masses of people were flocking to see him. That created a severe problem. The Jewish leaders hated John the Baptist because he taught the truth and thus condemned them, so you can imagine what they thought of Jesus Christ. The more people came to see Jesus, the more uncomfortable the religious leaders grew. In fact, from this point on in the ministry of Christ, his running battle with the Pharisees is a constant theme. It finally culminated in their putting him to death.

Jesus left Judea, not because he was afraid of the Pharisees, but because it was not God's time for a confrontation. He also had a positive reason for leaving: "He had to pass through Samaria" (v.4). This was not a geographical necessity. In fact, traveling through Samaria was not normal for a Jew. The Samaritans were so offensive to them that they wanted nothing less than to set foot in Samaria. Although the most direct route went straight through Samaria, the Jews never went that way. They had their own trail, which went to the north of Judea, east of the Jordan, then back into Galilee. Jesus could have followed that well-traveled route from Judea to Galilee.

But by journeying instead through Samaria, our Lord was displaying his love for sinners. The Samaritans were hybrid Jews who had married into the surrounding nations when Israel was taken into captivity in 722 B.C. (cf. 2 Kings 17:23–25). They rejected Jerusalem as the center of worship and built their own temple on Mount Gerizim in Samaria. Their intermarriage and idolatry were crimes so gross that orthodox Jewish people ordinarily had no dealings with them (v. 9). Samaria had essentially become a separate nation, viewed by the Jews as more abhorrent than the Gentiles. This hatred and bitterness between the Jews and the Samaritans had gone on for centuries. Merely by traveling through Samaria, our Lord was shattering age-old barriers.

The reason he *had* to go that way was to fulfill a divine appointment at Jacob's well. He had come to seek and to save the lost (Luke 19:10), and even if it meant a serious breach of cultural protocol, he would be there when the time was right. And his timing was critical. Had he arrived at that well ten minutes early or late, there may have been no woman. But his schedule was perfect; he wrote the script himself even before the foundation of the world.

Christ arrived at the appointed place, a plot of ground Jacob had purchased and given to Joseph. John 4:6 says, "Jesus therefore, being wearied from his journey, was sitting thus by the well. It was about the sixth hour." Here we get a glimpse of the humanity of Christ. Because he was a man in every sense, he was weary. The writer of Hebrews says he was touched with the feelings of our infirmities (Heb. 4:15).

John probably used the Roman system of marking time. Roman time began at noon, so the sixth hour would be six o'clock. The people in Sychar would be finished with their work, and the women would be doing the daily chore of drawing water. Our Lord had reached the end of a long, hot journey under the sun, and he was tired and thirsty. He was at the appointed place, in God's timing, determined to do God's will. He was there to seek and to save a single pathetic, wretched woman.

The Lesson of the Woman:
God Is No Respecter of Persons

"There came a woman of Samaria to draw water" (v. 7). This woman was a moral outcast, ostracized from society. Imagine her shock when Jesus, who did not have a utensil to draw water with, said to her, "Give Me a drink" (v. 7). She was surely startled. Not only was she used to being shunned by everyone, but in that culture, men did not speak publicly with women—even their wives. Furthermore, Jesus had shattered the racial barrier. She was startled that Jesus had spoken to her and even more shocked that he would ask for a drink from her "unclean" vessel. She asked, "How is it that You, being a Jew, ask me for a drink since I am a Samaritan woman?" (v. 9).

God is no respecter of persons (Acts 10:34), and Jesus was not ashamed to take a drink from the vessel of a woman for whom he had come to die. Nobody—not this woman, not a Pharisee like Nicodemus, not even the most loathsome leper—was beyond the reach of his divine love.

The Lesson of the Water: Everyone Who Thirsts May Come

"Jesus answered and said to her, 'If you knew the gift of God, and who it is who says to you, "Give Me a drink," you would have asked Him, and He would have given you living water'" (v. 10). Suddenly he turned the situation around. At first he was thirsty and she had the water. Now he was speaking to her as if she were the thirsty one and he had the water. Instead of asking for a drink, he declared that she needed a drink from his fountain. The issue was no longer his physical thirst, but her spiritual need. Though she apparently did not understand yet, he was offering living water for her dry soul.

As we have seen, those who hold the view that saving faith is unrelated to obedience or commitment often point to this account as proof that no surrender to divine authority is required. One author goes so far as to say:

> The synonyms for "faith" in the New Testament cannot mean "commit." For example, in John 4:14 Jesus said, "But whosoever drinketh of the water that I shall give him shall never thirst." Later, Jesus said, "Whoso eateth my flesh and drinketh my blood, hath eternal life." (John 6:54). Obviously, these statements suggest 'appropriation,' not commitment."[2]

Can we concede that the verb *drink* conveys the idea of appropriation apart from commitment? Certainly not. Matthew 20:22 ("Are you able to drink the cup that I am about to drink?") and John 18:11 ("The

[2]G. Michael Cocoris, *Lordship Salvation—Is It Biblical?* (Dallas: Redención Viva, 1983), 12–13.

cup which the Father has given Me, shall I not drink it?") both use *drink* in a way that clearly implies full compliance and surrender. Furthermore, to attempt to define faith with a metaphor is unwarranted selectivity. What do we then do with verses such as John 3:36 ("He who does not obey the Son shall not see life"), and Hebrews 3:18–19 ("Those who were disobedient . . . were not able to enter because of unbelief"), which clearly equate disobedience with unbelief?

The fact that Jesus offered this woman living water does not in any way minimize the factor of commitment ever present in true faith. The living water he held out to her was the gift of salvation, including all that is inherent in the reality of redemption—freedom from sin, the commitment to follow Jesus, the ability to obey God's law, and the power and desire to live a life that glorifies him.

Unfortunately, she still seemed to be thinking in terms of literal water. "She said to Him, 'Sir, You have nothing to draw with and the well is deep; where then do You get that living water? You are not greater than our father Jacob, are You, who gave us the well, and drank of it himself, and his sons, and his cattle?' " (vv. 11–12).

If only she knew—he was *incomparably* greater than Jacob and his water was *infinitely* better than Jacob's water. He tried to explain more about the unique properties of his living water: "Jesus answered and said to her, 'Everyone who drinks of this water shall thirst again; but whoever drinks of the water that I shall give him shall never thirst; but the water that I shall give him shall become in him a well of water springing up to eternal life' " (vv. 13–14). This was water to quench a parched soul.

Her response was immediate: "Sir, give me this water, so I will not be thirsty, nor come all the way here to draw" (v. 15). Apparently she still was somewhat confused about whether he meant literal water or something spiritual. Either way, she wanted this living water!

One writer says of this exchange:

It is hard not to be impressed with the magnificent simplicity of the transaction which Jesus proposes to this sin-laden Samaritan woman. Its very lack of complication is part of its grandeur. It is all a matter of giving and receiving and no other conditions are attached. . . . There is no effort to extract from the woman a promise to correct her immoral life. If she wants this water, she can have it. It is free! . . . It must be emphasized that there is no call here for surrender, submission, acknowledgement of Christ's Lordship, or anything else of this kind. A gift is being offered to one totally unworthy of God's favor. And to get it, the woman is required to make no spiritual commitment whatsoever. She is merely invited to ask.[3]

But that interpretation misses the point entirely. At this juncture, even though she did ask for it, Jesus did not simply give her the water of life. She asked for it and presumably would have accepted it had he given it outright. But Jesus was not looking for a cheap pseudoconversion. He knew she was not yet ready for living water. There were two issues that needed to be addressed first: Her sin and his true identity.

Jesus never sanctioned any form of cheap grace. He was not offering eternal life as an add-on to a life cluttered with unconfessed sin. It is inconceivable that he would pour someone a drink of living water without challenging and altering that individual's sinful lifestyle. He came to save his people *from their sin* (cf. Matt. 1:21), not to confer immortality on people in bondage to wickedness (cf. Gen. 3:22–24).

The Lord went right to the heart of the issue—by letting her know she could not cloak her sin: "Go, call your husband, and come here" (v. 16). It was a loaded remark. G. Campbell Morgan, commenting on this passage, writes, "How did He reply? 'Go, call thy husband.' Why that? If she was to have that well of water springing up in her, there must first be moral investigation and correction."[4] Willingness to confess the reality and odiousness of one's sin is an essential manifestation of genuine spiritual thirst. But the web of this woman's adulteries was so complex and her sin so great that she did not even try to explain. "I have no husband" (v. 17) was all she replied.

Jesus knew the full truth anyway: "You have well said, 'I have no husband'; for you have had five husbands; and the one whom you now have is not your husband; this you have said truly" (vv. 17–18). Imagine the woman's shame when she realized he knew all about her sin! Certainly she would have preferred to keep it hidden. She had not lied to him, but she had not told the whole truth, either. It is as if

---

[3]Zane C. Hodges, *The Gospel Under Siege* (Dallas: Redención Viva, 1981), 14. Hodges adds this comment: "It is precisely this impressive fact [that the Lord asks for no spiritual commitment] that distinguishes the true Gospel from all its counterfeits." But again, it is a mistake to presume that the words of Jesus recorded in this passage represent a model gospel presentation. Nothing in Jesus' message to this woman even hints at the truths of his death, burial, or resurrection. He does not mention the idea of substitutionary atonement or even of faith itself. No one—including Hodges, I presume—would argue that the gospel excludes all those truths.

[4]G. Campbell Morgan, *The Gospel According to John* (Old Tappan, N.J.: Revell, 1931), 75.

Jesus said, "All right, if you're not going to confess your own sin, I'm going to confront you by telling you what it is."

Then the woman did confess her sin. By saying, "Sir, I perceive that You are a prophet" (v. 19), she was, in effect, saying, "You are right. That's me. That's my sinful life. What you said about me is true."

Here she must have realized that whoever this Person was, he knew all the details of her sinful life. He had peeled back the camouflage on all of it. And yet, even with full knowledge of her depravity, he was offering her the water of life! If she had known the Scriptures well, Isaiah 55:1 might have come to mind: "Ho! Every one who thirsts, come to the waters." The offer of living water is not just to religious people like Nicodemus—everyone who thirsts is invited to drink deeply of the living water—even an adulterous woman whose life is fraught with sin.

Isaiah adds a charge to sinners, along with a wonderful promise that would have gladdened the Samaritan woman's heart:

> Let the wicked forsake his way,
> And the unrighteous man his thoughts;
> And let him return to the Lord,
> And He will have compassion on him;
> And to our God, for *He will abundantly pardon.*
>
> Isaiah 55:7 (emphasis added)

The Lesson of True Worship: Now Is the Acceptable Time

Having recognized Jesus as more than a mere traveling man, the woman asked the first spiritual question that came to mind: "Our fathers worshiped in this mountain; and you people say that in Jerusalem is the place where men ought to worship" (John 4:20). Since he was a genuine prophet, he ought to know which group was right!

Jesus' response, like his answer to Nicodemus, cut through the woman's misplaced interest and confronted her with her real need—forgiveness. "Woman, believe Me," He told her, "an hour is coming when neither in this mountain, nor at Jerusalem shall you worship the Father" (v. 21). Then, almost incidentally, he told her that the Jews were right and the Samaritans were wrong: "You worship that which you do not know; we worship that which we know; for salvation is from the Jews" (v. 22). If only she had known it, the Jew she was speaking to was the One who came to bring salvation!

The *where* of worship is not really the issue; it is *who, when,* and *how* that really count. Jesus said, "An hour is coming, and now is, when the true worshipers shall worship the Father in spirit and truth; for such people the Father seeks to be his worshipers. God is spirit; and those who worship him must worship in spirit and truth" (vv. 23–24). True worship occurs not on a mountain or in a temple, but in the inner person.

The phrase "an hour is coming and now is" gave Jesus words' a sense of urgency and personal meaning to this woman. It was as if he were saying, "You don't have to go up to the mountain or down to Jerusalem to worship. You can worship here and now." Having brought her to the threshold of eternal life, he was affirming the urgency of salvation that Paul spoke of: "Behold, now is 'the acceptable time,' behold now is 'the day of salvation'" (2 Cor. 6:2). The Messiah was present, the day of salvation had arrived, and this was not only Messiah's time but her time too.

It is significant that Jesus used the expression "true worshipers" to refer to the body of redeemed people. All who are saved are true worshipers. There is no possibility of being saved and yet not worshiping God in Spirit and truth. God's objective in salvation is to create a true worshiper[5] (cf. Phil. 3:3). Our Lord had come into the world to seek and to save the lost. He revealed to a Samaritan woman that his objective in seeking and redeeming sinners is to fulfill God's will in making them true worshipers. Then he invited her to become one.

When Jesus said the Father was seeking true worshipers, it was more than a statement of fact. It was a personal invitation to the Samaritan woman. Do not miss the importance of that invitation. It debunks the notion that Jesus was offering eternal life without making any demand for a spiritual commitment. The Lord of glory does not say "come to the waters" apart from the command, "let the wicked forsake his way" (cf. Isa. 55:1, 7). The call to worship the Father in spirit and in truth was a clear summons to the deepest and most comprehensive kind of spiritual submission.

But the woman was still confused, and one can hardly blame her. She had come to the well to get a simple pot of water, and in a brief conversation, her sin had been exposed and she was challenged to become a true worshiper of the living God. Her heart longed for someone who could take her tangled thoughts and emotions and make some sense out of everything. So she told Jesus, "I know that

[5]For a detailed presentation on true worship, see John F. MacArthur, *The Ultimate Priority* (Chicago: Moody Press, 1983).

Messiah is coming . . . ; when that One comes, He will declare all things to us" (John 4:25).

Jesus' reply must have shaken her to the core of her being: "I who speak to you am He" (v. 26). What a dynamic confrontation! This Man who had asked her for a simple cup of water was now standing there, claiming to be the true Messiah, holding forth living water and promising to forgive her sin and transform her into a true worshiper of the living God!

Although the text does not specifically tell us that the Samaritan woman became a believer, it seems obvious that she did. I believe she embraced him as Messiah and Savior, somewhere in the white space between verses 26 and 27. The hour of salvation had come for her. She would willingly become a true worshiper. She would drink of the Water of Life. The irresistible grace of the Messiah had penetrated her heart. Step by step he had opened her sinful heart and disclosed himself to her, and apparently she responded with saving faith.

The Lesson of the Witness: This Man Receives Sinners

The disciples had been in the village buying food, and John tells us they returned "at this point" (v. 27). The Greek expression means "precisely at this moment." Apparently they came back just when the Lord said, "I who speak to you am He." Had they arrived any later, they would not have heard Jesus' declaration of his Messiahship. It must have shocked them to hear him telling this outcast Samaritan woman that he was the Messiah, since he had never previously told anyone that. John says "they marveled that He had been speaking with a woman; yet no one said, 'What do You seek?' or, 'Why do You speak with her?'" (v. 27).

The woman's actions at this point strongly indicate that she had become a believer. She "left her waterpot, and went into the city, and said to the men, 'Come, see a man who told me all the things that I have done; this is not the Christ, is it?'" (vv. 28–30). She evidenced all the characteristics of genuine conversion. She had sensed her need, confessed her guilt, and recognized Jesus as Messiah, and now she was showing the fruit of her transformed life by bringing other people to him.

It is significant that the Samaritan woman's first impulse as a new believer was to go and tell others about Christ. The desire to proclaim one's faith is a common experience of new believers. In fact, some of the most zealous witnesses for Christ are brand-new believers. That is because their minds are fresh with the memory of the weight of their guilt and the exhilaration of being loosed from it. That was the case with this woman. The first thing she declared to the men of the town was that Jesus had told her everything she ever did. He had held her sin up to the light and compelled her to face who she really was. Then he had released her from the shame. That she talked so freely about it shows she had been liberated from the bondage of her guilt.

Jesus had given the woman a drink of the Water of Life, and she had begun to worship God in spirit and truth. She did not need to conceal her guilt anymore; she was forgiven.

The way the woman phrased her question seems to imply a negative answer: "This is not the Christ, is it?" But it was not an expression of doubt. If she had come into town and said, "Men, I've found the Messiah," the men would have either ignored her or laughed her out of town. She, an outcast adulteress, was not the most qualified person in town to identify the Messiah. Besides, women did not tell men anything in that society. So she put it in the form of a question—really a discreet challenge to them. That way they would meet him with an open mind. She knew Christ would do the rest.

The woman's testimony had a profound impact on the village. Scripture tells us, "From that city many of the Samaritans believed in him because of the word of the woman who testified, 'He told me all the things that I have done'" (v. 39). It was the news of how he had uncovered her sin that made such a deep impression. Others, too, responded to Jesus with zeal (vv. 40–42).

The reason for such a zealous reaction was that the people were Samaritans. In a sense, they all were in the same boat as the woman. They knew the Messiah was coming to set things right, and most of them probably anticipated his coming with fear. Their perspective was just the opposite of the Pharisees. The Jewish leaders were looking for a conquering victor who would take up their cause and destroy their enemies. The Samaritans had no such expectation. If the Jews were right, they would be the targets of Messiah's wrath.

So when this woman came and announced to the people of Sychar that One claiming to be the Messiah had dealt mercifully with her although he knew all her sin, their hearts embraced him enthusiastically.

Contrast their reaction with that of the Pharisees, described in Luke 15:2: "Both the Pharisees and the scribes began to grumble, saying, 'This man receives sinners.'" In essence, that is precisely what the Samaritan woman told the men of Sychar: "He is the Messiah, but He receives sinners!" What was repugnant to the scribes and Pharisees was good news to these Samaritans, because they were willing to admit they were sinners.

It was Jesus himself who said, "I did not come to call the righteous, but sinners" (Matt. 9:13). Those who refused to acknowledge their sin found him to be a Judge, not a Savior. He never gave such people any encouragement, any comfort, or any reason to hope. The water of life he held forth was given only to those who acknowledged the hopelessness of their sinful state.

God seeks people who will submit themselves to worship him in spirit and in truth. That kind of worship is impossible for those sheltering sin in their lives. Those who confess and forsake their sin, on the other hand, will find a Savior eager to receive them, forgive them, and liberate them from their sin. Like the woman at the well, they will find a source of living water that will quench forever even the strongest spiritual thirst.

The final chapter of the Bible closes with this invitation, which evokes a picture of the Samaritan woman: "Let the one who is thirsty come; let the one who wishes take the water of life without cost" (Rev. 22:17). While it is free, it is not cheap; the Savior himself paid the ultimate price so that thirsty, repentant seekers can drink as deeply as they like.

4

He Receives Sinners,
But Refuses the Righteous

One of the most malignant by-products of the debacle in contemporary evangelism is a gospel that fails to confront individuals with the reality of their sin. Even the most conservative churches are teeming with people who, claiming to be born again, live like pagans. Contemporary Christians have been conditioned never to question anyone's profession of faith. Multitudes declare that they trust Christ as Savior while indulging in lifestyles that are plainly inconsistent with God's Word—yet no one dares to challenge their testimony.

I once spent time with a fellow minister who drove me through his city. We passed a large liquor store, and I happened to mention that it was an unusual-looking place.

"Yes," he said. "There is a whole chain of those stores around the city, all owned by one man. He is a member of my Sunday school class."

I wondered aloud how such a thing could be, and the minister replied, "Oh, he's quite faithful. He is in class every week."

"Does it bother him that he owns all those liquor stores?" I asked.

"We've talked about it some," he said. "But he feels people are going to buy liquor anyway, so why not buy it from him?"

I asked, "What is his life like?"

"Well, he did leave his wife and is living with a young girl," the minister replied. Then after several minutes of my bewildered and uncomfortable silence, he added, "You know, sometimes it's hard for me to understand how a Christian can live like that."

I must confess that it is hard for me to understand how someone who teaches the Bible can assume that a man living in wanton rebellion against God's standards is a Christian merely because he claims to be—even if he attends Sunday school every week.

Coming to Grips with Sin

The contemporary church has the idea that salvation is only the granting of eternal life, not necessarily the liberation of a sinner from the bondage of his iniquity. We tell people that God loves them and has a wonderful plan for their lives, but that is only half the truth. God also hates sin and will punish unrepentant sinners with eternal torment. No gospel presentation is complete if it avoids or conceals those facts. Any message that fails to define and confront the severity of personal sin is a deficient gospel. And any "salvation" that does not alter a lifestyle of sin and transform the heart of the sinner is not the salvation that God's Word speaks of.

Sin is no peripheral issue as far as salvation is concerned; it is the issue. In fact, the distinctive element of the Christian message is the power of Jesus Christ to forgive and conquer our sin. Of all the realities of the gospel, none is more wonderful than the news that the enslaving grasp of sin has been broken. This truth is the heart and the very lifeblood of the Christian message. No message that excludes it can purport to be the gospel according to Jesus.

It is absurd to suggest that a person can encounter the holy God of Scripture and be saved without also coming to grips with the heinousness of sin and consequently longing to turn from it. In the Bible, those who met God were invariably confronted with an overwhelming sense of their own sinfulness. Peter, seeing Jesus for who he was, said, "Depart from me, for I am a sinful man, O Lord!" (Luke 5:8). Paul wrote, "It is a trustworthy statement, deserving full acceptance, that Christ Jesus came into the world to save sinners, among whom I am foremost of all" (1 Tim. 1:15). Job, whom God himself identified as a righteous man (Job 1:1, 8), said after seeing God face to face, "I abhor myself, and repent in dust and ashes" (Job 42:6 KJV). Isaiah, seeing God, gasped, "Woe is me, for I am ruined! Because I am a man of unclean lips, and I live among a people of unclean lips; for my eyes have seen the King, the Lord of hosts" (Isa. 6:5).

There are many other examples of men and women in Scripture who, having seen God, feared for their own lives—always because they were smitten with the weight of their own sin. It is appropriate, then, that when Matthew relates his own conversion experience, the central truth that emerges is Christ's mercy to sinners.

Matthew 9:9–13 describes the incident, along with the controversy that ensued. In one of the most important statements ever recorded in the Bible, the Lord says, "I did not come to call the righteous, but sinners" (v. 13). This statement contains a full perspective on Jesus' ministry, a summary of the message of Christianity, a close-up of the nucleus of the gospel, and the basic rationale behind the Incarnation.

Why did Jesus come into the world? To call sinners—those who know they have a terminal disease, those who are hopeless and desperate, those who are hurting, those who are hungry and thirsty, those who are weak and weary, those who are broken, those whose lives are shattered—sinners who know they are unworthy yet long to be forgiven.

Jesus' words were aimed at the self-righteous Pharisees, who, like many today, thought they were righteous and without any real spiritual need. The truth is that unless people realize they have a sin problem, they will not come to Christ for a solution. People do not come for healing unless they know they have a disease; they do not come for life unless they are conscious that they are under the penalty of death; they do not come for salvation unless they are weary of the bondage of sin.

Thus Jesus came to expose us all as sinners. That is why his message was so penetrating, so forceful. It tore our self-righteousness away and exposed our evil hearts, so that we might see ourselves as sinners.

Receiving Sinners

Throughout his gospel, Matthew argues that Christ is the Messiah of Israel. In chapters 8 and 9 he describes a series of Jesus' miracles categorically selected to show the range of the Messiah's credentials. He lists nine miracles, showing Jesus' power over sickness (8:1–17), over nature (8:23–27) over demons (8:28–34), over death (9:18–26), over blindness (9:27–31), and over a silent tongue (9:32–34).

Matthew's conversion itself falls in among those miracles, right after a spectacular miracle designed to demonstrate Jesus' power over sin (9:1–8). Christ had just forgiven a paralyzed man's sins, and in a monumental display of his divine authority, confirmed his deity before the Pharisees by commanding the disabled man to take up his bed and walk. Following immediately on the heels of that narrative, verse 9 describes the call and salvation of Matthew: "As Jesus passed on from there, He saw a man, called Matthew, sitting in the tax office; and He said to him, 'Follow Me!' And he rose, and followed Him."

By this account, which is consistent with Mark's and Luke's versions, Jesus spoke only two words to him: "Follow Me!" And Matthew obeyed. Luke 5:28 adds this significant statement: "And he left everything behind." He forsook all to follow Christ. Matthew was too humble to say that about himself, but Luke did—and it speaks volumes about the nature of Matthew's conversion. He paid a great price, perhaps a higher price than any of the other disciples. A fisherman who followed Jesus could always go back to fishing, but a tax collector who left his station was finished, because the next day Rome would have someone else to take his place. Yet Matthew forsook everything immediately. He did not say, "Well, I'm coming Lord—but, hey, I could finance this whole operation if You'd just let me grab these bags!" He turned his back on it all, forsaking everything he had.

Matthew was a major sinner, and everyone knew it. By the standards of his day, he was unequivocally the vilest, most wretched sinner in Capernaum. He was a publican, a willing tool of the Roman government, employed in the odious task of squeezing tax money out of his own people. Publicans would buy franchises from Rome. That gave them the right to collect taxes in a certain town or district. By buying into the Roman system, Matthew had revealed himself as a traitor to Israel. Nothing in the mind of the Jewish people was more offensive. He had hired on to the conquering pagans who oppressed his own people and in doing so established his reputation as the worst kind of turncoat, heretic, and renegade.

Rome required each publican to collect a certain amount of taxes. Anything they acquired over that they could keep. The Roman government, in order to keep their tax collectors happy and productive, supported them in the wildest excesses and abuses. They virtually had a free hand to overcharge people and extort whatever they could from their countrymen. A shrewd publican could amass a huge fortune in very little time—all at the expense of his own oppressed people. Understandably, publicans were regarded with the utmost contempt by all Israel.

Publicans were so despised by the Jews that they were barred from the synagogues. They were regarded as unclean beasts, treated like swine. They could not be witnesses in any court of law because they were not to be trusted. They were known as flagrant liars, classified with robbers and murderers.

Most Jews believed it was wrong to pay taxes to Rome. Looking backward to an Old Testament theocracy, they believed only God should receive their money. That is why the Pharisees tested Jesus, attempting to bring him into disfavor with the people by asking him whether it was right to pay taxes (Matt. 22:15–22).

Matthew had authority to collect taxes on almost everything. In addition to import and export taxes, he was free to assess bridge tolls, harbor fees, and road-use taxes. He could open every package coming along the road. He could even open private letters to see if business was being conducted. If so, he could also tax that.

His office was located at the confluence of two roads, probably right at the north port of the Sea of Galilee. That would have put him at a strategic point on the road from Damascus and the Orient, where he could tax everyone going east and west. He also could tax the area's highly productive fishing industry.

Note that Matthew was sitting at the tax table. Some publicans, concerned about their reputations, stayed out of the public eye byhiring others to collect taxes for them. But the really brash ones— the ones who did not care what people thought of them—actually sat at the table themselves, rather than pay someone else to do it. It was one thing to be a publican; it was worse to flaunt it. Rabbinical tradition said it was impossible for a man in Matthew's position to repent. You can imagine the gasps from the crowd when Jesus stopped before Matthew and said, "Follow Me."

Matthew must have been a man under conviction. Deep down in his heart he must have longed to be free from his life of sin, and that must have been why he virtually ran to join Christ. He would never have followed Jesus on a whim; he would have given up too much. He surely knew what he was getting into. Jesus had ministered publicly all over that area; everyone in the vicinity of Capernaum knew who he was and what he taught. They had seen his miracles, signs, and wonders. Matthew was familiar with Jesus' rigorous demands for discipleship (Matt. 8:18–22). He knew what he was being recruited for. He had counted the cost and was prepared to follow.

Eating with Tax-Gatherers and Sinners

Matthew decided to have a banquet to introduce Jesus to his friends. Like most new believers, he wanted to bring everyone he knew to Christ. Luke 5:29 reveals that Matthew (who was also known as Levi) held the banquet in his own house. Jesus was the honored guest. This gathering was attended by some of the most notorious, base, villainous people in the history of banquets. The only people Matthew knew were sordid types, wretched sinners, because no one else would associate with him. The respectable people despised him. His friends were thieves, blasphemers, prostitutes, con artists, swindlers, and other tax collectors—the riffraff of society.

Supercilious religious types would say, of course, that Jesus should not go to a banquet with such degenerates. That is exactly what the Pharisees thought. But that was not the way of the Savior. Matthew

11:19 indicates that he was known among the people as "a friend of tax-gatherers and sinners." This very banquet probably gave rise to that perception. The Pharisees meant it derisively, but it was nonetheless a fitting title for the Son of Man.

Matthew 9:10 sets the scene: "It happened that as He was reclining at the table in the house, behold, many tax-gatherers and sinners came and were dining with Jesus and His disciples." This was so scandalous to the self-righteous Pharisees that they could hardly conceal their shock. *If he were really the Messiah,* they thought, *he would be having a dinner for us!*

Apparently the Pharisees lingered outside until the banquet was over. Avoiding a head-on confrontation with Jesus, they cornered the disciples and asked, "Why is your Teacher eating with tax-gatherers and sinners?" (v. 11). Rather than an honest question, this was a veiled rebuke, a venting of their bitterness.

On overhearing their conversation Jesus had his own rebuke: "It is not those who are healthy who need a physician, but those who are sick. But go and learn what this means, 'I desire compassion, and not sacrifice,' for I did not come to call the righteous, but sinners" (vv. 12–13). Jesus' answer is a powerful threefold argument, first appealing to human experience, then arguing from Scripture, and finally resting on his own divine authority.

Jesus' appeal to experience compares sinners to sick people who need a doctor. The analogy is simple: a physician can be expected to visit the ill (or at least that was the case in Jesus' day), so a forgiver should be expected to visit people who sin. It came as a stinging rebuke to the hardheartedness of the Pharisees: "If you're so perceptive as to diagnose them as sinners, what are you going to do about it? Or are you doctors who give diagnoses but no cure?" Thus he exposed the Pharisees as pious critics who freely defined others as sinners but were utterly indifferent to their plight.

Jesus' argument from Scripture blasted the Pharisees' pride: "Go and learn" (v. 13). This phrase was used in the rabbinic writings to reprove students who were ignorant about something they should have known. It was like saying, "Go back through the books and come again when you've got the basic information." He quotes Hosea 6:6, "I delight in loyalty [Heb., *ḥésed,* 'lovingkindness'] rather than sacrifice." In other words, God is not concerned with ritual (ceremony) but with compassion, mercy, and lovingkindness (character). The Pharisees, good at ritual, had no love for sinners. God had instituted the sacrificial system and had ordered Israel to follow prescribed rituals, but that was pleasing to God only when it was the expression of a broken and contrite heart (Ps. 51:16–17). When the heart was not right, the ritual was an abomination. God is never pleased with forms of religion apart from personal righteousness.

The third argument, from Jesus' own authority, leveled the Pharisees: "I did not come to call the righteous, but sinners" (v. 13). Luke 5:32 adds the words "to repentance." Luke 18:9 describes the Pharisees as "certain ones who trusted in themselves that they were righteous, and viewed others with contempt." Here, in essence, Jesus is saying to them, "You say you're righteous, and I accept that as your self-evaluation. But if that's the case, I have nothing to say to you, for I have come to call sinners to repentance."

The Greek word translated "call" here is *kaleō*, a word often used for inviting a guest into one's home. Such an invitation is found in Matthew 22:1–14, a parable that fits perfectly with Jesus' words to these Pharisees. There, Jesus pictured his kingdom as a banquet. A king sent invitations calling all his friends to a wedding banquet for his son, but everyone who was invited refused to come. So the king told his servants to get anyone they could find and invite them. These pious, cold-hearted, self-righteous Pharisees were like those who refused to come to the banquet. They would not acknowledge their sin, so they could not respond to Jesus' call.

This is the theme of the gospel according to Jesus: He came to call sinners to repentance. The corollary is that until people have been brought to see that they are sinners, until they realize their thirst, until they feel the weight of sin and long to be rid of it, the Lord will not give them salvation.

Refusing the Righteous

God receives sinners. The flip side of that truth is that he refuses the righteous. Not that there are any truly righteous people, of course (Rom. 3:10). But those who think they are good enough—those who do not understand the seriousness of sin—cannot respond to the gospel. They cannot be saved, for the gospel is a call to sinners to repent and be forgiven. These are frightening words: "I did not come to call the righteous." The unmistakable message is that Christ's gracious call to salvation is not extended to those who view themselves as righteous.

The gospel according to Jesus is first of all a mandate for repentance. I mentioned that in relating this account of Matthew's conversion, Luke includes two words Matthew omitted: "I have not come to call the righteous but sinners *to repentance*" (Luke 5:32, emphasis added). From the beginning of Jesus' ministry, the heart of his message was a call to repentance. In fact, when our Lord first began to preach, the opening word of his message was *Repent* (Matt. 4:17). It was also the first word of John the Baptist's message (Matt. 3:2) and the basis of the gospel the apostles preached (Acts 3:19; 20:21; 26:20). No one who neglects to call sinners to repentance is preaching the gospel according to Jesus.

Now and then a preacher will smugly say that he does not preach on sin because it is too negative. A few years ago, a nationally known preacher sent me a book he had written in which he redefined sin as nothing more than a poor self-image. The way to reach people, he said, is to bolster their self-esteem, not to make them think of themselves as sinful. There is no gospel in a message like that! Rather than bringing people to salvation, it confirms them in the self-condemning vanity of their own egos.

The truth of the gospel according to Jesus is that the only ones who are eligible for salvation are those who realize they are sinners and are willing to repent. Christ's call is extended only to sinners who in desperation realize their need and desire transformation. Our Lord came to save sinners. But to those who are unwilling to admit their sin, he has nothing to say—except to pronounce judgment.

5

He Opens Blind Eyes

A Christian magazine recently published an article arguing that Jesus' lordship is an inappropriate topic to bring up in the course of witnessing to the lost. The decision to "make Christ Lord" is possible only for those who have already trusted him as Savior, the article said, and so it argued that the gospel presentation should contain nothing about yielding one's life to the lordship of Christ. A member of my church was disappointed to find such an article in a normally trustworthy magazine and wrote a letter of concern to the editor.

The editor wrote back, saying, "The article that we published in no way questions that Jesus is Lord, that is, Jehovah God. It raises the question whether a lost sinner must become a theologian before he can become a Christian."[1]

Is that really the issue? Does the lordship controversy have to do with whether people must become theologians to be saved?

Certainly not. But it is a revealing statement. Those who argue against lordship salvation have a tendency to identify the object of faith as a basic set of biblical facts. To them, the gospel is largely an academic issue, historical and doctrinal data about Christ's death, burial, and resurrection. Trusting those things alone constitutes saving faith, they say. Everything else is peripheral. Any talk of

[1]Near the end of his letter the editor wrote, "Certainly a sinner must know that Jesus Christ is God—the Lord Jehovah—because only God can save a lost sinner." Thus he agrees, and rightfully so, that there is a core of theological truth to be known and affirmed before an individual is saved. My question is, what kind of faith is it that permits a person, having affirmed Jesus Christ as Jehovah God, to continue in an unbroken pattern of sin and rebellion? Is that not demonic faith (James 2:19), orthodox but not efficacious?

obedience, submission, or Jesus' right to rule is refuted as adding to the gospel, an illegitimate attempt to turn a pagan into a theologian.

Lest you think I am unfairly presenting someone else's position, let me quote from an essay written to argue that lordship salvation corrupts the gospel: "This [referring to 1 Cor. 15:3–4] is the essential message of good news that must be believed for salvation. It contains these facts: (1) man is a sinner, (2) Christ is the Savior, (3) Christ died as man's substitute, and (4) Christ rose from the dead."[2] The writer then goes on to argue that surrender to Christ's authority has no place in the gospel message:

> Everyone who believes the gospel believes that Jesus is the Savior (1 Cor. 12:3). But not everyone who believes the gospel realizes that the Savior has the right to be sovereign over his life. The Child of God should also let Christ be sovereign over his life (Rom. 12:1–2), but obedience to that command is not a condition for salvation. . . . All that is required for salvation is believing the gospel message.[3]

And so informing an unbeliever that "the Savior has the right to be sovereign over his life" is challenged as extraneous doctrine added to the gospel. It is, we are told, tantamount to trying to make a theologian out of an unbeliever.

I reject that. A cultist who denies the deity of Christ could wholeheartedly affirm those four truths from 1 Corinthians 15:3–4, but that does not make him a true believer. Along with everyone else who rejects the Savior's right to be sovereign, that person is an unbeliever, no matter what other points of evangelical doctrine he or she might accept. True faith embraces not only the data of the gospel, but the Person of Christ as well. It comprehends not merely the truth that Jesus died and rose again, but also the corresponding implication: that he did this to deliver us from our sins in order to be the sovereign Master of our lives (Rom. 14:9).

The gospel is not a sterile set of facts; it is the dynamic through which God redeems sinners from the bondage of sin (Rom. 1:16). It calls not simply for the acquiescence of the mind, but for the full surrender of the heart, soul, mind, and strength (cf. Mark 12:30). Its work is not to make a theologian of a heathen, but to open the eyes of the spiritually blind.

John 9 is a clear case in point. There Jesus heals a man born blind, and in a second encounter with the same man, opens his spiritual eyes. In the interim, confronted by hostile Pharisees, the man—

[2]Thomas L. Constable, "The Gospel Message," *Walvoord: A Tribute* (Chicago: Moody Press, 1982), 203–4.
[3]Ibid., 209.

clearly no theologian—nevertheless gave a forceful and accurate testimony on behalf of Christ. Yet he was unregenerate, having not yet come to full faith in Christ. In fact, though Jesus had healed his sightless physical eyes, he was still in the dark about who Jesus was (9:25). But when Jesus finished opening his spiritual eyes, he worshiped Christ as Lord (v. 38). It was not a theology lesson that brought about this transformation, but a miracle of divine grace.

The Physical Miracle

The man in John 9 was born blind. It is noteworthy that this is the only miracle recorded in the Gospels where Scripture specifically states Jesus healed a congenital illness or disability. There was no way for skeptics to dismiss this miracle as a psychological healing or any kind of trickery on Jesus' part. Everyone who knew this man knew he had been blind from birth. His blindness was a birth defect, not a temporary affliction from which he could hope to recover—such is the case with the sin of the human race.

We might expect the witnesses to this healing to say, "That settles it! This must be the Christ." But they did not. They were locked into unbelief. Instead, this incident became a turning point in the ministry of Christ. From here on, he began to withdraw from the Jewish crowds and their unbelieving leaders. Instead, he turned his attention to the Gentiles.

Note carefully the setting in which the miracle took place. At the end of John 8, Jesus was engaged in a toe-to-toe confrontation with the religious leaders in the temple, where he made a dramatic proclamation of his deity: "Before Abraham was born, I am" (John 8:58). The next verse says the Jews were so incensed that they tried to stone him. In the midst of the confusion, Jesus was able to get out of the temple.

John 9 picks up the narrative just as Jesus left the temple: "As He passed by, He saw a man blind from birth" (v. 1). Although our Lord's life was in danger, and the mob from the temple would almost certainly be looking for him, Jesus stopped to deal with this blind man. Even though he was dodging bloodthirsty men, he took time to stop and minister to a blind sinner.

The man was a beggar (v. 8), yet he did not initiate contact with Jesus. He did not ask Jesus to heal him. It seems unlikely that he even knew who Jesus was. But the Lord saw him (v. 1). Sovereign grace had chosen him to receive a miracle.

The disciples raised an interesting theological question: "Rabbi, who sinned, this man or his parents, that he should be born blind?"

(v. 2). As far as they were concerned, those were the only possible options. That was standard rabbinical teaching. As far back as the time of Job, the common assumption was that suffering and illness were always traceable to an individual's specific acts of sin. In fact, some of the rabbis taught that a child could sin in the womb and then pay the penalty all his life for his prenatal sin.

Jesus, avoiding a lengthy discussion on the relationship of sin and suffering, simply answered, "It was neither that this man sinned, nor his parents; but it was in order that the works of God might be displayed in him. We must work the works of Him who sent Me, as long as it is day; night is coming, when no man can work" (vv. 3–4). In only a matter of months Jesus would be crucified. The time for discussing theological trivia was long past. What our Lord could do by healing this man would speak volumes more than a discourse on the theology of sin and suffering. The blind man was a miracle waiting to happen! He had been selected in eternity past and specially prepared for Jesus to pass by him and manifest his glory.

Although Jesus and the disciples were discussing him, the Lord had not yet said anything to the blind man, who just sat there. The beggar was not asking for any favors or seeking to enlist Jesus' power. He probably did not realize who Jesus was or what he was doing. Without even speaking to him, Jesus "spat on the ground, and made clay of the spittle, and applied the clay to his eyes" (v. 6).

We cannot attribute any special significance to the method Jesus used to heal this man. It is not the way he healed others who were blind. But his sovereign choice for this particular man was an amazingly simple miracle. No flash of bright light, no angels singing, no sound of trumpets. Just a little clay made from spittle.

Jesus told him simply, "Go, wash in the pool of Siloam" (v. 7). This must have made a very strange sight—a blind man with mud on his eyes crossing Jerusalem. But something, possibly the authority with which Jesus spoke, compelled him to obey. He responded with unquestioning obedience. Scripture says, "He went away and washed, and came back seeing" (v. 7). Through this act of obedience, God opened the man's physical eyes. Thus the man began a pattern of response to Christ that would culminate in his seeing spiritually.

The Inquisition

The miracle stirred up an extraordinary furor. When the man returned and the people realized who he was and what had happened to him, they were understandably perplexed. Some asked, " 'Is this not the man who used to sit and beg?' Others were saying, 'This is he,' still others were saying, 'No, but he is like him.' He kept saying, 'I am the one'" (vv. 8–9). This was very hard to believe!

"How then were your eyes opened?" they asked (v. 10). No one had ever witnessed a miracle like this.

Notice the man's theological naivete. They wanted an explanation, but all he could provide was a reciting of the events: "The man who is called Jesus made clay, and anointed my eyes, and said to me, 'Go to Siloam, and wash'; so I went away and washed, and I received sight" (v. 11). He was unsure of who Jesus was, did not know where he was, and had no logical or theological explanation for what had happened to him. After questioning the man at length, his neighbors bundled him off to the Pharisees.

Suddenly the story turns nasty. When the formerly blind man told the Pharisees, "He applied clay to my eyes, and I washed, and I see" (v. 15), they were indignant. Jesus had violated their Sabbath tradition.

"This man is not from God, because he does not keep the Sabbath" (v. 16), they concluded.

A few of the Pharisees tried to be more reasonable. "How can a man who is a sinner perform such signs?" they asked (v. 16). And they began to argue among themselves. The militant unbelievers among the Pharisees were not about to let up. Most of John 9 describes how they went to everyone they could find, arguing desperately that Jesus had sinned by violating the Sabbath, furiously looking for evidence to corroborate their unbelief. It makes a pathetic picture—these legalistic, unbelieving zealots, groping around trying to investigate a miracle without the capacity to see or believe it.

What a contrast! The beggar, devoid of any theological explanation or rationale for what had happened, simply rejoiced in what Jesus had done. The Pharisees, fat with theological information, wanted only to deny what had obviously happened, because they could not harmonize it with their predetermined system.

They turned to the blind man again and asked: "What do you say about Him, since He opened your eyes?" (v. 17). It was a challenge, not an honest question.

Theologically uninformed though he was, this man was not about to be intimidated by a group of Pharisees. "He is a prophet," was his candid appraisal.

Almost frantic in their passion to disprove the validity of the miracle, the Pharisees sought out the man's parents. "Is this your son, who you say was born blind? Then how does he now see?" (v. 19). They were asking the same question over and over, not looking for an answer, but rather desperately seeking some way to dismiss the unwelcome miracle.

The parents acknowledged that this was their son and that he had indeed been born blind, but they dodged the second question. Verse 22 says they were afraid of the Pharisees, who had threatened to put anyone out of the synagogue who affirmed that Jesus was the Christ. Excommunication was a terrible thing. The synagogue was the center of the Jewish community. Those who were excommunicated were cut off from everything. They could not buy or sell, and they were excluded from religious life. They became total outcasts. And when they died, they were given no funeral.

This man's parents were not taking any chances. They replied to the Pharisees, "Ask him; he is of age, he shall speak for himself" (v. 21).

These Pharisees were militant unbelievers. They went back to the man again, and said to him, "Give glory to God; we know that this man [Jesus] is a sinner" (v. 24). Of course they had no evidence that he had sinned—for he was without sin (Heb. 4:15). But they had already passed judgment, using their artificial standards in an attempt to justify what they had already concluded. Exposed to all the evidence, unbelief always remains resolute. Their minds were made up, and they were not going to be confused with the facts.

The blind man's reply was tinged with sarcasm: "Whether He is a sinner, I do not know; one thing I do know, that, whereas I was blind, now I see" (v. 25). He challenged their certainty that Jesus was a sinner, almost as if he said, "I'm not sure He's a sinner. I'm not that informed. But I do know that I couldn't see before He came along, and now I can."

What response did they offer for that? None. It is hard to argue against the simplicity of the obvious. Frantic, they repeated the same questions the man had already answered: "What did He do to you? How did He open your eyes?" (v. 26).

"Why do you want to hear it again?" he shot back. "You do not want to become His disciples, too, do you?" (v. 27).

Now the Pharisees were furious. They began to revile the man, to curse at him. "You are His disciple, but we are disciples of Moses. We know that God has spoken to Moses; but as for this man, we do not know where He is from" (vv. 28–29).

The calm, simple, obvious logic of the blind man vanquished the Pharisees' attack. Clearly, he was in control of this debate:

"Well, here is an amazing thing, that you do not know where He is from, and yet He opened my eyes. We know that God does not hear sinners; but if anyone is God-fearing, and does His will, He hears him. Since the beginning of time it has never been heard that anyone opened the eyes of a person born blind. If this man were not from God, He could do nothing" (vv. 30–33).

As they became more and more antagonistic, he became more and more convinced that Jesus was from God! The more they challenged him, the clearer his testimony became.

Finally, when the Pharisees had no more to say, they turned to mockery: "You were born entirely in sins [as if they were not], and are you teaching us?" Scripture adds, "And they put him out" (v. 34). That means they threw him out of the building and excommunicated him from the synagogue. Thus this once-blind beggar became the first person recorded in Scripture to be put out of the synagogue for Christ's sake. This incident began the breach that finally resulted in the separation of the church and Israel.

The Pharisees' inquisition was over. They had heard the testimony, they had seen the miracle, and still they were not swayed. Theirs was hardened, vicious, determined unbelief. Ultimately their hatred of Christ would ascend to such a fever pitch that they would sell their souls to put him to death.

Meanwhile, the beggar's faith was still incomplete. He had responded positively to Christ, even defended him against the Pharisees. But he was as yet unregenerate. His physical eyes were healed, but his spiritual blindness still needed to be removed.

The Spiritual Miracle

When Jesus heard that the man had been put out of the synagogue, he sought him out. Again, the Lord made the overture; the beggar did not come looking for him. Though his trade was begging, neither of the two miracles he received from Christ—the physical healing nor his subsequent salvation—came in response to his asking.

This episode illustrates perfectly the working of divine sovereignty. Salvation always results because God first pursues sinners, not because sinners first seek God. In John 15:16 Jesus said to his disciples, "You did not choose Me, but I chose you, and appointed you." Luke 19:10 says, "The Son of Man has come to seek and to save that which was lost. In Scripture, Christ is always portrayed as the seeking Savior. His divine initiative made redemption possible, and it is through his initiative that individuals are sought out and saved.

No one seeks God unless God has first sought that person (cf. Rom. 3:11). Salvation is first of all a work of God and in no sense the result of human enterprise or individual longing. A blind man has no capacity to give himself sight. Spiritual sight depends on God's initiative and God's power, offered in divine and sovereign grace.

Here is an important point. This blind man in John 9 did not gain his sight because he was exposed to the light. No amount of light affects blindness. A blind man in daylight is equally blind in the dark. All the light in the world will not make blind eyes see. The only things that can cure physical blindness are either surgery or a miracle. And the only thing that can change spiritual blindness is a divine miracle—not mere exposure to light.

Teaching theology to a heathen will not bring him to faith in Christ. He may learn the evangelical vocabulary and verbally affirm the truth. He may intellectually accept a list of gospel facts. But without a divine miracle to open his blind eyes and give him a new heart, he will only be a theologically informed pagan, not a Christian.

If, on the other hand, salvation is truly a work of God, it cannot be deficient. It cannot fail to impact an individual's behavior. It cannot leave his desires unchanged or his conduct unaltered. It cannot result in a fruitless life. It is the work of God and will continue steadfastly from its inception to ultimate perfection (Phil. 1:6).

Obviously God had begun to work in this blind man's heart. He stood up for Christ before the Pharisees and paid a great price for it. He was excommunicated from the synagogue and disfellowshiped from the life of Israel. Though he did not yet know the fullness of who Christ was, he was totally committed to him.

Christ asked him, "Do you believe in the Son of Man?" (John 9:35).[4] The beggar was willing and responsive. His heart was completely open: "Who is He, Lord, that I may believe in him?" (v. 36). His confidence in Jesus was such that he would have responded immediately to anyone Jesus pointed out as the Son of Man. Contrast his attitude with that of the Pharisees, who thought they knew it all and were not about to take direction from Jesus. They were learned in the Word of God, full of theological knowledge, but their hearts were blinded by willful unbelief. The beggar did not yet believe, but he was open.

Faith is the necessary complement to the sovereignty of God. Though divine initiative is ultimately responsible for redemption—although men and women are elected, predestined, chosen before the foundation of the world—there must still be on our part a submissive response of personal faith in Jesus Christ.

[4]The King James Version reads, "Dost thou believe on the Son of God?" "Son of Man" and "Son of God" are both terms Jesus used to emphasize his incarnate deity. The blind man evidently understood that Jesus was claiming to be God, because his response was to worship him (v. 38).

This man's simple response of faith is instructive. "Jesus said to him, 'You have both seen Him, and He is the one who is talking with you.' And he said, 'Lord, I believe'" (vv. 37–38). He did not hesitate. He did not ask for proof. Christ had given sight to his spiritual eyes, and the moment they were opened, he saw Christ and responded to him in faith.

Like the physical healing, this was a divine miracle. When someone understands the truth about Christ, it is always a divine miracle. Remember Peter's great confession? Jesus asked, "Who do you say that I am?" and Peter answered, "Thou art the Christ, the Son of the living God" (Matt. 16:15–16). How did he know? Jesus said, "Flesh and blood did not reveal this to you, but My Father who is in heaven" (v. 17). There is no way to recognize Jesus Christ for who he is apart from a miracle of God to open spiritually blind eyes. But when Christ opens the eyes of a soul, suddenly truth becomes recognizable.

This poor, blind beggar, who had never seen anything in his life, clearly recognized the Son of God. Meanwhile, the religious leaders who thought they knew everything could not even recognize their own Messiah. Spiritual sight is a gift from God that makes one willing and able to believe.

What did this man first see with his newly opened eyes of faith? He saw Christ as sovereign Lord. Verse 38 says, "He worshiped Him." He fell on his knees right there and worshiped. It is a beautiful climax to the story. It was not a question of "making" Christ his lord; when the scales fell off his spiritual eyes, he saw him for who he was, and the only possible response was to sink to his knees.

John 9 closes with these words: "And Jesus said, 'For judgment I came into this world, that those who do not see may see; and that those who see may become blind.' Those of the Pharisees who were with Him heard these things, and said to Him, 'We are not blind too, are we?' Jesus said to them, 'If you were blind, you would have no sin; but since you say, "We see," your sin remains'" (vv. 39–41).

It is a tragic thing to be spiritually blind, but it is more tragic still to be blind and not know it. These Pharisees thought they could see. After all, in terms of theological knowledge, they were far beyond this beggar. But unlike him, they had never had the blindness removed from their spiritual eyes, so they could not recognize Jesus for who he was. They knew doctrine, but they could not even recognize the Messiah. They were blind, and they did not even know it.

The result of spiritual sight is a surrendered, worshiping heart. The result of spiritual blindness is more blindness, more sin, and ultimately certain doom. Mere doctrine is no help for spiritual blindness; light cannot cure blindness. The only hope for those locked in the darkness of spiritual sightlessness is a miracle of God to open their eyes. That is what God does through his Spirit in salvation (1 Cor. 2:9–10). Those who would be saved do not require in-depth theological instruction to know that Christ is Lord and that they should obey him; the truth becomes self-evident when their spiritual blindness is removed.

Salvation is a supernatural, divine transformation—no less than a miracle that takes place in the soul. It is a true work of God, and it must make a difference in the life of the one whose eyes have been opened. The believing person will see Christ for who he is— sovereign Lord of all—and that revelation, to one who formerly could not see, will inevitably provoke worship, adoration, and a heart that desires to do the will of God. None of that is the result of theological tutoring; it is the work of God's Spirit in the heart of the redeemed.

6

He Challenges an Eager Seeker

Many years ago, in the early days of my ministry, I was on a cross-country flight. The man seated next to me noticed I was reading the Bible. He introduced himself and then surprised me by asking, "You wouldn't happen to know how I could have a personal relationship with Jesus Christ, would you?"

Of course, hot prospects like that do not approach me very often, so I did not want to lose this one! I said, "Well, yes, you simply believe in the Lord Jesus Christ and accept Him as your Savior." I explained that Jesus had died and risen again so that we might have eternal life. I told him all he needed to do was receive Christ as his personal Savior.

"I'd like to do that," he said. So I led him in a prayer, and he asked the Lord to be his Savior. Later that month I baptized him. I was very excited about what had happened and was eager to follow him up in discipleship. After a short time, however, he broke off contact with me. I recently discovered he has no continuing interest in the things of Christ.

What happened? Why is this such a common experience? Most people who regularly witness for Christ would admit that it is relatively easy to get people to profess faith. Getting them to follow the Lord is a much more frustrating experience. All of us have known "converts" who seem initially to embrace the idea of salvation enthusiastically but never really follow the Lord. Why?

I really did not understand the reasons myself until I studied the account of the rich young ruler in Matthew 19. There we read of a young man who asks in the clearest possible terms how he can lay hold of eternal life. If there was ever a place to look for a straightforward presentation of the gospel according to Jesus, we would expect it here. What we find is a startling discourse:

> Behold, one came to Him and said, "Teacher, what good thing shall I do that I may obtain eternal life?" And He said to him, "Why are you asking Me about what is good? There is only One who is good; but if you wish to enter into life, keep the commandments." He said to Him, "Which ones?" And Jesus said, "You shall not commit murder; You shall not commit adultery; You shall not steal; You shall not bear false witness; Honor your father and mother; and You shall love your neighbor as yourself." The young man said to Him, "All these things I have kept; what am I still lacking?" Jesus said to Him, "If you wish to be complete, go and sell your possessions and give to the poor, and you shall have treasure in heaven; and come, follow Me." But when the young man heard this statement, he went away grieved; for he was one who owned much property (vv. 16–22).

At first sight, we might wonder what kind of message Jesus was trying to give this man. A closer look reveals clearly what it was. If we could condense the truth of this entire passage into a single statement, it would be Luke 14:33: "So therefore, no one of you can be My disciple who does not give up all his own possessions."

Our Lord gave this young man a test. He had to choose between his possessions and Jesus Christ. He failed the test. No matter what points of doctrine he might affirm, because he was unwilling to turn from what else he loved most, he could not be a disciple of Christ. Salvation is only for those who are willing to give Christ first place in their lives.

The issue here was clearly this man's salvation, not some higher level of discipleship subsequent to conversion. His question was about how to obtain eternal life.

The term *eternal life* is used about fifty times in Scripture. It always refers to conversion, evangelism, the new birth—the entire salvation experience. In fact, the most familiar gospel verse of all, John 3:16, uses the expression: "For God so loved the world, that He gave His only begotten Son, that whoever believes in Him should not perish, but have eternal life."

Much of the work in evangelism is getting people to come to the point where they sense their need for salvation. This young man had come to that point before he ever asked Jesus the question. He was the perfect evangelistic target. He was ready to sign the card, raise his hand, walk the aisle, or whatever. He passed over the whole process of preevangelism. There was no need to explain to him how we know God exists, why we can trust the Bible, or why he should be concerned about eternity. Like that young man who approached me on the airplane, he appeared ready. To the human eye, he looked like the hottest evangelistic prospect the Lord had encountered so far. He was ripe. He was eager. There was no way he would get away without receiving eternal life.

But he did. He left not because he heard the wrong message, not even because he did not believe, but because he was unwilling to forsake what he loved most in this world and commit himself to Christ as Lord. Instead of taking him from where he was and getting him to make a "decision," Jesus had laid out terms that were unacceptable to him. In a sense, Jesus drove him away.

What kind of evangelism is this? Jesus would have failed personal evangelism in almost every Bible college or seminary I know! He began by preaching law to the young man and at this point did not even mention faith or the facts of redemption. He did not challenge the man to believe. He failed to get closure. He did not draw the net. After all, when a man comes along saying he wants eternal life, you cannot let him get away, right?

Wrong. Our ideas of evangelism cannot indict Jesus; rather, he must judge contemporary methods of evangelism. Modern evangelism is preoccupied with decisions, statistics, aisle-walking, gimmicks, prefabricated presentations, pitches, emotional manipulation, and even intimidation. Its message is a cacophony of easy-believism and simplistic appeals. Unbelievers are told that if they invite Jesus into their hearts, accept him as personal Savior, or believe the facts of the gospel, that is all there is to it. The aftermath is appalling failure, as seen in the lives of millions who have professed faith in Christ with no consequent impact on their behavior. Who knows how many people are deluded into believing they are saved when they are not?

What went wrong with this young man? Why did he seem to start so well yet turn away from Christ without receiving eternal life? He seemed to have the right motive and the right attitude; he came to the right source; and he asked the right question. But he went away unredeemed.

He Had the Right Motive

This man came seeking eternal life. He knew what he wanted, and he knew he did not have it. He had just about everything else, but not eternal life.

Nothing was wrong with the young man's motivation. It is good to desire eternal life. He was not looking for more wealth, but for something far more important—spiritual life. Jesus said, "Seek first

His kingdom and His righteousness; and all these things shall be added to you" (Matt. 6:33).

This man was young (Matt. 19:20) and rich (v. 22). In Luke 18:18 we learn that he was a ruler (*archōn* in the Greek text), which most likely means he was a ruler of the synagogue (cf. the same use of the word in Matt. 9:18). Thus it appears that he was a Jewish religious leader—devout, honest, young, wealthy, prominent, highly respected, and influential. He had everything. The words "and behold" (v. 16) are an exclamation indicating wonder and amazement. Matthew must have been astonished that this man would seek out Jesus and admit he needed eternal life.

Here was a man undoubtedly in turmoil. All his religion and wealth had not given him confidence, peace, joy, or settled hope. There was a restlessness in his soul, and he felt the absence of assurance in his heart. He came on the basis of a deeply felt need. He knew what was missing: eternal life.

Biblically, eternal life speaks not only of the promise of life in the ages to come, but also of the quality of life that is characteristic of the redeemed. It signifies quality as much as duration (cf. John 17:3). It is not just living forever; eternal life is being alive to the realm where God dwells. It is walking with the living God in unending communion.

This seems to be what the rich young ruler wanted. Apparently he perceived that he did not have that caliber of life. He knew that he did not walk with God or commune with God. Perhaps he sensed an inability to respond to God fully. He was not experiencing God's love, rest, peace, hope, joy, or security. At any rate, he knew he did not possess spiritual life or the assurance that he belonged to God.

In this the young man was very perceptive. Spiritually, he had gone far beyond the Pharisees, who were content with their own musings and praying for show. He was not. He knew he was missing eternal life, and he wanted to have it. No one can fault his motivation in approaching Christ.

He Had the Right Attitude

Not only was the young man's motivation correct, but his attitude was commendable as well. He was not haughty or presumptuous; he seemed to feel his need deeply. Many people know they do not have eternal life, but they also feel no need for it. They realize they do not sense the divine dimension, but they are not really interested in it. Not this young man. He was desperate. One can feel the urgency in his question, "Teacher, what good thing shall I do that I might have eternal life?" Without prologue or warmup, he just blurted it out.

Mark 10:17 says the man came running. He also came publicly. Unlike Nicodemus, who came by night, this man came in broad daylight and in front of other people. Mark says that the Lord was on the road, having just set out on a journey. No doubt there was the usual crowd around him. This fellow ran right through the crowd, unhampered by the fact that the people knew who he was. He was bold enough to confess publicly and openly that he did not possess eternal life. For a man in his position to ask such a question took tremendous courage. He had a lot to lose by openly admitting that he lacked eternal life.

Mark also tells us that this rich young ruler knelt at Jesus' feet. In a position of humility before the Lord, he acknowledged the undesirable situation he was in. He had the integrity not to hide it. He wanted eternal life so badly that he risked losing face with all those who looked to him as a spiritual giant already. Nevertheless, in frustration over his inability to find peace, he asked, "What am I still lacking?" We sense his anxiety, lack of fulfillment, and great consternation. He had been religious all his life, yet something was missing. This is the cry of a heart in deep need.

What are we to make of the young man's claim that he had kept all of the law? Of course he exaggerated, but apparently he did live an exemplary life outwardly. He was a moral man, not a gross sinner. He conformed to the strict standards of his religion.

But the man felt a deep void. If someone had approached him and asked, "How would you like peace, joy, happiness, and love?" he would certainly have responded. Had he been in an evangelistic service, there would have been no need to sing additional verses of "Just As I Am" for this man. He was ready. He was enthusiastically in pursuit of eternal life, and he seemed to have the right attitude.

What an opportunity! This fellow was eager, seeking, a "can't-miss" convert. He was young, rich, intelligent, and influential. Think of what he could do for the Lord! He could give his testimony, write a book, and be a large donor to the Christian cause. No evangelist worth his salt would muff an opportunity like this.

He Came to the Right Source

But the young ruler had not come to just an evangelist—this was the Source of eternal life himself. Here was the right place to be pursuing what he wanted. Some people look in the most bizarre places for eternal life. Satan is a master counterfeiter when it comes to false assurance. Most people never find eternal life because they spend their entire lives looking in the wrong places.

First John 5:11 says, "The witness is this, that God has given us eternal life, and this life is in His Son." Verse 20 says of Jesus, "This is the true God and eternal life." Not only is Jesus the source of eternal life; he is eternal life. So the rich young ruler was looking in the right place.

No doubt this man had heard about the power of Jesus. He addressed him as *didaskalos*, "master," or "teacher." With that title, he acknowledged that Jesus was a teacher of divine truth. Mark and Luke tell us he called him "good," using the Greek word *agathos*, which implies that he saw the Lord as good in nature and in essence. He would have used the word *kalos* if he had meant to denote strictly external goodness or good form. So in saying "good teacher," he was not just calling Jesus a capable teacher—he was affirming that he believed in the Lord's essential goodness.

That is not to say that he believed Jesus was God. He probably did not even realize that Jesus was the Messiah, let alone God in human flesh. It is likely that he was captivated by the authority of Jesus' teaching and the power of his virtuous life. He wanted to get this teacher's guidance on the issue of eternal life because he believed Jesus had it. It seems that Jesus' reply, "Why are you asking Me about what is good? There is only One who is good" (v. 17), was meant to prod him into realizing who he really was.

Nevertheless, though he did not acknowledge that Christ was Messiah or God in the flesh, he certainly had come to the right Person. "There is salvation in no one else; for there is no other name under heaven that has been given among men, by which we must be saved" (Acts 4:12).

He Asked the Right Question

Many readers of Matthew 19 have taken the young man to task for his question. They say his mistake was in asking "What good thing shall I do?" In other words, he had a works-oriented mind-set. And, of course, it is true that he was attuned to a religion based on works. He had been raised in a Pharisaic system of tradition. He was trained to think of religion as a system to earn divine favor. But with all that in his background, he asked a fair question. It was not a calculated bid to trap Jesus into condoning self-righteousness. It was a simple, honest question, asked by one in search of the truth: "What good thing shall I do that I may obtain eternal life?"

After all, there is something we have to do to inherit eternal life:

we have to believe. This man's question was not much different from the question of the multitudes in John 6:28: "What shall we do, that we may work the works of God?" Jesus answered those people with a simple and straightforward reply: "This is the work of God, that you believe in Him who He has sent" (v. 29).

But this is where the story takes an extraordinary turn. Jesus' answer to this young man seems preposterous: "If you wish to enter into life, keep the commandments" (Matt. 19:17). Our Lord revealed nothing of himself or the facts of the gospel. He did not invite the man to believe. He did not ask for a decision. Instead, Jesus erected a wall in front of him, which drew the inquirer to a sudden stop.

Strictly speaking, Jesus' answer was correct. If a person could keep the law all his life and never violate a single jot or tittle, he would be perfect, sinless (cf. James 2:10). But no one except the Savior alone is like that; we are born in sin (Ps. 51:5). To suggest that the law is a means to eternal life clouds the issue of faith. So why in the world would Jesus tell the man that? If he had come with the right motive and the right attitude to the right source, asking the right question, why was it that Jesus did not simply tell him the way of salvation through faith?

He Was Filled with Pride

In spite of all the young man had going for him, he was missing an important quality. Jesus knew the young ruler was utterly lacking a sense of his own sinfulness. His desire for salvation was based on an emptiness in his soul, perhaps with a desire to get rid of anxiety and frustration and to attain joy, love, peace, and hope. This is a good desire, but it does not constitute a valid reason for committing oneself to Christ.

Much of contemporary evangelism is woefully deficient when it comes to confronting people with the reality of their sin. Preachers offer people happiness, joy, fulfillment, and everything positive. Present-day Christians are taught that all they have to do is find a person's psychological needs then offer Jesus as a panacea for whatever the problem is. It is very easy to get a response, because people are looking for quick solutions to their felt needs. But if that is all we do, it is not legitimate evangelism.

Our Lord offered no relief for the rich young ruler's felt need. Instead, his answer confronted the ruler with the fact that he was a living offense to God. It was imperative that he perceive his sinfulness. Recognition of personal sin is a necessary element in understanding the truth of salvation. One cannot come to Jesus Christ for salvation only on the basis of psychological needs, anxieties, lack of peace, a sense of hopelessness, an absence of joy, or a yearning for happiness. As we have seen, salvation is for people who hate their sin and want to turn away from the things of this life. It is for individuals who understand that they have lived in rebellion against a holy God. It is for those who want to turn around, to live for God's glory. Salvation is not a mere psychological phenomenon.

Jesus' answer took the focus off the young man's felt need and put it back on God: "There is only One who is good." Then he slammed the man up against the divine standard, not because keeping the law would merit eternal life, but so that he would see how far he fell short: "If you wish to enter into life, keep the commandments." But the young man ignored and rejected the point. He was utterly unwilling to confess his own sinfulness.

As I think back to my conversation with the man on the airplane, I realize that this is where I failed. Too hastily I offered him Christ for his psychological needs without compelling him to acknowledge his sinfulness.[1] The salvation I described to him had a manward focus, rather than a Godward focus.

Evangelism must measure sinners against the perfect law of God so that they can see their deficiency. A gospel that deals only with human needs, only with human feelings, only with human problems, lacks the true balance. That is why churches are full of people whose lives are essentially unchanged after their supposed conversion. Most of these people, I am convinced, are unregenerate and grievously misled.

The pattern of divine revelation confirms the importance of comprehending one's sinfulness. In Romans, Paul spends three full chapters declaring the sinfulness of humanity before he begins to discuss the way of salvation. John 1:17 says, "The law was given through Moses; grace and truth were realized through Jesus Christ." Law always precedes grace: it is the tutor that leads us to Christ (Gal. 3:24). Without the law and its effect on us that God designs, grace is meaningless. And without an understanding of the reality and gravity of sin, there can be no redemption.

We need to adjust our presentation of the gospel. We cannot dismiss the fact that God hates sin and punishes sinners with eternal torment. How can we begin a gospel presentation by telling people on their way to hell that God has a wonderful plan for their lives?

---

[1] If the Holy Spirit had really prepared his heart for salvation, he would have been under great conviction of sin (cf. John 16:9–11). I should have looked for evidence of such conviction before leading him in a prayer for salvation.

Scripture says, "God is angry with the wicked every day" (Ps. 7:11 KJV). A righteous, holy, pure God cannot tolerate evil. He will not save those who try to come to him harboring sin.

The rich young ruler asked Jesus which commandments he should keep. The Lord responded by giving him the second half of the Ten Commandments: "You shall not commit murder; You shall not commit adultery; You shall not steal; You shall not bear false witness; Honor your father and mother." And then he added, "You shall love your neighbor as yourself" (Matt. 19:18–19). We have no way of knowing why the Lord chose those particular commandments to highlight; maybe he knew that the young man was not honoring his parents—a common sin among the religious rulers of that day (cf. Matt. 15:3–6). But the significant thing to note is that Jesus preached law to him.

We have no business preaching grace to people who do not understand the implications of God's law. It is meaningless to expound on grace to someone who does not know the divine demand for righteousness. Those who do not even sense their own guilt cannot possibly comprehend God's mercy. You cannot preach a gospel of grace to someone who has not heard that God requires obedience and punishes disobedience.

Jesus' words should have awakened a realization within the rich young ruler that he had fallen short. That was the whole point. But he rejected it entirely.

He Did Not Confess His Guilt

Scripture says, "The young man said to Him, 'All these things I have kept; what am I still lacking?'" (v. 20). That indicates how he perceived the law. Maybe he had never murdered anyone. Maybe he had never committed adultery. Giving him the benefit of the doubt, perhaps he did not steal or lie, and maybe he thought he had honored his father and his mother. It is quite possible that on the surface he had done all those things. But the emphasis in Jesus' teaching from the beginning had been to define all the law in such a way that no one—even those who adhered strictly to the law's external requirements—could look at the commandments and feel justified (cf. Matt. 5:20–48; Rom. 3:20).

The man could not escape the demands of the divine standard. The commandment to love your neighbor as yourself has an inescapable internal application. There was no way he could honestly say he had always kept *that* law. He could not have been telling the truth—if he was not lying, he was certainly deluded.

The Pharisees were accustomed to externalizing the law. They were very alert to the externals of ritual and conduct, but they never dealt with the heart. Jesus, on the other hand, taught that hatred was the moral equivalent of murder, that lust was tantamount to adultery, and that hating an enemy was as wrong as hating a neighbor (Matt. 5:21–47). The young ruler had missed the significance of Jesus' teaching. Boldly before a crowd of people, he claimed that he had kept the law. He must have felt that they would affirm that he was indeed a righteous man. After all, as far as they knew, he was. Externally, he *had* kept the law.

This confirms the truth that what he wanted was something to fill the emptiness in his heart. He acknowledged no sense of having violated God. He was saying, in effect, "I don't have any real sin. I've kept all the law. I look at myself, and I don't see any transgression." Self-righteous religion is deceiving. This man actually believed he was righteous. He believed he had obeyed the law. He thought he had kept the code. He had no idea how far he had fallen short.

There was no way this man could be saved while he clung to his self-righteous attitude. Salvation is not for people who want an emotional lift; it is for sinners who come to God for forgiveness. Those who are not ashamed of their sin cannot receive salvation.

At this point, Mark 10:21 tells us, "And looking at him, Jesus felt a love for him." That statement paints a pathetic picture. This young man was sincere, and his spiritual quest was genuine. He was an honestly religious person. Jesus loved him and was about to die for sinners like him. Jesus was not willing that any should perish, but that all should come to repentance. Yet that was one thing this man would not do.

The Lord Jesus does not take sinners on their own terms. As much as he loved the young man, he nevertheless did not grant him eternal life upon request.

He Would Not Submit to Christ

Finally, Jesus gave the young man the ultimate test: "If you wish to be complete, go and sell your possessions and give to the poor, and you shall have treasure in heaven; and come, follow Me" (Matt. 19:21). This challenged his claim to having kept the law. In effect, Christ told the young man, "You say you love your neighbor as yourself. OK, give him everything you've got. If you really love him as much as you love yourself, that should be no problem."

The ultimate test was whether this man would obey the Lord. Jesus was not teaching salvation by philanthropy. He was not saying that it is possible to buy eternal life with charity. In effect, he was saying, "Here is the test of true faith: Are you willing to do what I want you to do? Whom do you want to run your life, you or me?" The Lord was putting his finger on the very nerve of this man's existence. Knowing where the man's heart was, Jesus said, "Unless I can be the highest authority in your life, there is no salvation for you." By placing himself alongside the man's wealth and demanding that he make the choice, our Lord revealed the true state of the young man's heart.

Do we literally have to give away everything we own to become Christians? No, but we do have to give Christ first place (cf. Col. 3:18). That means we must be willing to forsake all for him (Luke 14:33)—that is, we cling to nothing that takes precedence over Christ. And the true believer will desire to do whatever he commands. Jesus' request of this man was simply to establish whether he was willing to submit to the sovereignty of Jesus over his life. Scripture never records another demand that anyone else sell everything and give it away. The Lord was making a frontal attack on the man's weakness—the sin of covetousness, indulgence, and materialism. He was indifferent to the poor. He loved his possessions. The Lord challenged that.

The rich young ruler failed the test. He was not willing to acknowledge Jesus as sovereign Lord over his life. Matthew 19:22 says, "When the young man heard this statement, he went away grieved; for he was one who owned much property." His possessions were more important to him than Christ, and he could not come to Jesus if it meant giving them up. It is interesting that he went away grieved. It seems he really did want eternal life, but he was unwilling to come the way Jesus specified—the way of confessing his sin and surrendering to Jesus' lordship. In other words, he remained in unbelief.

Contrast this man's response with that of Zaccheus in Luke 19. Zaccheus had a deep sense of sorrow for his sin. He was willing to do anything—including getting rid of all his wealth—to come to Jesus Christ on his terms. And Jesus' message to Zaccheus was, "Today salvation has come to this house. . . . For the Son of Man has come to seek and to save that which was lost" (Luke 19:9–10).

The rich young ruler left without the eternal life he sought. This is a tragic, heartbreaking story. Proverbs 13:7 says, "There is one who pretends to be rich, but has nothing; another pretends to be poor, but has great wealth." This young man thought he was rich, but he walked away from Jesus with absolutely nothing.

Salvation is by grace through faith (Eph. 2:8). That is the consistent and unambiguous teaching of Scripture. But people with genuine faith do not refuse to acknowledge their sinfulness. They sense that they have offended the holiness of God. They embrace the lordship of Christ. They desire him more than the things of this world. Real faith produces *all* those attributes. Saving faith does not recoil from the demand to forsake sin and self and follow Jesus Christ at all costs. Those who find his terms unacceptable cannot come at all. He will not barter away his right to be Lord.

I do not believe, and have never taught, that a person coming to Christ must understand fully all the implications of sin, repentance, or the lordship of Christ. Even after growing in understanding for years as a Christian, the seasoned believer will not know all these things in their full depth. Because we are sinful creatures, we can never understand or obey his lordship perfectly. But a person must have a willingness to obey. Furthermore, repentance and submission are no more human works than faith itself. They are every bit the work of God—essential aspects of God's work in a believing heart.

A message that offers mere psychological relief but does not require a turning from sin and an affirmation of the lordship of Christ is a false gospel that will not save. To come to Jesus Christ, a person must say yes to him. That means he takes first priority and becomes the supreme Lord of our lives.

If we learn anything from the account of the rich young ruler, it is the truth that although salvation is a blessed gift from God, Christ will not give it to one whose hands are filled with other things. Those who are not willing to turn from sin, possessions, false religion, or selfishness will find they cannot turn to Christ in faith.

7

He Seeks and Saves the Lost

There is no more glorious truth in the Bible than the words of Luke 19:10: "The Son of Man has come to seek and to save that which was lost." That verse sums up the work of Christ on earth. From the human viewpoint, it may represent the single most important truth ever recorded in Scripture.

Unfortunately traditional dispensationalism tends to miss that simple point. Some dispensationalists teach that "the gospel of the kingdom" Jesus proclaimed (Matt. 4:23) is distinct from "the gospel of the grace of God."[1] The substance of this "gospel of the kingdom," one popular source says, is "that God purposes to set up on earth the kingdom of Christ . . . in fulfillment of the Davidic Covenant."[2] Lewis Sperry Chafer wrote that the gospel of the kingdom was for the nation of Israel only "and should in no wise be confused with the gospel of saving grace."[3] Another early dispensationalist writer declared that the gospel Jesus preached had nothing to do with salvation but was simply an announcement that the time had come to set up the kingdom of Christ on earth.[4] That may fit neatly into a particular dispensational scheme, but Scripture does not support it. We must not forget that Jesus came to seek and to save the lost, not merely to announce an earthly kingdom.

When Jesus proclaimed his kingdom, he was preaching salvation. His conversation with the rich young ruler in Matthew 19 helps to clarify the terminology he used. The young man asked Jesus what he

[1]E. Schuyler English et al., eds., *The New Scofield Reference Bible* (New York: Oxford Univ. Press, 1967), 1366.
[2]Ibid.
[3]Lewis Sperry Chafer, *Grace* (Grand Rapids: Zondervan, 1922), 132.
[4]Clarence Larkin, *Rightly Dividing the Word* (Philadelphia: Larkin, 1918), 61.

could do to obtain eternal life. After the man left without receiving it, Jesus said to his disciples, "Truly I say to you, it is hard for a rich man to enter the kingdom of heaven" (v. 23). Thus, entering the kingdom of heaven is synonymous with obtaining eternal life. In the next verse the Lord said, "It is easier for a camel to go through the eye of a needle, than for a rich man to enter the kingdom of God" (v. 24). Obviously the kingdom of God, the kingdom of heaven, and eternal life all refer to salvation. The disciples clearly understood this, for they asked immediately, "Then who can be saved?" (v. 25).

Whatever terms Jesus employed—receiving eternal life, entering the kingdom, or being saved—the essence of his message was always the gospel of salvation. He said of his own mission, "I have not come to call righteous men but sinners to repentance" (Luke 5:32). The apostle Paul said in 1 Timothy 1:15, "It is a trustworthy statement, deserving full acceptance, that Christ Jesus came into the world to save sinners, among whom I am foremost of all."

Search and Rescue

The nature of God is to seek and to save sinners. From the opening pages of human history, it was God who sought the fallen couple in the Garden. In Ezekiel 34:16 God says, "I will seek the lost, bring back the scattered, bind up the broken, and strengthen the sick." The Almighty was portrayed as a Savior throughout the Old Testament (Ps. 106:21; Isa. 43:11; Hos. 13:4), so it is appropriate that when Christ entered the world of human beings as God in human flesh, he was known first of all as a Savior.

Even Jesus' name was divinely chosen to be the name of a Savior. An angel told Joseph in a dream, "You shall call His name Jesus, for it is he who will save His people from their sins" (Matt. 1:21). The very heart of all redemptive teaching is that Jesus entered this world on a search-and-rescue mission for sinners. That truth is what characterizes the gospel as good news.

But it is good news only for those who perceive themselves as sinners. The unequivocal teaching of Jesus is that those who will not acknowledge and repent of their sin are beyond the reach of saving grace. All are sinners, but not all are willing to admit their depravity. If they do, he becomes their Friend (cf. Matt. 11:19). If they will not, they will know him only as Judge (cf. Matt. 7:22).

Again, Jesus' parable in Luke 18:10–13 underscores this truth. He directed these words at "certain ones who trusted in themselves that they were righteous, and viewed others with contempt" (v. 9):

Two men went up into the temple to pray, one a Pharisee, and the other a tax-gatherer. The Pharisee stood and was praying thus to himself, "God, I thank Thee that I am not like other people: swindlers, unjust, adulterers, or even like this tax-gatherer. I fast twice a week; I pay tithes of all that I get." But the tax-gatherer, standing some distance away was even unwilling to lift up his eyes to heaven, but was beating his breast, saying, "God, be merciful to me, the sinner!"

Our Lord's assessment of those two men must have bewildered and infuriated his audience of self-righteous Pharisees: "I tell you, this man [the tax-gatherer] went down to his house justified rather than the other; for everyone who exalts himself shall be humbled, but he who humbles himself shall be exalted" (v. 14).

Humble repentance is the only acceptable response to the gospel according to Jesus. Those who fail to confess their sin—like the rich young ruler—he turns away. But he reaches out in grace to those who, like Matthew and the Samaritan woman, admit their sinfulness and seek deliverance. The worse the sinner, the more marvelously his grace and glory are revealed through that sinner's redemption.

Multitudes of repentant sinners responded during Jesus' earthly ministry. He continually ministered to tax collectors and other outcasts. Luke 15:1 indicates that a constant stream of such people approached him. In fact, the Pharisees' worst complaint about his ministry was, "This man receives sinners, and eats with them" (Luke 15:2). They set themselves in contrast and were condemned by their own comparison. They had no heart for the outcast, no love for the sinner, no compassion for the lost. Worse, they had no sense of their own sinfulness. Christ could do nothing for them.

The Setting for a Miracle

Like Matthew, Zaccheus was a tax-gatherer whose heart was divinely prepared to receive and follow Christ. His encounter with Jesus took place in Jericho, as the Lord was passing through on his way to Jerusalem to die. Jesus had for some time been ministering in Galilee. His home town, Nazareth, was there. He was now headed to Jerusalem for the final Passover, in which he would be the Paschal Lamb, giving his life on the cross for sinners. And as if to show exactly why he had to die, he paused in Jericho to reach out to a wretched tax-gatherer.

Along the journey the Lord had collected an entourage of pilgrims going to celebrate Passover in Jerusalem. His fame had spread throughout Palestine. Not long before this, he had raised Lazarus from the dead. That happened in Bethany, not far from Jericho. Word had spread, and people were curious about Jesus. Everyone in Jericho who could move lined the streets in preparation for his passing through. The city was buzzing. Was he the Messiah? Was he coming to take over? Was he coming to defeat the Romans and set up his kingdom?

Jericho is north and a little east of Jerusalem. It was an international crossroads, located where the main routes north, south, east, and west all came together. The customs house there, where taxes were collected, was a busy place, and Zaccheus was the publican in charge there.

Seeking the Savior

Zaccheus was despised by the whole community. Luke 19:7 says that everyone called him a sinner. Not only was he a tax-gatherer and a traitor to the nation, but this designation "sinner" probably meant that his personal character was debauched as well, as was the case with most publicans.

The Lord Jesus had a special love for tax collectors. Luke especially focuses on the numerous times Jesus encountered them. Luke's theme is the love of the Savior for the lost, and he repeatedly portrays Jesus reaching out to the riffraff of society. Every time Luke mentions a tax-gatherer (3:12; 5:27; 7:29; 15:1; 18:10–13; 19:2), it is in a positive sense. These were the outcasts of a religious society—flagrant public sinners—the very kind Jesus had come to save.

It might appear that Zaccheus was seeking Jesus on his own initiative, but the truth is that if Jesus had not first sought him, he never would have come to the Savior. Sinners never seek God on their own (Rom. 3:11). In our natural, fallen state we are dead in trespasses and sins (Eph. 2:1), excluded from the life of God (Eph. 4:18), and therefore totally unable and unwilling to seek God. Only when we are touched by the sovereign, convicting power of God do we move toward him (John 6:44, 65). And thus it is not until God begins to pursue a soul that the soul responds by seeking him. An anonymous hymn writer penned these words:

> I sought the Lord, and afterward I knew
> He moved my soul to seek Him, seeking me;
> It was not I that found, O Savior true;
> No, I was found of Thee.

Whenever someone seeks God, you can be certain it is a response to the prompting of a seeking God. We would not love him if he had not first loved us (cf. 1 John 4:19).

Nevertheless, God invites sinners to seek. Isaiah 55:6 says, "Seek the LORD while He may be found; call upon Him while He is near." Jeremiah 29:13 says, "You will seek Me and find Me, when you search for Me with all your heart." God says in Amos 5:4, "Seek Me that you may live." Jesus said, "Seek first His kingdom and His righteousness" (Matt. 6:33) and "Seek, and you shall find" (Matt. 7:7).

Being sought by God, Zaccheus was seeking. He had heard of Jesus but apparently had never seen him. Luke 19:3 says, "He was trying to see who Jesus was." The verb tense implies that he was continually making an effort to see Jesus. Why? Curiosity? Probably. Conscience? Surely. Desire for freedom from guilt? That could be. But beyond all these factors, the reality that he was ultimately saved demonstrates that the central force driving him to Christ was the irresistible convicting power of the Holy Spirit. It is apparent that the Spirit of God had begun in the heart of Zaccheus the process of drawing him to Christ. Zaccheus was not seeking God on his own initiative; the Spirit of God was moving his heart. In response he made an effort to see Jesus.

Here was an outcast, a hated man, a man whose hands were filled with money he had taken at the expense of poor people. He was a man with tremendous guilt. Yet instead of running and hiding, he desperately wanted to see Jesus. To do this, he overcame a number of obstacles. One was the crowd. The residents of Jericho were already lining the streets. Add to that his small stature. Zaccheus probably judiciously avoided crowds. A short man would have a problem in a crowd to start with. But a short man who was the chief tax commissioner risked getting a well-placed elbow in the jaw, a heavy boot on the big toe, or even a knife in the back.

On this day, Zaccheus was not concerned with such fears. He was not even concerned with his dignity. He was so determined to see Jesus that he ran ahead of the crowd and climbed up into a sycamore tree to await the Savior (v. 4). The sycamore was a short, fat tree with spreading branches. A little person could scurry up the trunk, get out on a limb, and hang over the road. And that is what Zaccheus did. The tree offered a perfect seat for the parade. It was not a dignified place for a man to be, but that was not important to Zaccheus at this point. He only wanted to see Jesus.

The Seeking Savior

What happened next must have staggered Zaccheus. Although Jesus had never met him before, he stopped in the middle of thousands of people, looked up in the tree and said, "Zaccheus, hurry and come down, for today I must stay at your house" (v. 5). That is known as the direct approach to evangelism! Nothing about Jesus' approach was subtle.

Our Lord had a divinely ordained appointment with the man. "Today I must stay at your house" suggests a mandate, not a request. He was not asking; he was saying, "I'm coming"—"I *must* come." Zaccheus's heart was prepared according to the divine timetable.

Zaccheus wanted to see Jesus, but he had no idea that Jesus wanted to see him. "And he hurried and came down, and received Him gladly" (v. 6). We might suppose that such a despicable sinner would be distressed to hear the perfect, sinless Son of God say, "I'm coming to your house," but he was glad. His heart was prepared.

The reaction of the crowd was predictable. Both the religious elite and the common people looked down on Zaccheus. "When they saw it, they all began to grumble, saying, 'He has gone to be the guest of a man who is a sinner' " (v. 7). They believed, as we have seen, that to go into the house of an outcast was to make oneself unclean. To eat with someone like Zaccheus was the worst possible defilement. They placed no value on Zaccheus's soul. They had no concern for his spiritual welfare. Their self-righteous eyes could see only his sin. They could not understand and would not see in their blind pride that Jesus had come to seek and to save sinners, and they condemned him for it. In doing so, they condemned themselves.

We are never told what happened at Zaccheus's house. Scripture does not say what he served for dinner or how long Jesus stayed or what they talked about. Nor do we know what Jesus said to Zaccheus in bringing him to salvation. As we have seen in other accounts where Jesus evangelized, the methodology he used is not the point. Conversion is a divine miracle, and there are no formulas that can bring it about or explain it. There is no four- or five-step plan of salvation, or any prefabricated prayer that can guarantee the salvation of a soul.

We can assume that Jesus dealt with the issue of Zaccheus's sin. No doubt Zaccheus already realized what a great sinner he was. Certainly Christ revealed to Zaccheus who he really was—God in the flesh. Whatever he said, he found in Zaccheus an open heart.

The Fruit of Salvation

The curtain seems to rise near the end of Jesus and Zaccheus's conversation in Luke 19: "And Zaccheus stopped and said to the Lord, 'Behold, Lord, half of my possessions I will give to the poor, and if I have defrauded anyone of anything, I will give back four times as much.' And Jesus said to him, 'Today salvation has come to this house, because he, too, is a son of Abraham'" (vv. 8–9).

Notice that Zaccheus addressed Jesus as Lord. That term can mean simply "sir," or "teacher." But here it certainly means more. In verse 9, Jesus said Zaccheus was saved. If so, he must have acknowledged Jesus as Lord God, confessing him as his own sovereign master. That is an affirmation he could not have made before Christ worked in his life, and he could not have denied it afterward (cf. 1 Cor. 12:3).

Here is a radically changed man. Deciding to give half his possessions to the poor was a complete reversal and is clear evidence that his heart was transformed. The taker had become a giver. The extortioner had become a philanthropist. He would repay those he had defrauded, giving back four times as much. His mind was changed, his heart was changed, and his clear intention was to change his behavior also. It was not so much that his heart had changed toward people, although that surely had happened. But first his heart had changed toward God. Now he wanted to obey God by doing what was just and righteous.

It was not necessary for Zaccheus to repay four times as much. Numbers 5:7 required a penalty of one-fifth as restitution for a wrong. But Zaccheus's generosity showed a transformed soul. It is a response typical of a newly redeemed person, the blessed fruit of redemption. He did not say, "Salvation is wonderful, but don't place any demands on my life." There is something in the heart of every newborn believer that wants to obey. The results are eager, generous obedience, a changed mind, and changed behavior.

All the evidence indicated that Zaccheus was a genuine believer. Jesus saw it and recognized a heart of faith. Luke 19:9, "He, too, is a son of Abraham," is a statement about his faith.

Zaccheus was a son of Abraham not because he was Jewish, but because he believed. Romans 2:28 says, "He is not a Jew who is one outwardly." Then what makes a true Jew? Romans 4:11 says that Abraham is the father of all who believe. Galatians 3:7 says, "It is those who are of faith who are sons of Abraham." All who trust in Christ are Abraham's offspring. Thus a true son of Abraham is the same as a believer.

Salvation did not come to Zaccheus because he gave his money away, but because he became a true son of Abraham; that is, a believer. He was saved by faith, not by works. But the works were important evidence that his faith was real. His experience harmonizes perfectly with Ephesians 2:8–10: "For by grace you have been saved through faith; and that not of yourselves, it is the gift of God; not as a result of works, that no one should boast. For we are His workmanship, created in Christ Jesus for good works, which God prepared beforehand, that we should walk in them" (cf. also James 2:14–26).

This is the purpose of salvation: to transform an individual completely. Genuine saving faith changes behavior, transforms thinking, and puts within a person a new heart. Second Corinthians 5:17 says, "If any man is in Christ, he is a new creature; the old things passed away; behold, new things have come." Zaccheus's response to Christ confirms the truth of that verse. He would have had a hard time understanding contemporary people who claim to be born again but whose lives challenge everything Christ stands for.

In Luke 3 John the Baptist rebuked the multitudes who came to be baptized: "Bring forth fruits in keeping with your repentance" (v. 8). It is a striking picture—a prophet of God, chiding those who have responded positively to his ministry, calling them a brood of vipers. He was actually trying to turn them away!

We might do well to imitate John's example. Contemporary Christianity often accepts a shallow repentance that bears no fruit.

The conversion of Zaccheus argues against any such superficial response. His instant and dramatic transformation is the expected result of true faith.

This was the purpose for which Christ came: "To seek and to save that which was lost" (Luke 19:10). As we see in Zaccheus's conversion, the necessary result of God's saving work is a transformed person. When a soul is redeemed, Christ gives a new heart (cf. Ezek. 36:26). Implicit in that change of heart is a new set of desires—a desire to please God, to obey, and to reflect his righteousness. If such a change does not occur, there is no reason to think genuine salvation has taken place. If, as in the case of Zaccheus, there is evidence of faith that desires to obey, that is the mark of a true son of Abraham.

8

He Condemns
a Hardened Heart

Opponents of lordship salvation admit that one of the reasons they exclude obedience from their concept of saving faith is to make room in the kingdom for professing believers whose lives are filled with sin. "If only committed people are saved people, then where is there room for carnal Christians?" one leading advocate of the antilordship view pleads.[1]

This eagerness to accommodate so-called carnal Christians[2] has driven some contemporary teachers to define the terms of salvation so loosely that virtually every profession of faith in Christ is regarded as the real thing.[3] All who say they have "accepted Christ" are enthusiastically received as Christians, even if their supposed faith later gives way to a persistent pattern of disobedience, gross sin, or hostile unbelief. One antilordship writer perfectly distills the utter absurdity of his own view:

[1]Charles C. Ryrie, *Balancing the Christian Life* (Chicago: Moody Press, 1969), 170.

[2]Paul's words to the Corinthians, "Are ye not carnal, and walk as men?" (1 Cor. 3:3 KJV) were not meant to establish a special class of Christianity. These were not people living in static disobedience. Paul does not suggest that carnality and rebellion were the rule in their lives. In fact, he said of these same people, "You are not lacking in any gift, awaiting eagerly the revelation of our Lord Jesus Christ, who shall also confirm you to the end, blameless in the day of our Lord Jesus Christ" (1 Cor. 1:7–8). Nevertheless, by having taken their eyes off Christ and created religious celebrities (3:4–5), they were behaving in a carnal way. Contrast Paul's words about the incestuous man in chapter 5. Paul calls him a "so-called brother" (v. 11). Because of the man's pattern of gross immorality, Paul could not affirm him as a brother.

[3]In an otherwise positive review of Zane Hodges' *The Gospel Under Siege*, J. A. Witmer noted Hodges' "failure to recognize that profession of faith can be less than saving faith" (*Bibliotheca Sacra* 140 [January–March 1983], 81–82).

It is possible, even probable, that when a believer out of fellowship falls for certain types of philosophy, if he is a logical thinker, he will become an "unbelieving believer." Yet believers who become agnostics are still saved; they are still born again. You can even become an atheist; but if you once accept Christ as saviour, you cannot lose your salvation, even though you deny God.[4]

That is a damning lie. No one who denies God should be deceived into thinking that because he once professed faith in Christ, he is eternally secure (cf. Matt. 10:33—"Whoever shall deny Me . . . I will also deny him" and 2 Tim. 2:12—"If we deny Him, He also will deny us").

I am committed to the biblical truth that salvation is forever.[5] Contemporary Christians have come to refer to this as the doctrine of *eternal security*. Perhaps the Reformers' terminology is more appropriate; they spoke of the *perseverance of the saints*. The point is not that God guarantees heaven to everyone who professes faith in Christ, but rather that those whose faith is genuine will never totally or finally fall away from Christ. They will persevere in grace unto the very end. Even if they fall into grievous sins or continue in sin for a time, they will never abandon the faith completely. A. W. Pink, writing on this subject, says:

[God] does not deal with [believers] as unaccountable automatons, but as moral agents, just as their natural life is maintained through their use of means and by their avoidance of that which is inimical to their well-being, so it is with the maintenance and preservation of their spiritual lives. God preserves his people in this world through their perseverance.[6]

True believers *will* persevere. Professing Christians who turn against the Lord only prove that they were never truly saved. As the apostle John wrote, "They went out from us, but they were not really of us; for if they had been of us, they would have remained with us; but they went out, in order that it might be shown that they all are not of us" (1 John 2:19). No matter how convincing a person's testimony might seem, once that person becomes apostate, he or she demonstrates irrefutably that the testimony was hypocritical and the professed salvation was spurious. God will keep his own. He "is able

[4]R. B. Thieme, *Apes and Peacocks or the Pursuit of Happiness* (Houston: Thieme, 1973), 23.
[5]For a complete discussion of the issue of the believer's security, see John F. MacArthur, *Saved Without a Doubt* (Wheaton, Ill.: Victor, 1992).
[6]Arthur W. Pink, *Eternal Security* (Grand Rapids: Guardian, 1974), 15.

to keep [them] from stumbling, and to make [them] stand in the presence of His glory blameless with great joy" (Jude 24).[7]

Judas is a prime example of a professing believer who fell into absolute apostasy. For three years he followed the Lord with the other disciples. He appeared to be one of them. Presumably he thought of himself as a believer, at least at the outset. It is doubtful that he joined Christ's band with the intention of turning against him. Although somewhere along the line he became greedy, that could hardly have been his motive in the beginning, since Jesus and the disciples never had anything of material value (Matt. 8:20). Apparently Judas initially shared the hope of Christ's kingdom. He likely believed that Jesus was the Messiah. After all, he also had left everything to follow the Lord. In modern terminology, he had "accepted" Jesus.

For three years, day in and day out, he occupied himself with Jesus Christ. He saw the Lord's miracles, heard his words, even participated in his ministry. In all that time, no one ever questioned his faith. He had the same status as the other disciples. Except for the Savior himself, who knew the thoughts of Judas's heart, no one ever suspected that this man would betray Christ.

Yet while the others were growing into apostles, Judas was quietly becoming a vile, calculating tool of Satan. Whatever his character seemed to be at the beginning, his faith was not real (John 13:10–11). He was unregenerate, and his heart gradually hardened so that he became the treacherous man who sold the Savior for a fistful of coins. In the end, he was so prepared to do Satan's bidding that the devil himself possessed Judas (John 13:27).

Judas was so skilled at hypocrisy that he stayed on the inside right

---

[7]Cf. Zane C. Hodges, *The Gospel Under Siege* (Dallas: Redención Viva, 1981), 68–69. Hodges writes, "It is widely held in modern Christendom that the faith of a genuine Christian cannot fail. But this is not an assertion that can be verified from the New Testament." Then, on the basis of 2 Timothy 2:17–18, which he calls "a fundamental passage on the defectibility of human faith," Hodges argues that Scripture teaches genuine believers may indeed succumb to apostasy.

This passage proves no such thing. The apostle Paul was not implying that people whose supposed faith had been overthrown were genuine believers. The gnostic heresies of Hymenaeus, whose faith Paul described as shipwrecked (cf. 1 Tim. 1:19–20), were the doctrines of unregenerate false teachers. Those who forsook the faith for such teachings were not to be considered brethren (cf. 1 John 2:19). Whatever faith they had was only "human faith"—to use Hodges' expression—and that is not saving faith.

The next verse, "Nevertheless, the firm foundation of God stands, having this seal, 'The Lord knows those who are His'" (2 Tim. 2:19), underscores the truth that saving faith, which is wrought by God, cannot fail. We cannot always see whose faith is genuine and whose is a sham, but God knows.

up to the very end. On the night he betrayed the Lord of glory, he was there in the Upper Room, seated next to Jesus. He even let the Savior wash his feet. And that was after he had made his bargain to betray Jesus for thirty pieces of silver!

Jesus knew it all the time. In John 13:18 he said, "I know the ones I have chosen; but it is that the Scripture may be fulfilled, 'He who eats My bread has lifted up his heel against Me.'" Why did the Lord choose him? To fulfill Scripture. Jesus was quoting Psalm 41:9. Another psalm that prophesied about Judas is 55:12–14:

> It is not an enemy who reproaches me,
> Then I could bear it
> Neither is it one who hates me who has exalted himself
> against me,
> Then I could hide myself from him.
> But it is you, a man mine equal,
> My companion and my familiar friend.
> We who had sweet fellowship together,
> Walked in the house of God in the throng.

That is a perfect picture of Judas. He was as close as anyone could get to the Savior but as far from salvation as it is possible to be. It would have been better for Judas if he had never been born (Matt. 26:24).

Judas and his life of treachery stand as a solemn warning to anyone who casually professes faith in Christ. We learn from his story that it is not enough to be close to Jesus Christ. One may "accept" him and still fall short. The individual who responds positively but not wholeheartedly risks being lost and damned forever. In the words of Psalm 55, one who is friendly to Jesus and enjoys his sweet fellowship may yet turn against him and thus condemn himself. Judas is proof of that.

One of You Will Betray Me

It was not the will of God apart from Judas's own choice that he should betray Christ. At every opportunity, Jesus warned Judas and entreated him to repent and be saved, but at every point Judas turned away. Judas had heard the gospel according to Jesus, yet he refused to turn from his sin and selfishness. Jesus' words in John 13 represent his final, loving appeal to this man. In the end, however, the Savior's merciful entreaty would condemn Judas in the hardness of his heart.

John 13:21 describes a dramatic moment during the Lord's last supper on the night he was betrayed: "Jesus . . . became troubled in spirit, and testified, and said, 'Truly, truly, I say to you, that one of you will betray Me.'" Imagine the shock that must have rattled that group—all except for Judas.

What was it that troubled Jesus? Probably a lot of things. He might have been troubled because of his unreciprocated love for Judas; or because of the ingratitude in Judas's heart; or because he had a deep hatred of sin, and the incarnation of everything sinful was sitting right next to him. Surely he was troubled by Judas's cold-hearted hypocrisy and imminent betrayal; and because he knew Satan was moving in on Judas; and because Judas was a classic illustration of the wretchedness of sin, which he would bear in his body the next day. But perhaps most of all, our Lord was troubled by the knowledge that Judas was about to make—or had already made—a decision that would condemn him to eternal torment. Judas, one of Jesus' own disciples, had never really been saved (cf. vv. 10–11) and was about to be lost forever.

The hearts of the disciples must have raced when Jesus said one of them would betray him. They did not know whom he was talking about. Matthew 26:22 says they all asked, "Surely not I, Lord?" Even Judas, always playing the part, said, "Surely it is not I, Rabbi?" Jesus' reply, "You have said it yourself" (v. 25), told Judas that the Lord knew his heart.

Who Is It?

It is interesting that the disciples were perplexed. Apparently Jesus had treated Judas the same as the other disciples. For three years the Lord had been gentle, loving, and kind to Judas—exactly as he had been to the other eleven. Any rebukes from Jesus for Judas's unbelief had been private and personal. Publicly he had treated him like one of the group. All the disciples would have known if Jesus had treated Judas any differently. If Judas had in any way been thought of as the black sheep of the group, someone would surely have suggested his name as the betrayer. But no one did. In fact, Judas was the treasurer of the group. The disciples all trusted him.

Contrast the hatred Judas harbored for Jesus with the love John had for the Savior. John reclined at the table next to Jesus. This was normal posture for a banquet. The table was a low platform, and all the guests reclined on the floor, resting on their left elbows, using their right hands to eat. John, reclining to the right of Jesus, had his head at chest level to Jesus. When he turned to speak with him, Christ's head would be just above his. Because of his great love for the Savior, John loved to be there, near the Lord's heart.

Peter signaled to John to ask Jesus who would betray him. "He,

leaning back thus on Jesus' breast, said to Him, 'Lord, who is it?'"
(John 13:24–25). Peter and John may be the only ones who heard the
answer. Verse 26 says, "Jesus therefore answered, 'That is the one for
whom I shall dip the morsel and give it to him.' So when He had
dipped the morsel, He took and gave it to Judas, the son of Simon
Iscariot."

The Guest of Honor

This was not only an answer to John's question; it was yet another
loving appeal to Judas. The morsel was a piece of unleavened bread,
broken from the cakes prepared for the meal. On the table during the
Passover feast was a dish filled with bitter herbs, vinegar, salt, dates,
figs, and raisins. Those ingredients were mashed into a paste with a
little water, and it made a kind of dip. The host would put a piece of
unleavened bread in the dip, and give it to the guest of honor. Jesus,
in a gesture of love toward Judas, dipped the morsel and handed it to
Judas on his left, as if Judas were the guest of honor. Jesus had
already washed Judas's feet; now he treated him as an honored
friend. That should have broken Judas's heart, but it didn't. His heart
was like granite; he had made his final decision.

John 13:27 portrays the sinister nature of Judas's final rejection:
"After the morsel, Satan then entered into him." There is an eternity
in that verse. Judas had been beguiled by Satan, flirting with evil
while pretending to follow Christ. Now Satan entered his heart and
took full control. In that awful moment, the evil will of Judas resisted
the final offer of Jesus' love. The day of salvation thus expired for
him. Judas was damned to hell by his own choice; his doom was
sealed.

Do It Quickly

Jesus was through with Judas. All he wanted to do now was get
him out of the room. "Jesus therefore said to him, 'What you do, do
quickly'" (v. 27). Judas was confirmed in his unbelief, and Jesus had
no more to say to him. He was an intruder on Jesus' time alone with
his disciples.

Scripture says, "Now no one of those reclining at the table knew
for what purpose He had said this to him. For some were supposing,
because Judas had the money box, that Jesus was saying to him, 'Buy
the things we have need of for the feast'; or else, that he should give
something to the poor" (vv. 28–29). None of them, except possibly
Peter and John, yet knew that Judas would be the betrayer. His

testimony had been so convincing, his hypocrisy so slick, that none of them yet realized he was capable of such treachery. Yet he was possessed by Satan himself. How wrong appearances can be! How deceiving is a carnal person's profession of faith!

Into the Night

Off Judas went into the night (v. 30). It was the beginning of eternal night in his soul as well. Judas, who had been privy to the greatest spiritual advantages afforded any person, had squandered that wonderful opportunity just to fulfill his illicit passion. Why? Because his faith was never genuine. In the beginning he had responded positively to Christ, but never with a heart of sincere, penitent faith. His life, lived in the unclouded light of Jesus' presence, ended in a night of despair. That frightening potential exists for every person who comes to Christ without a committed heart.

Kiss of Death

It is a bitter irony that Judas's final contact with Jesus was a kiss. It was the kiss of death—not for Jesus, but for Judas. It happened later the same night, in the garden where the Savior went to pray. That kiss was the prearranged signal by which Judas had agreed to identify Jesus.

Kisses between men were part of the culture of Jesus' time. Slaves would kiss the feet of their masters. Those who sought mercy from an angry monarch would kiss his feet, begging for pardon. Great reverence was expressed by kissing the hem of a superior's garment. Students kissed their teacher's hand as a sign of respect. But an embrace and a kiss on the cheek was a sign of close affection, warm love, and intimacy. Such a gesture was reserved for the closest of friends.

And so the kiss of Judas became the most despicable of all acts. He could have kissed Jesus' hand or the hem of his garment, but he chose instead to feign affection for Christ. Thus he not only gave his conspirators a sign, but he also made his act all the more repugnant. Perhaps he thought he could still deceive Christ and the disciples. But Luke 22:48 records that Jesus said, "Judas, are you betraying the Son of Man with a kiss?" Even those sorrowful words could not stop this deranged man. Mark 14:45 says Judas only said, "Rabbi!" and kept kissing him.

The Lord Jesus had to endure those despicable kisses. His final response, recorded in Matthew 26:50, was, "Friend, do what you have come for." The Greek word translated "friend" in this verse is *hetairos,* which literally means, "comrade," or "fellow." Jesus was not addressing Judas as a warm friend at this point. "Friend" is a name he reserves for those who obey him (John 15:14).

That was Jesus' farewell to the son of perdition. Judas must still hear these words ringing in his ears, as he will for all eternity: "Judas, are you betraying the Son of Man with a kiss?" (Luke 22:48). "Do what you have come for" (Matt. 26:50).

They All Forsook Him and Fled

The behavior of the rest of the disciples at this point raises the question of how they differed from Judas. Matthew 26:56 says, "All the disciples left Him and fled." Jesus had predicted this earlier when he said, "You will all fall away because of Me this night" (v. 31). They did turn away from Jesus. Peter even denied Christ three times and sealed his denials with a curse. How did that act differ from Judas's betrayal?

For one thing, it was motivated differently. The disciples fled out of fear and in the pressure of the moment; Judas's betrayal was a calculated act of treachery. The disciples failed in the face of a great trial; Judas's act of treason was something he plotted and schemed to carry out, the response of a greedy heart. The disciples later turned from their sins and humbly accepted Jesus' forgiveness; Judas was resolute in unbelief and hatred; he even confirmed it with the sinful act of suicide (Matt. 27:5). The disciples' denial was a lapse of normally faithful behavior; Judas's sin manifested an utterly depraved soul.

The mark of a true disciple is not that he never sins, but rather that when he does sin he inevitably returns to the Lord to receive cleansing and forgiveness. Unlike a false disciple, the true disciple will never turn away completely. He may occasionally turn back to his fishing nets, but ultimately he will be drawn again to the Master. When Christ confronts him, he will return to a life of service for the Savior.

The Marks of a False Disciple

Judas illustrates false discipleship. Note carefully the characteristics of his hypocrisy. First, he loved temporal gain more than eternal riches. He wanted glory; he wanted success; he wanted earthly treasures. Perhaps he was disappointed that Christ did not fulfill all his political expectations for the Messiah. He may have had his heart set on a high position in Christ's earthly kingdom. It is typical of false disciples that they get on board with Jesus to get what they want, but when instead of delivering he makes demands on them, they turn away. Such people reveal that they never had genuine faith to begin with. They are like the seed that springs up in rocky soil. It grows well for a while, but when the sun comes out, it withers and dies (cf. Matt. 13:20–21). They follow Christ for a season but eventually sell him for selfish desire, money, prestige, or power.

Second, Judas was marked by deceit. His show of faith was only a masquerade. False disciples are masters of subtle deception, adept at deluding others. They pretend to love the Lord, but their kisses are the kisses of betrayal.

Finally, Judas and all false disciples are in it for what they receive. They are satisfied with a salved conscience, peace of mind, a good reputation, or spiritual self-satisfaction. Some of them profess Christ because it is good for business or because they think that trusting Christ will bring health, wealth, or prosperity. But they will sell the Savior just as Esau sold his birthright for a mess of pottage. Like Judas, they love the world and they love darkness. Their half-hearted faith turns inevitably to hard-hearted unbelief.

I fear there are multitudes like Judas in the contemporary church. They are friendly to Jesus. They look and talk like disciples. But they are not committed to him and are therefore capable of the worst kind of betrayal.

A real disciple, on the other hand, may fail Christ but will never turn against him. A true Christian might temporarily fear to stand up for the Lord but would never willingly sell him out. Inevitably, true disciples will falter, but when they fall into sin, they will seek cleansing. They will not wallow in the mire (cf. 2 Peter 2:22). Their faith is neither fragile nor temporary; it is a dynamic and ever-growing commitment to the Savior.

9

He Offers a Yoke of Rest

It may surprise you to learn that Scripture never once exhorts sinners to "accept Christ."[1] The familiar twentieth-century evangelistic appeal in all its variations ("make a decision for Christ"; "ask Jesus into your heart"; "try Jesus"; "accept Jesus Christ as your personal Savior"), violates both the spirit and the terminology of the biblical summons to unbelievers.[2]

The gospel invitation is not an entreaty for sinners to allow the Savior into their lives. It is both an appeal and a command for them to repent and follow him. It demands not just passive acceptance of Christ but active submission to him as well. Those unwilling to surrender to Christ cannot recruit him to be part of a crowded life. He will not respond to the beckoning of a heart that cherishes sin. He will not enter into partnership with one who loves to fulfill the passions of the flesh. He will not heed the plea of a rebel who simply wants him to enter and by his presence sanctify a life of continued disobedience.

The great miracle of redemption is not that we accept Christ, but that he accepts us. In fact, we would never love him on our own (1 John 4:19). Salvation occurs when God changes the heart and the

[1]Receiving Christ in the biblical sense is more than simply "accepting" him or responding positively to him. John 1:11–12 contrasts those who "received" him with those who rejected him as Messiah. Those who received Christ were people who embraced him and all his claims without reservation—they "believed on His name" (v. 12 KJV; cf. Col. 2:6).

[2]Dr. Winn Arn of the Institute for American Church Growth, commenting on the failure of contemporary methods of evangelism, said, "Nowhere in Scripture is the concept for 'decisions' found. The bottom line was a transformed life and an active Christian—a disciple . . . one who becomes a follower" (quoted in *Eternity*, September 1987, 34).

unbeliever turns from sin to Christ. God delivers the sinner from the domain of darkness into the kingdom of light (Col. 1:13). In the process Christ enters the heart by faith to dwell there (cf. Eph. 3:17). Thus conversion is not simply a sinner's decision for Christ; it is first the sovereign work of God in transforming the individual.

The portrait of Jesus in the Gospels is altogether different from the picture contemporary evangelicals typically imagine. Rather than a would-be redeemer who merely stands outside anxiously awaiting an invitation to come into unregenerate lives, the Savior described in the New Testament is God in the flesh, who invades the world of sinful humanity, challenging sinners to turn from their iniquity.[3] Rather than waiting for an invitation, he issues his own—in the form of a command to repent and take on a yoke of submission.

Not surprisingly, Jesus' personal invitation to sinners stands in stark contrast to the evangelistic message we are accustomed to hearing. Matthew 11:25–30 records these words, spoken by our Lord immediately after he pronounced condemnation on the Galilean cities that refused to repent:

> At that time Jesus answered and said, "I praise Thee, O Father, Lord of heaven and earth, that Thou didst hide these things from the wise and intelligent and didst reveal them to babes. Yes, Father, for thus it was well-pleasing in Thy sight. All things have been handed over to Me by My Father; and no one knows the Son, except the Father; nor does anyone know the Father, except the Son, and anyone to whom the Son wills to reveal Him. Come to Me, all who are weary and heavy-laden, and I will give you rest. Take My yoke upon you, and learn from Me, for I am gentle and humble in heart; and you shall find rest for your souls. For My yoke is easy, and My load is light."

That is an invitation to salvation, not just an appeal for believers to move into a deeper experience of discipleship. The people our Lord spoke to were weighted down with sin and legalism, laboring in their own energy to find spiritual rest.

It is significant that our Lord began his invitation with a prayer recognizing God's sovereignty. He said it aloud in the presence of the people. Thus the truth it contained was a critical part of the message to them. It was a statement to all who heard—an affirmation that everything was going according to the divine plan, even though the mass of people had rejected their Messiah.

The Savior emphasized that God himself is the determinative

---

[3]Note that Jesus' invitation in Revelation 3:20, "Behold, I stand at the door and knock . . ." immediately follows his command in verse 19: "Be zealous, therefore, and repent."

factor in salvation. We who witness for Christ are not ultimately responsible for how people respond to the gospel. We are only responsible to preach it clearly and accurately, speaking the truth in love. Some will turn away, but it is God who either reveals the truth or keeps it hidden, according to what is well-pleasing in his sight. His plan cannot be stymied. Though the gospel according to Jesus may offend, its message must not be made more palatable by watering down the content or softening the hard demands. In God's plan, the elect will believe despite the negative response of the multitudes.

Considering the overwhelming rejection swirling around Jesus when he uttered these words, we might conclude that things were at a low point in his ministry. His work in Galilee was coming to a close. Although he had demonstrated irrefutably that he was the Messiah, a majority of the people were unresponsive. Yet Jesus never wavered in his confidence that all things were under the Father's control. He continued to pursue his Father's will and reach out to the unregenerate. He had come to seek and to save the lost. Negative circumstances never deterred him from that purpose.

Jesus' offer of rest for the weary is a call to conversion. It is a masterpiece of redemptive truth—a synopsis of the gospel according to Jesus. It outlines five essential elements of genuine conversion, all so inextricably linked that it is impossible to eliminate any one of them from the biblical concept of saving faith.

Humility

First is humility. Jesus prays: "Thou didst hide these things from the wise and intelligent and didst reveal them to babes" (Matt. 11:25). He did not mean that "these things"—the spiritual realities of the kingdom—are hidden from smart people. Spiritual understanding has nothing to do with one's mental capacity. He is condemning people whose knowledge of spiritual truth is limited only to what they can discover with their own intelligence—those who are ultimately dependent on human wisdom. Their sin is not their intellect; it is their intellectual pride.

This warning was especially applicable to the Pharisees, the rabbis, and the scribes. They were closed to the revelation of God in Christ because they thought they already knew everything God had to say. Unaware that they were spiritually blind, they depended on human reason to interpret spiritual reality. Instead of finding truth, they had erected a system of theological error.

Human intellect cannot understand or receive spiritual truth. The things of the Spirit of God are not accessible through human wisdom or clever reasoning. This is the same truth the apostle Paul cited in 1 Corinthians 2:9. The eye cannot see spiritual truth and the ear cannot hear it—it is not empirically or objectively discernible. Nor has it entered into the heart of man—it is not perceivable by intuition.

Jesus' point in Matthew 11 was not that God has withheld the truth from intelligent people, but rather that those who rely on their own cleverness cut themselves off from the truth. Their wisdom and intelligence are corrupted by pride. They have rejected God's truth, and he may seal their rejection by closing their minds to spiritual truth once and for all. God reveals the truth not to the proud and sophisticated but to "babes." This parallels Jesus' statement in Matthew 18:3, "Unless you are converted and become like children, you shall not enter the kingdom of heaven." A childlike response is the antithesis of human wisdom and stubborn pride. It requires the humility of one who has limited skill, no education, and little human ability. One word best sums up the child—*dependent.*

Who can enter into salvation? Those who, like children, are dependent, not independent. Those who are humble, not proud. Those who recognize that they are helpless and empty. Aware that they are nothing, they turn in utter dependency to Christ. Psalm 138:6 says: "For though the LORD is exalted, yet He regards the lowly; but the haughty he knows from afar." Those with true humility, the "babes," have access to God and his truth. But the proud, the "wise and intelligent," have no knowledge of him whatsoever.

The contrast between the wise and the childlike is actually a contrast between works and grace. The Galileans who rejected Christ were oriented to a system of works-righteousness. They were prosperous, self-sufficient, and egotistical. Jesus stood in opposition to all they loved, so they rejected him. Less sophisticated people, deeply distressed over their own emptiness, humble and broken, were open to him. They had no righteousness of their own to rely on. And so it seemed good in God's sight to reveal the truth to them.

Isaiah 57:15 says: "For thus says the high and exalted One who lives forever, whose name is Holy, 'I dwell on a high and holy place.'" That statement places Jehovah on as high a level as we can envision him. But then he adds, "[I dwell] also with the contrite and lowly of spirit in order to revive the spirit of the lowly and to revive the heart of the contrite." The word *revive* in that verse is translated in the Septuagint (the Greek version of the Hebrew Scriptures) with the same Greek word translated "give you rest" in Matthew 11:28. God gives rest—salvation—to humble people, people filled with contrition, brokenness, and a sense of dependency. There is no place for the proud.

First Corinthians 1:26–28 says, "Consider your calling, brethren, that there were not many wise according to the flesh, not many mighty, not many noble; but God has chosen the foolish . . . and the weak . . . and the base." They are the ones who sense their need, and are not proud. Pride says, "I can do it on my own. I have my own resources." The wise and prudent who take that position are shut out from the kingdom.

Revelation

A second essential element of conversion is revelation. Salvation comes to one who is childlike but only on the basis of revelation from God through Christ. Jesus said, "All things have been handed over to Me by My Father; and no one knows the Son, except the Father; nor does anyone know the Father, except the Son, and anyone to whom the Son wills to reveal Him" (Matt. 11:27). What is revealed is a personal knowledge of the Father and the Son. The only people who receive it are those who are sovereignly chosen.

That verse is one of the most profound passages in all of Scripture. It begins with a declaration of Jesus' deity: "All things have been handed over to Me by My Father." Two elements of that statement would have been especially offensive to those steeped in the teaching of the Pharisees. First, Jesus called God "My Father." This is the first time Scripture records Jesus' use of that name in his public ministry. He had often called God "Father" and "Our Father," but never before had he publicly said "My Father." "My Father" underscores the Son's uniqueness as the only begotten of God, and it places him in a position of absolute equality with the Father. The other offensive element in this verse is his claim, "All things have been handed over to Me." It is an affirmation of his sovereignty and again a clear claim of deity. A parallel statement is found in Matthew 28:18, where Jesus said, "All authority has been given to Me in heaven and on earth."

Jesus had already demonstrated his authority over Satan, demons, illness, the elements, the body, the soul, life, death, and even his disciples. He had showed his authority to save, to forgive sin, and to judge. He had proved that he had authority over people, earth, heaven, hell—even time. His ministry was dramatic proof that everything in the universe is under his sovereignty.

Verse 27 of Matthew 11 continues, "No one knows the Son, except the Father." No one with mere human perception can ever know the

Father like the Son does. Such knowledge is unavailable to finite beings. That is why philosophy and man-made religion are fruitless and vain. How then can we know God? Only by revelation from the Son of God himself: "Nor does anyone know the Father, except the Son, and anyone to whom the Son wills to reveal Him." Thus God chooses to reveal truth to babes. Fully dependant and emptied of human wisdom, they receive his revelation of divine truth.

Repentance

If you are troubled by the fact that God's sovereign grace determines the recipients of saving revelation, note that those words are immediately followed by an all-inclusive invitation: "Come to Me, all who are weary and heavy-laden, and I will give you rest" (v. 28).

The tension here echoes John 6:37, where the Lord said, "All that the Father gives Me shall come to Me," and then immediately added, "The one who comes to Me I will certainly not cast out." God is sovereign in election, but he issues an open invitation. We must affirm both truths, despite the difficulty in harmonizing them.

The word *weary* in Greek is *kopiaō*. It signifies labor to the point of sweat and exhaustion. As Jesus used it here, it is a reference to the futility of attempting to please God through human effort. It describes one weary of the search for truth, one who has despaired of trying to earn salvation.

"Heavy-laden" brings to mind the pitiable image of someone working hard, with a heavy burden on his back that continually gets heavier. The rabbis said the way to find spiritual rest was by keeping the minutiae of their religious laws. But the law created a yoke that was too heavy to bear (cf. Acts 15:10). And the legacy of the rabbis' teaching was a whole nation of people utterly spent and desperately in need of relief from the crushing load of a sin-laden, guilt-ridden conscience.

Although the word *repentance* is not specifically used here, that is what our Lord is calling for. "Come to Me" demands a complete turnaround, a full change of direction. The invitation is for people who know they have no answers. Overpowered and overburdened by sin, they have failed to gain entry into the kingdom through self-effort. They know they are lost. He says, "Turn around. Leave your futile despair and come. I offer the gift of God's grace."

No one is invited to bring the load and simply add Jesus to it. The invitation applies only to those who know they are at the end of their own resources, people desperate to turn from self and sin to the Savior. This is not an invitation to people who enjoy their sin.

When Jesus blasted in fury at the cities of Chorazin, Bethsaida, and Capernaum back in verses 20–24, he did it because they had refused to repent. Now, moments later, he invites those who are weary of their sin and their self-righteous, works-based religion to turn to him and lay down the load they are carrying.

Faith

Another essential element of genuine conversion is faith. "Come to Me" is tantamount to saying "Believe in Me." In John 6:35 Jesus said, "I am the bread of life; he who comes to Me shall never hunger, and he who believes in Me shall never thirst." To come to Jesus is to believe in him.

Faith is the flip side of repentance. Repentance means turning from sin, and faith means turning to the Savior—one turning. Salvation occurs when a heart is humbled by a sovereign God who reveals his truth. In desperation the soul turns from sin and embraces Christ. It is not an intellectual exercise (which would appeal to "the wise and intelligent"); it is a turning of the whole heart to Christ.

Submission

Salvation does not end there. Another element of genuine conversion is submission. Jesus' invitation does not end with the words "I will give you rest." He goes on to say, "Take My yoke upon you, and learn from Me, for I am gentle and humble in heart; and you shall find rest for your souls. For My yoke is easy, and My load is light" (Matt. 11:29). The call to surrender to Jesus' lordship is part and parcel of his invitation to salvation. Those unwilling to take on his yoke cannot enter into the saving rest he offers.

Jesus' hearers understood that the yoke was a symbol of submission. In Israel yokes were made of wood, carefully fashioned by the carpenter's hand to fit the neck of the animal that was to wear it. Undoubtedly Jesus had made many yokes as a young man in Joseph's carpentry shop in Nazareth. It was a perfect illustration of salvation. The yoke was worn by the animal to bear a load, and used by the master to direct the animal.

The yoke also signified discipleship. When our Lord added the phrase "and learn from Me," the imagery would have been familiar to Jewish listeners. In ancient writings, a pupil who submitted himself to a teacher was said to take the teacher's yoke. One writer records this proverb: "Put your neck under the yoke and let your soul receive instruction." Rabbis spoke of the yoke of instruction, the yoke of the Torah, and the yoke of the law.

It is a yoke that also implies obedience. The imagery of the yoke itself argues against the notion that one can take Jesus as Savior and not as Lord. Jesus does not bid people come to him if they are unwilling to receive his yoke. True salvation occurs when a sinner in desperation turns from his sin to Christ with a willingness to have him take control.

Salvation is by grace through faith. It has nothing to do with meritorious human works. But the only possible response to God's grace is a broken humility that causes the sinner to turn from his old life to Christ. The evidence of such a turning is the willingness to submit and obey. If cold-hearted disobedience and deliberate rebellion continue unabated, there is good reason to doubt the reality of a person's faith.

The yoke of the law, the yoke of human effort, the yoke of works, and the yoke of sin are all heavy, chafing, galling yokes. They represent large, unbearable burdens carried in the flesh. They lead to despair, frustration, and anxiety. Jesus offers a yoke we can carry, and he also gives the strength to carry it (cf. Phil. 4:13). Therein is true rest.

The yoke Jesus offers is easy, and the burden he gives is light, because he is meek and lowly. Unlike the Pharisees and scribes, Jesus does not desire to oppress us. He does not want to pile burdens on us that we cannot bear. He is not trying to show how hard righteousness can be. He is gentle and tender, and he gives a light burden to carry. Obedience under his yoke is a joy. It is when we disobey that the yoke chafes our neck.

The yoke of submission to Christ is not grievous; it is joyous. It means liberation from the guilt and burden of sin—"rest for your souls." This is an echo of Jeremiah 6:16, where the prophet says, "Stand by the ways and see and ask for the ancient paths, where the good way is, and walk in it; and you shall find rest for your souls. But they said, 'We will not walk in it.'"

Jesus received an identical response. Subsequent events in his ministry show that the hatred for Christ only intensified—to the point that the rejecting crowd finally crucified him. His yoke was easy, but for hypocritical, rebellious, stubborn, sin-laden hearts, the demand to come to him was too much. His invitation was spurned. His salvation was rejected. These people loved the darkness of their sin more than the brightness of his glory. And thus by their unbelieving rejection of his lordship, they condemned themselves.

PART THREE

———

JESUS ILLUSTRATES
HIS GOSPEL

10

The Soils

Jesus' invitation, "Come to Me. . . . Take My yoke upon you . . . and you shall find rest" (Matt. 11:28–30) signaled the end of one phase of his public teaching ministry and the beginning of a much broader, yet more personal, evangelistic emphasis.

Matthew 12 describes in detail what happened immediately after he spoke those words. That Sabbath day the religious leaders' festering hatred for Jesus finally erupted. The Pharisees, epitomizing the nation's response to their Messiah, accused him of using Satan's power to cast out demons (Matt. 12:24). Israel had rejected their King and refused the kingdom he offered. It was a full and final renunciation.

From that day on, the tenor of Jesus' ministry changed. He no longer proclaimed to Israel that the kingdom was at hand. Now the call he issued was for individuals—Jews as well as Gentiles—to surrender in faith to the yoke of his lordship.

Even the style of his teaching changed. Beginning that very day (Matt. 13:1), he taught in parables—everyday stories that illustrated spiritual reality. Rather than openly proclaiming his message, he thus obscured the truth from those who had rejected it already (vv. 11–15). Those who hungered to understand—the genuine believers—found him eager to explain every detail (cf. Mark 4:34). Those who hated the truth did not bother to ask.

The parables that begin in Matthew 13 describe "the mysteries of the kingdom of heaven" (v. 11). Our Lord was revealing a dimension of his kingdom heretofore undisclosed. The kingdom envisioned by the Jews was hardly mysterious. It was a permanent, earthly political regime that would bring the whole world under the rule of Israel's Messiah. After all, that is how they saw the kingdom described in the

123

Old Testament.[1] Up to this point, Jesus had taught nothing markedly different. But when the Israelites saw no signs of any earthly kingdom, they had rejected their Messiah's rule. Thus they had forfeited the kingdom altogether and had no right to be privy to the truths he was now teaching.

And so the parables beginning Matthew 13 were given to reveal the mystery of God's kingdom to his true disciples while concealing the truth from those outside the kingdom (cf. Mark 4:11). The parables describe the nature of God's rule during the period between Israel's rejection of Christ and the ultimate consummation of the earthly millennial kingdom. This phase of the kingdom in which we are now living is a mystery, not revealed in the Old Testament.

What is the kingdom? In Scripture it is usually called the kingdom of God; Matthew often refers to it as the kingdom of heaven.[2] The kingdom—God's rule over the earth and in the hearts of people—exists now in mystery form. Christ does not exercise his full divine will as King over all the earth, though he is ultimately sovereign. He rules as King only among those who believe. His kingdom encompasses all the redeemed, but not in a form that is visible to an unbelieving world. This aspect of God's kingdom was utterly missed by those who were looking for a political monarchy.

As always, Jesus' preoccupation was with seeking and saving the lost. That is also one of the main activities in the mystery kingdom. It is no surprise, then, that the first parable he told focused on preaching the gospel:

> Behold, the sower went out to sow; and as he sowed, some seeds fell beside the road, and the birds came and devoured them. And others fell upon the rocky places, where they did not have much soil; and immediately they sprang up, because they had no depth of soil. But when the sun had risen, they were scorched; and because they had no root, they withered away. And others fell among the thorns, and the thorns came up and choked them out. And others fell on the good soil,

[1]The Jewish concept of the kingdom was rooted in such Old Testament promises as Daniel 2:44, "The God of heaven will set up a kingdom which will never be destroyed, and that kingdom will not be left for another people; it will crush and put an end to all these kingdoms, but it will itself endure forever."

[2]There is no biblical support for the teaching of some that the kingdom of heaven and the kingdom of God are separate entities. "The kingdom of heaven" is used in the Gospels only by Matthew, who employs it some twenty-two times. Cross references, such as Matthew 13:11 with Mark 4:11 and Luke 8:10, show that the terms are interchangeable. The Jews used *heaven* as a euphemism for the name of God. Thus the distinction seems to reflect the sensitivities of the Jewish audience Matthew wrote to.

and yielded a crop, some a hundredfold, some sixty, and some thirty. He who has ears, let him hear (Matt. 13:3–9).

The Lord was using a familiar metaphor. Agriculture was the heart of Jewish life. Everyone understood the sowing of seed and the process of growing crops. It is even likely that from where Jesus was teaching, the multitude could see men sowing seed. The sower would drape a bag of seed over his shoulder. As he walked up and down the furrows, he would take handfuls of seed and broadcast it. The seed he threw would fall on four kinds of soil.

The Wayside Soil

First was the hard-packed dirt of the road bordering the field: "And as he sowed, some seeds fell beside the road, and the birds came and devoured them" (v. 4). Palestine was covered with fields. No fences or walls surrounded them; the only boundaries were narrow paths. Travelers from all over used the paths; Matthew 12:1 describes how the Lord Jesus and his disciples plucked grain to eat as they were walking through the fields, no doubt on one of these paths.

The method of sowing by broadcasting caused some of the seed to fall on the paths. The soil of the paths would be beaten hard, packed down, uncultivated, never turned over or loosened. The continual pounding of travelers' feet, along with the dry climate, would so compact the soil on these paths that the surface would be as hard as pavement. Any seed the farmer threw beyond the furrow and onto that hard ground could not penetrate the ground. It would lie there until the hovering birds ate it. What they did not eat, Luke 8:5 says, was trampled. Thus the birds and travelers obliterated the seed that landed on the wayside.

The Shallow Soil

Verse 5 describes the shallow soil: "And others fell upon the rocky places, where they did not have much soil; and immediately they sprang up, because they had no depth of soil. But when the sun had risen, they were scorched; and because they had no root, they withered away."

"Rocky places" did not refer to soil with stones in it; any farmer who cultivated a field would remove all the stones he could. In Israel, however, strata of limestone rock bed runs through the land. In places, the rock bed juts up so close to the surface that it lies only inches beneath the topsoil. As seed fell on these shallow places and began to germinate, the descending roots would soon reach rock and have nowhere to go. With roots unable to probe deeper, the young plants would generate tremendous foliage, making them more spectacular than the surrounding crop. But when the sun came out, those plants would be the first to die, because their roots could not go deep for moisture. This part of the crop would shrivel to nothing long before it could bear fruit.

The Weedy Soil

Verse 7 talks about weedy soil: "And others fell among the thorns, and the thorns came up and choked them out." This soil looked good. It was deep, rich, tilled, and fertile. At sowing time it looked clean and ready. The seed that landed there began to germinate, but the fibrous roots of weeds hidden under the surface also sprouted. They inevitably choked out the grain crop.

Weeds that are indigenous to an area always have an advantage over cultivated crops. The weeds are where they flourish naturally. The planted crop is a foreign element that needs cultivation and care. If the weeds in their natural habitat get a foothold, they will dominate the ground. The weeds grow faster and send out their leaves, which shade the planted crop from the sun. Their stronger roots also soak up all the moisture. In the end, the good plants are choked out.

The Good Soil

Finally, verse 8 describes good soil: "And others fell on the good soil, and yielded a crop, some a hundredfold, some sixty, and some thirty." This soil is soft, unlike the hard wayside soil. It is deep, unlike the shallow ground. And it is clean, unlike the weed-infested soil. Here the seed bursts into life and brings forth a tremendous harvest, a hundredfold, sixtyfold, or thirtyfold.

The Parable

On the face of it, the story of the sower and the seed is simple. The only clue that it has a deeper meaning is Jesus' admonition in verse 9: "He who has ears, let him hear." In other words, if you can understand this, then heed its message. Who *can* understand it? Only those who have the King to teach them. The disciples must have realized that this simple story about planting and harvesting grain concealed some rich spiritual truth. Mark 4:10 records that they came to Jesus when he was alone with them and asked him to explain the parable. And he did.

Note the bridge from "He who has ears, let him hear" in verse 9 to "Blessed are . . . your ears, because they hear" in verse 16. This was glorious truth from the Master's lips: "Many prophets and righteous men desired to see what you see, and did not see it; and to hear what you hear, and did not hear it. Hear then the parable of the sower" (vv. 17–18).

The Seed and the Sower

Now alone with the disciples and other inquisitive believers (Mark 4:10), the Lord took what seemed like a simple, obvious story and used it to unveil the magnificent reality of the kingdom. The seed he spoke of was not literal seed, but rather the gospel: "When anyone hears the word of the kingdom . . ." (v. 19). The seed is the message about the King and his kingdom. Luke 8:11, a parallel account, is even more explicit: "The seed is the Word of God." Thus the sower is anyone who plants the seed of the gospel by the Word of God (cf. 1 Peter 1:23) in the heart of an individual. The prototype of all sowers is the Lord himself.

Seed is an appropriate illustration of the gospel. It cannot be created; it is only reproduced. Spreading the gospel is a process of taking that which has been sown and reproduced, and sowing it again. God does not call on us to create our own seed, or message. His Word is the only good seed. There is no such thing as evangelism apart from God's Word.

The Condition of the Soil

The point of this parable is not that something is wrong with the sower or his method. Nothing is wrong with the seed. Nothing is fundamentally wrong with the *composition* of the soil either. The problem is the *condition* of the soil.

The soil illustrates the human heart. Verse 19 confirms this: "When anyone hears the word of the kingdom, and does not understand it, the evil one comes and snatches away what has been sown in his *heart*" (emphasis added). The heart of the hearer is the spiritual equivalent of soil receiving a farmer's seed.

In their essential makeup, all the soils in Jesus' parable are the same. The dirt in and around a field is the same dirt, no matter that it is hard, soft, shallow, or weedy. The difference in the soils has to do with how they have been conditioned. All the soils *could* receive the seed if they were properly prepared. But soil that is not properly prepared will never bear a crop.

It is the same with human hearts. We are all exactly the same in essence but conditioned differently according to the influences that are permitted to shape us. This is indeed an important point in the spiritual lesson of the parable: a person's response to the gospel depends primarily on the preparation of his or her heart. A heart not properly prepared will never bear spiritual fruit.

The Unresponsive Heart

The soil by the wayside pictures a hardened, unresponsive hearer. "When anyone hears the word of the kingdom, and does not understand it, the evil one comes and snatches away what has been sown in his heart. This is the one on whom seed was sown beside the road" (v. 19). Here is the hard-hearted individual—one whom the Old Testament would call stiff-necked (e.g., Prov. 29:1). He is unresponsive, unconcerned, inattentive, indifferent, negligent, and often hostile. He wants nothing to do with the gospel. It just bounces off him. Satan is portrayed as a ravenous bird, hovering over the hardened soil, eager to pluck up the seed the moment it lands. Luke 8:12 makes the meaning indisputable; these are unsaved people: "The devil comes and takes away the word from their heart, so that they may not believe and be saved."

Here our Lord warns that the human heart can be so pounded and beaten down with the traffic of sin that it becomes completely insensitive to the gospel. This is the heart that knows no repentance, no sorrow over sin, no guilt, and no concern for the things of God. It allows itself to be trampled by an endless procession of evil thoughts, cherished sins, and ungodly activities. It is careless, callous, indifferent—never broken up or softened by conviction or sorrow for wrongdoing. This is the heart of the fool described in Proverbs. He hates knowledge, resists instruction, and despises wisdom. He says in his heart there is no God. He will not hear for his mind is closed. And he does not want to be bothered with a gospel invitation.

Many people have hearts like that. You can shower them with seed, but it just lies there and does not penetrate. And it does not stay very long before Satan comes and takes it away completely. Each time you try to witness to such a person, you must start again at the beginning.

Dry, hard soil on the edge of the field does not necessarily signify someone who is antireligious. Some of the hardest individuals in the world stay on the fringes of true religion. But because sin has so hardened their hearts, they are utterly unproductive and unresponsive to God. They are very close to the truth, very close to the good soil, often receiving handfuls of seed, but the seed will not sprout in their lives.

The Superficial Heart

The shallow soil pictures the response of a superficial, impetuous heart. "And the one on whom seed was sown on the rocky places, this is the man who hears the word, and immediately receives it with joy; yet he has no firm root in himself, but is only temporary, and when affliction or persecution arises because of the word, immediately he falls away" (Matt. 13:20–21). This kind of heart is enthusiastic but shallow. It responds positively but not with saving faith. There is no thought involved, no counting the cost. It is quick, emotional, euphoric, instant excitement without any understanding of the actual significance of discipleship. That is not genuine faith.

The superficial response is epidemic in twentieth-century Christianity. Why? Because the gospel is usually presented with the promise of joy, warmth, fellowship, and a good feeling, but without the hard demand to take up one's cross and follow Christ. "Converts" are not confronted with the real issues of sin and repentance. Instead, they are encouraged to jump on the Jesus bandwagon for the good things they are promised. Yet underneath the shallow layer of apparently fertile topsoil is an unyielding rock bed of rebellion and resistance to the things of God. There is no true repentance, no brokenness, and no contrition. The slab of defiance under the soft surface is even harder than the roadside soil. And the eternal consequence is just as tragic. The initial enthusiasm is mere emotion; the germinating seed quickly dies. These people are not saved (cf. 1 John 2:19).

Shallow responders like this constitute one of the greatest disappointments of the ministry. I have spent hours discipling some of them. On the surface, their faith looks encouraging. In fact, when you look at the field, you might think these people stand taller and stronger than everyone else. But they have no root to support such lush growth, and as soon as a trial or persecution comes, they dry up and wither away.[3]

Be on guard against conversions that are all smiles and cheers with no sense of repentance or humility. That is the mark of a superficial

[3]A sidelight of this truth is the encouraging assurance that suffering and persecution play an important dual role in the kingdom of God. First, such trials expose false believers, and second, they strengthen true believers. First Peter 5:10 says, "After you have suffered for a little while, the God of all grace . . . will Himself perfect, conform, strengthen and establish you."

heart. A person with such a heart lacks the root system needed to endure harsh weather. If a profession of faith in Christ does not grow out of a deep sense of lostness; if it is not accompanied by an inner conviction of sin; if it does not include a tremendous desire for the Lord to cleanse and purify and lead; if it does not involve a willingness to deny self, to sacrifice, and to suffer for Christ's sake, then it is without a proper root. It is only a matter of time before the flourishing growth withers and dies.

The Worldly Heart

Weedy soil represents a heart preoccupied with worldly matters. Verse 22 says, "The one on whom seed was sown among the thorns, this is the man who hears the word, and the worry of the world, and the deceitfulness of riches choke the word, and it becomes unfruitful."[4] That is a perfect description of a worldly person—one who lives for the things of this world. He or she is consumed with the cares of this age. Such a person's chief pursuit is a career, a house, a car, a hobby, or a wardrobe. Prestige, looks, or riches are everything to the weedy heart.

Have you known people who fit this category? For a while they look just like the rest of the field. They come to church, identify with the people of God, even show signs of growth. But they never bear spiritual fruit. They are uncommitted and preoccupied with the world's pleasures, money, career, fame, fortune, or the lusts of the flesh. They say they are Christians, but they care nothing about a pure life. That is the response of weedy soil. The germinating seed that looks so good will ultimately be overwhelmed by the thorns of worldliness, and eventually the weedy heart will show no evidence that good seed was ever sown.

What happens when the seed that once looked so promising is choked out? Has such a person lost his salvation? No, he never had it. The Word of God fell on a heart that was unprepared because it was full of malignant weeds. That person received the seed of the gospel but not into clean soil. The gospel germinated but was choked out before it could come to fruition. The person with the weedy heart was never saved in the first place. Weedy hearts may be willing to accept Jesus as Savior, but not if it means letting go of the world. That is not salvation. Jesus said, "You cannot serve God and mammon" (Matt.

---

[4]"Becomes unfruitful" does not imply that this soil once bore fruit. Mark 4:7 shows that there was never fruit at all: "The thorns came up and choked it, and it yielded no crop."

6:24). And the apostle John wrote, "If anyone loves the world, the love of the Father is not in him" (1 John 2:15). Soil must be cleansed of the weeds and thorns if it is to produce a crop.

The Enemies

The weeds, the sun, and the birds of this parable represent our enemies. The weeds are "the worry of the world and the deceitfulness of riches" (v. 22). The sun that scorches the improperly rooted plants is "affliction [and] persecution" (cf. vv. 6, 21), which challenges the comfort that appeals so much to the flesh. The birds portray "the evil one" (cf. vv. 4, 19), Satan, who does everything he can to steal the seed of the gospel even before it can germinate. These are the three constant enemies of the gospel: the world, the flesh, and the devil.

Here is an important lesson for the sower: you will face resistance and hostility. There will be shallow, short-term converts. And you will encounter double-minded people who want Christ but will not let go of the world. The hardness of the road, the shallowness of the soil, and the aggressiveness of the weeds will frustrate your efforts to sow a good crop.

Nevertheless, be encouraged. The Lord of the harvest can break up even the hardest ground and rid it of the most stubborn weeds. Hard soil, shallow soil, or weedy soil may not always stay that way. God can till the soil of the most stubborn heart. One ancient Palestinian method of farming was to throw the seed first and then plow it under. That sometimes happens in evangelism. We sow the seed, and even when it seems the hovering birds are about to snatch it away, the Holy Spirit plows it under so that it can sprout and bear glorious fruit.

The Receptive Heart

Knowing there are three kinds of soil that produce undesirable results might be discouraging. But there is still the good soil, which illustrates the receptive heart. "And the one on whom seed was sown on the good soil, this is the man who hears the word and understands it; who indeed bears fruit, and brings forth, some a hundredfold, some sixty, and some thirty" (v. 23). This is the climax of the parable. It is a promise to the discouraged disciples that there is good soil in the field. Lest they be shaken by the people's negative response, Jesus wanted them to know that there is a huge field cultivated and ready to receive the seed. It will bear abundant fruit.

The Fruit

Fruit-bearing is the whole point of agriculture. It is also the ultimate test of salvation. Jesus said, "Every good tree bears good fruit; but the rotten tree bears bad fruit. A good tree cannot produce bad fruit, nor can a rotten tree produce good fruit. Every tree that does not bear good fruit is cut down and thrown into the fire. So then, you will know them by their fruits" (Matt. 7:17–20). If there is no spiritual fruit, or if the fruit is bad, the tree must be rotten. Or, translating the imagery to the metaphor of a field, if the soil does not produce a crop, it is worthless ground, symbolic of an unredeemed heart.

Taken at face value, the message of the parable of the soils is clear: of four soils, only one is good. Only one produces fruit, and thus it alone is of any value to the farmer. This good soil pictures the believer. The weedy soil and the shallow soil are pretenders. The soil by the wayside is an absolute rejecter.

Fruit, not foliage, is the mark of true salvation. Those who miss that point confuse the meaning of the parable. Much has been written in recent years attempting to argue that the shallow soil or weedy soil represent true believers, albeit unproductive ones. For example, Zane Hodges writes:

> From the roadside—and from the roadside alone—the Word of God had been retrieved. By the Saviour's own explicit observation this retrieval was for the purpose that salvation might not occur. Here, *but here alone*, Satan had triumphed completely. . . . The inference from this was plain. *Into all of the remaining hearts, whatever the character of their soil, new life had come.*[5]

That misses the point completely. The seed in the parable is not symbolic of eternal life; it is the message of the gospel. The sprouting of the seed in the shallow soil and the weedy soil simply means that the Word had been received and had begun to operate, not that eternal life had been conferred. Warren Wiersbe understands the issue clearly:

> It is important to note that none of these first three hearts [the soil by the wayside, the shallow soil, and the weedy soil] underwent salvation. The proof of salvation is not listening to the Word, or having a quick emotional response to the Word, or even cultivating the Word so that it

[5]Zane C. Hodges, *The Hungry Inherit* (Portland: Multnomah, 1980), 68–69, emphasis added.

grows in a life. The proof of salvation is *fruit,* for as Christ said, "Ye shall know them by their fruits" (Matt. 7:16).[6]

Indeed, fruit is the ultimate test of true salvation. In the harvest, weedy soil is no better than the hard road or shallow ground. All are worthless. Seed sown there is wasted, and the ground is fit for nothing except burning (cf. Heb. 6:8). It cannot picture salvation.

Notice that not all the good ground is equally productive. Some bears quantities of a hundredfold, some sixtyfold, and some thirtyfold. Not every Christian will bear as much fruit as he or she ought to or could. But each one is fruitful to some degree. Christians are sometimes disobedient, and of course they still sin. But ultimately, believers are identifiable by their fruit. Whether it is a hundredfold, sixtyfold, or thirtyfold, the spiritual fruit of true believers sets them apart from the hard dirt of the road or the uselessness of a weed patch. Their fruit comes in varying amounts—some are more fruitful than others—but all are fruitful. It is that fruit-bearing capability that makes the good soil stand out clearly from the rocky, thorny, and barren earth.

As sowers, we are called to broadcast the seed of the unadulterated gospel, even if some of it falls on unprepared soil. Wayside soil, shallow soil, and weedy soil will always exist, but so also will good soil that will bring forth crops thirty-, sixty-, or a hundredfold. That prepared soil needs only to have the right seed thrown on it.

[6]Warren W. Wiersbe, *Meet Yourself in the Parables* (Wheaton: Victor, 1979), 27.

11

The Wheat and Tares

Christians are not supposed to live like unsaved people.

That may not sound especially profound, but many evangelicals today do not seem to understand it. I am chagrined at the way Christians tolerate flagrant sin in their midst. Like the Corinthian church, who arrogantly welcomed a brazen fornicator to their fellowship (1 Cor. 5:1–2),[1] some Christians today seem to take perverse pride in never challenging the lifestyle of anyone who claims to be a believer.

Sin that was unheard of in the church only a generation ago is now commonplace. Divorce and immorality are epidemic among Christians. Churches claiming to be evangelical smugly offer the right hand of fellowship to unmarried couples openly living together. One fast-growing denomination consists almost entirely of practicing homosexuals. Many in the church believe them to be Christians because they affirm faith in Jesus. Worst of all, the state of leadership in some of the most obvious segments of the church is pathetic. Recent news headlines have made that clear to the world.[2]

[1]Paul rebuked the Corinthians for their cockiness about the sin in their congregation (1 Cor. 5:2). He implied they had no right to assume an incestuous fornicator was a true believer—his sin was so wicked that even pagan Gentiles would not do such things openly (v. 1). He demanded that the Corinthians excommunicate the man (vv. 2, 5, 13) and referred to him as a "so-called brother" (v. 11). Paul clearly doubted that a regenerate person would live so contemptuously.

[2]It is embarrassing that the scandals of the 1980s and 1990s have exposed even worse sin in the church than in the secular political arena. Ironically, however, many Christians seem more willing than the world to restore their disqualified leaders to positions of prominence, violating the cardinal requirement that a leader be above reproach (1 Tim. 3:2, 10; Titus 1:6).

I am convinced that the popularized gospel of the twentieth-century church has made all this possible—even inevitable. The notion that faith is nothing more than believing a few biblical facts caters to human depravity. If repentance, holiness of life, and submission to the lordship of Christ are all optional, why should we expect the redeemed to differ from the heathen? Who is to say that someone might not be a believer, just because that person lives in stubborn rebellion against God? If people say they believe, shouldn't we just take their word for it?

The tragic result is that many people think it is fairly normal for Christians to live like unbelievers. As I noted in chapter 1, contemporary theologians have devised an entire category for this type of person—the "carnal Christian." Who knows how many unregenerate persons have been lulled into a false sense of spiritual security by the suggestion that they are merely carnal?

Please don't misunderstand me. Christians can and do behave in carnal ways. But nothing in Scripture suggests that a real Christian might pursue a lifestyle of unbroken indifference or antagonism toward the things of God. Christians do not masquerade as children of the devil. The reverse is true; Satan pretends to be an angel of light, and his servants imitate the children of righteousness (2 Cor. 11:14–15).

When Scripture acknowledges the difficulty of telling the sheep from the goats, the point is not that Christians may seem ungodly, but rather that the ungodly often appear to be righteous. To switch metaphors slightly, the flock is supposed to be on the lookout for wolves in sheep's clothing, not tolerant of sheep that act like wolves. In this regard, Jesus' parable about the wheat and tares (Matt. 13:24–30) has often been misunderstood.

This parable uses imagery similar to that of the parable of the soils, but here our Lord makes a completely different point:

> He presented another parable to them, saying, "The kingdom of heaven may be compared to a man who sowed good seed in his field. But while men were sleeping, his enemy came and sowed tares also among the wheat, and went away. But when the wheat sprang up and bore grain, then the tares became evident also. And the slaves of the landowner came and said to him, 'Sir, did you not sow good seed in your field? How then does it have tares?' And he said to them, 'An enemy has done this!' And the slaves said to him, 'Do you want us, then, to go and gather them up?' But he said, 'No; lest while you are gathering up the tares, you may root up the wheat with them. Allow both to grow together until the harvest; and in the time of the harvest I will say to the reapers,

"First gather up the tares and bind them in bundles to burn them up; but gather the wheat into my barn"'" (Matt. 13:24–30).

Oversowing another's grain crop with weeds was a common enough act that Rome had a law against it. It was an almost certain way to ruin one's neighbor, because it rendered his crop useless and thus nullified his chief source of income.

In this parable, a man's enemy had sowed tares in his field. "Tares" refers to darnel, a wheatlike plant that produced useless seed instead of grain. It so closely resembled wheat that it was known as bastard wheat. Until its seed head was mature, it was nearly impossible to distinguish from real wheat, even under the most careful scrutiny.

The landowner in Jesus' parable chose not to risk destroying any of the legitimate crop while trying to pull out the tares. Instead, he decided to let both wheat and weeds grow together until harvest, at which time the reapers would separate the good crop from the bad when the difference would be obvious.

What can this story mean? It is surprising that the multitudes did not ask, but they were more interested in seeing miracles and being fed than in knowing the truth (John 6:26). The disciples, however, did want to know. Matthew 13:36 says that after the Lord had left the multitudes and entered a house—very likely Simon Peter's house in Capernaum—the disciples said to him, "Explain to us the parable of the tares of the field."

The Players

Jesus' explanation begins simply: "The one who sows the good seed is the Son of Man." That is the title the Lord used more than any other to refer to himself. Only once in the New Testament is "the Son of Man" used by someone else to describe Jesus; every other time it appears, he uses it of himself. It identifies him in his humanness as the incarnate One who was the perfection of all that a man could be. It speaks of him as the second Adam, the sinless representative of the race. It also associates him with messianic prophecy (Dan. 7:13).

According to Matthew 13:38, "The field is the world." By implication the sower—the Son of Man—owns the field. He holds in his hand the title deed to it. He is its sovereign monarch. And he cultivates his crop there. What does he sow? "As for the good seed, these are the sons of the kingdom" (v. 38). The children of his kingdom are believing people, those submissive to the King. And he sows them throughout his field, the world.

"The tares are the sons of the evil one; and the enemy who sowed them is the devil" (vv. 38–39). These are unbelievers. The phrase "Sons of the evil one" is similar to the terminology Jesus used in John 8:44, when he castigated the religious leaders: "You are of your father, the devil." First John 3:10 indicates that all who are not children of God are children of the devil.

The Plot

The meaning of this parable is not at all complicated. The Son of Man—Jesus—sowed the children of his kingdom in the world. The enemy—Satan—ruined the purity of the crop, mingling his children with those the Son of Man had sowed. These unbelieving children of the Evil One live together with believers in the world. In the final judgment God will separate the wheat from the weeds.

As simple as that is, many Bible students miss the point entirely. Although the field is clearly said to represent the world, a surprising number of commentators see the field as the church. To them, the parable is a message about false elements in the church and divine permission to leave them alone until the Lord and the angels sort out the true from the false in the final judgment.

Obviously, that is not the point of this parable at all. Such a teaching would violate everything the New Testament teaches about church discipline. Satan likes to sow his tares as close to the wheat as he can, and he does sow some of them in the church. But this parable is not teaching Christians that they should tolerate unbelievers in the fellowship. We are to have nothing to do with false teachers and sham believers (2 John 9–11). We are clearly commanded to purge such influences from the church (1 Cor. 5:2, 7).

This parable contains instructions for the church in the world, not a free pass for the world in the church. Satan sows his people everywhere. We who belong to the kingdom exist in the same realm as unbelievers. We breathe the same air, we eat the same food, we drive the same highways, we live in the same neighborhoods, we work at the same factories, we go to the same schools, we visit the same doctors, we shop at the same stores, we enjoy the same warm sun, and we are all rained on by the same rain. What we can never share, however, is spiritual fellowship (2 Cor. 6:14–16), and this parable does not teach otherwise.

The message of the wheat and the tares is simply that God does not sanction any effort that would rid the world of unbelievers by force. The disciples were ready to put in the sickle and get rid of the children of the devil. We understand their passion. We can certainly relate to the prayer of the psalmist, "Let the wicked perish before

God" (Ps. 68:2). We can understand why James and John, the Sons of Thunder, would ask Jesus, "Lord, do you want us to command fire to come down from heaven and consume them?" (Luke 9:54).

In essence, that is what the slaves of the landowner were asking when they said, "Do you want us, then, to go and gather them [the tares] up?" (v. 28). The landowner wisely told them not to pull them up, because rooting out the tares might destroy the wheat also.

World history confirms the wisdom of such a plan. Whenever there has been a religious movement to rid the world of paganism, it is the true church that has suffered the most. Read, for example, *Foxe's Book of Martyrs*. Many of those slaughtered for their faith throughout church history have been faithful believers put to death by misguided zealots claiming to represent God. The Inquisition was responsible for the deaths of untold numbers of Christians, killed because they held God's Word as a higher authority than the teachings of church leaders. One of my friends owns a sixteenth-century Bible stained with the blood of a martyr, put to death simply for owning it. Religious fanatics always see genuine believers as the enemy.

God does not call his people to a ministry of inquisition. Now is not the time to rip the tares out. Our mission is not a political or military crusade, and this is not a time of judgment. Moreover, we are not called to dole out retribution. We are sent out rather to be ambassadors for Christ, emissaries of his mercy and grace.

We are not here by accident. We are planted by the Lord, in the world. We should never try to escape that. We are not told to sequester ourselves in a monastery or escape with other believers into a holy commune. We are to stay where we are planted and bear fruit. We might even have a positive effect on the tares.

Here, of course, is where the symbolism breaks down. Real tares cannot become wheat, but a son of the Evil One can be transformed into a child of the kingdom. That is the whole point of salvation. In Ephesians 2 Paul wrote, "We . . . were by nature children of wrath, even as the rest" (v. 3). Salvation gives us a new nature and turns us from "sons of disobedience" (v. 2) into members of God's household (v. 19), from tares into wheat. "We are His workmanship," Paul wrote in verse 10 of that same chapter. And we are "created in Christ Jesus for good works, which God prepared that we should walk in them." In the spiritual sense, all wheat begins as tares.

We are not to root out the tares or demand that they live by the spiritual principles of the kingdom. It is futile trying to make tares produce good harvest. Without a divine rebirth, a tare will never be wheat. Grooming a weed to look like wheat will not make it produce good grain. In Matthew 7:6, during the Sermon on the Mount, Jesus said, "Do not throw your pearls before swine." In other words, do not take kingdom principles and try to enforce them on a society that lives outside the kingdom.

Christians are not to condemn the world or force external reform upon it, though we must preach against its sins. We are commanded to teach the gospel (cf. Matt. 28:19–20) and live as examples of righteousness. But we are not God's executioners.

The Plan

At harvest time, the wheat and the tares will be separated. "The reapers are angels" (Matt. 13:39). They will carry out judgment at the end of the age. The tares—the sons of the Evil One—will be gathered and burned (v. 40). Hell will be their eternal abode. The reapers "will cast them into the furnace of fire" (v. 42). The picture is terrifying: "there shall be weeping and gnashing of teeth"—literally, "grinding of the teeth and piercing shrieks." The sons of the kingdom—"the righteous" (v. 43)—will eternally inhabit the kingdom.

How will the reapers know the wheat from the tares? The issue, as always, is the spiritual fruit they bear. Tares may look similar to wheat, but tares cannot produce wheat kernels. The mature grain clearly sets wheat apart from tares. So it is in the spiritual world. The sons of the Evil One can imitate the children of the kingdom, but they cannot produce true righteousness: "A rotten tree [cannot] produce good fruit" (Matt. 7:18). The language of the parable confirms this. The tares are called "stumbling blocks . . . those who commit lawlessness" (v. 41). The wheat are called "righteous" (v. 43). Clearly, character and behavior are what separate the wheat from the tares. In the Judgment the difference will be fully manifest.

Yet this parable is not saying we should be unconcerned with the difference between wheat and tares until the final judgment. It does not encourage us to accept tares as wheat. It does not sanction indifference about the sins of the lost. Nor does it suggest we forget there are weeds in the field and be inattentive to the peril they pose. It simply tells us to leave final judgment and retribution in the hands of the Lord and his angels.

In the end, real wheat will inevitably be identified by the crop it produces. Wheat will not produce dandelion heads. It will not grow to look like a tumbleweed. Because of its inherent nature, it will produce wheat grain, though it be cultivated in a field overgrown with tares.

The children of the kingdom are like that as well. They live in the

world, where children of the Evil One flourish. But the children of
the kingdom have a heavenly nature. The fruit they bear will be
different from the fruit borne by the children of the Evil One. You
can count on it.

12

The Treasure of the Kingdom

A Calvinist friend once remarked that the contemporary church often fails to present the gospel clearly enough for the nonelect to reject it. He has a point. The gospel our age has popularized is a sugar-coated placebo designed more to soothe sinners than to convert them.

The gospel according to Jesus stands in stark contrast. Our Lord frequently chased the most enthusiastic inquirers away. We have already studied his challenge to the rich young ruler. That was no isolated episode in his evangelistic ministry. Luke 9:57–62, for example, relates how Jesus ran off three other hot prospects. Think also of the crowds that followed Jesus during the early days of his ministry. Why did so many of them turn away (cf. John 6:66)? Because Jesus repeatedly made difficult demands. He commanded those who sought eternal life to deny themselves, forsake all, and follow him. He never held forth the hope of salvation to anyone who refused to submit to his sovereign lordship. His words to the multitudes in Mark 8:34–37 could hardly have been more straightforward: "If anyone wishes to come after Me, let him deny himself, and take up his cross, and follow Me. For whoever wishes to save his life shall lose it; and whoever loses his life for My sake and the gospel's shall save it. For what does it profit a man to gain the whole world, and forfeit his soul? For what shall a man give in exchange for his soul?"

Some have tried to soften that demand by interpreting it as a call for saved people to take a further step of commitment.[1] But similar words from the Lord in John 12:24–25 make his meaning unmistak-

---

[1]Cf. Zane C. Hodges, *The Hungry Inherit* (Portland: Multnomah, 1980), 77–91.

141

able. The subject here is explicitly eternal life and salvation: "Truly, truly I say to you, unless a grain of wheat falls into the earth and dies, it remains by itself alone; but if it dies, it bears much fruit. He who loves his life loses it; and he who hates his life in this world shall keep it *to life eternal*" (emphasis added). Forsaking oneself for Christ's sake is not an optional step of discipleship subsequent to conversion; it is the *sine qua non* of saving faith.

The Savior consistently set forth his gospel on those terms. Faith as he characterized it is nothing less than a complete exchange of all that we are for all that he is. Two brief parables in Matthew 13:44–46 illustrate precisely this truth. They show the incomparable worth of the kingdom of heaven and the nature of the commitment required of everyone who would enter:

> The kingdom of heaven is like a treasure hidden in the field, which a man found and hid; and from joy over it he goes and sells all that he has, and buys that field. Again, the kingdom of heaven is like a merchant seeking fine pearls, and upon finding one pearl of great value, he went and sold all that he had, and bought it.

Both parables make the same point: a sinner who understands the priceless riches of the kingdom will gladly yield everything else he cherishes in order to obtain it. The corresponding truth is also clear by implication: those who cling to their earthly treasures forfeit the far greater wealth of the kingdom.

Some students of Scripture object to this interpretation of these parables. They see Christ—not the sinner—as the one who sells all to buy the precious treasure and pearl. C. I. Scofield, for example, wrote:

> The interpretation of the parable of the treasure, which makes the buyer of the field to be a sinner who is seeking Christ, has no warrant in the parable itself. The field is defined (v. 38) to be the world. The seeking sinner does not buy, but forsakes, the world to win Christ. Furthermore, the sinner has nothing to sell, nor is Christ for sale, nor is he hidden in a field, nor, having found Christ, does the sinner hide him again (cf. Mk. 7:24; Acts 4:20). At every point the interpretation breaks down.
>
> Our Lord is the buyer at the awful cost of his blood (1 Pet. 1:18), and Israel . . . hidden in "the field," the world (v. 38), is the treasure."[2]

For similar reasons, Scofield wrote, "The Church is the pearl of great cost."[3]

---

[2]C. I. Scofield, ed., *The Scofield Reference Bible* (New York: Oxford Univ. Press, 1909), 1017.
[3]Ibid.

We cannot be dogmatic about the meaning of parables not specifically explained by the Lord, but I reject that view for several reasons. First, the field in this parable is not said to be the world. Verse 38 ("the field is the world") applies to the parable of the tares. The seed strewn there pictures "the sons of the kingdom" (v. 38). By contrast, the field in the parable of the soils represents a cultivated heart and the seed is the Word. The imagery is not at all the same. One parable cannot be used to interpret another.

Second, Scofield rejects the classic interpretation of these parables because he is trying to read too much into them. Symbolism in a parable is not meant to be carried out to the Nth degree. Most parables have one main lesson, and if you allegorize, stretch the symbolism too far, or try to squeeze meaning from peripheral details, you will inevitably find a point where the metaphor breaks down. In fact, a close look at the interpretation Scofield proposes reveals it has its own inconsistencies—some that strain the doctrine of grace Scofield is hoping to preserve. For example, Christ did not stumble across Israel by accident or discover the church after a long time of searching. Furthermore, the Lord did not purchase Israel and the church because they were rare treasures worthy of great sacrifice. They were, like all sinners, useless debris until *after* Christ redeemed them (cf. 1 Cor. 1:26–29). He did not discover inherently priceless commodities and then purchase them; rather, he bought what was utterly worthless and made it precious.

Third, and most important, Jesus was giving these parables to unveil the mysteries of the kingdom of heaven—not to explain the Atonement. Biblical interpreters know that the simplest and most obvious interpretation is the normal one. And in these stories the most obvious interpretation is that they portray the kingdom of heaven as a treasure more valuable than the sum of all our possessions. That interpretation is consistent with everything Jesus ever taught about the way of salvation.[4] If you are not convinced, compare these parables with Jesus' words to the rich young ruler in Mark 10:21: "Go and sell all you possess, and give to the poor, and you shall have treasure in heaven." The parallels are striking. The

---

[4]J. C. Macaulay, whose interpretation of these parables is similar to Scofield's, nevertheless makes this excellent observation: "While 'the gift of God is eternal life,' entering the kingdom of heaven is costly business, for which reason Christ Himself warns us to count the cost, and adds, 'whosoever he be of you that forsaketh not all he hath, he cannot be my disciple' (Luke 14:28–33). Whatever else the parable of the hidden treasure has to teach us, it certainly reminds us that it costs to enter the kingdom of God, but that it is more than worth the cost" (*Behold Your King* [Chicago: Moody Press, 1982], 114).

man who sells all to obtain treasure pictures the one who enters the kingdom of heaven.

Hidden Treasure

It was common in Palestine for people to bury valuables in a secret place. Israel was a land of war. Jewish history is filled with battles, sieges, and conquering armies who came to steal and to plunder. Josephus, a Jewish historian of the first century, wrote of "the gold and the silver and the rest of that most precious furniture which the Jews had, and which the owners treasured up underground against the uncertain fortunes of war."[5]

Matthew 13:44 is a complete parable in one verse: "The kingdom of heaven is like a treasure hidden in the field, which a man found and hid; and from joy over it he goes and sells all that he has, and buys that field." Jesus did not say how the man in the parable found this store of wealth. Perhaps he was employed by the field's owner to cultivate it, or maybe he just happened to pass through and stumbled over part of the treasure protruding above the ground. Immediately he put it back where he found it. Then he sold everything he owned in the world and bought the field so the treasure would be his.

Was this unethical? Didn't the treasure legally belong to the owner of the field? No. Rabbinic law said that if a man found scattered fruit or money, it was his. Obviously this cache did not belong to the landowner, or he would have dug it up before selling the field. It undoubtedly belonged to a previous landowner now deceased. It may have been there for generations without being discovered. The man who uncovered it had a rightful claim to it.

In fact, this man's actions show how fair and honest he was. He could have walked away with the treasure, and no one would have been the wiser. Or he might have quietly pilfered just enough to buy the field. But he didn't. Instead, he liquidated everything he owned and bought the entire field so that no one could accuse him of obtaining the treasure unethically.

A Costly Pearl

The parable of the costly pearl is only slightly different: "Again, the kingdom of heaven is like a merchant seeking fine pearls, and upon finding one pearl of great value, he went and sold all that he

[5]Quoted in William Barclay, *The Gospel of Matthew*, vol. 2 (Philadelphia: Westminster, 1958), 93–94.

had, and bought it" (Matt. 13:44–45). Here we read of a wholesale merchant who specialized in pearls. Unlike the man in the first parable, he did not make his discovery by accident.[6] His life was one long search for the finest pearls, which he would then sell to retailers—until the day he discovered one pearl that he wanted more than anything else in the world.

Pearls were the costliest of gems, and wealthy people purchased them as investments. The Talmud speaks of pearls as being beyond price. The Egyptians actually worshiped them. First Timothy 2:9 refers to women who flaunted their wealth by putting pearls in their hair. And when Jesus warned against casting pearls before swine (Matt. 7:6), he was contrasting the lowest unclean animal with what was perceived to be the most valuable jewel. Even prophecy emphasizes the value of pearls; John's vision of the heavenly city revealed gates that are giant pearls (Rev. 21:21).

This merchant was a pearl expert. He bought and sold fine pearls for a living. Yet a single priceless pearl, the finest one he had ever seen, stirred in his heart such a passion that he was willing to give up everything he owned to buy it.

Acquiring the Kingdom

In relating these parables, the Lord debunked some cherished presuppositions in the minds of his Jewish listeners. They believed they were destined to gain entrance to the kingdom of God because of their lineage—the same way they had become members of their tribes or citizens of the nation. These parables cautioned them not to take the kingdom for granted. No one gets in automatically. This is the gist of both parables: the kingdom of heaven is only for those who perceive its immeasurable value and are willing to sacrifice everything else to acquire it. It is not enough to lodge in the branches or be touched by the kingdom's influence;[7] one must embrace the kingdom with a whole heart—with the zeal of one who gladly forsakes everything to buy one treasure more precious than anything else he or she could possess.

The kingdom of heaven is rich beyond comparison. It encompasses Christ and all that he offers—eternal life and unending blessing. It is

---

[6]Some men stumble upon the kingdom as if by accident, like the man who found the treasure. Others discover it only after diligent searching, like the man who bought the pearl. But in either case, once they see its value, they are willing to sacrifice everything to have it.

[7]Cf. verses 31–35. This was the point of the parables of the mustard seed and leaven.

incorruptible, undefiled, unfading, and infinite. Its value far exceeds that of the world's richest treasures or finest pearls. Yet its richness eludes most people. Like the treasure hidden in the field, the riches of the kingdom are passed over by multitudes who never know they are there. First Corinthians 2:14 acknowledges this: "A natural man does not accept the things of the Spirit of God, for they are foolishness to him, and he cannot understand them, because they are spiritually appraised." That verse follows a quotation adapted from Isaiah: "Things which eye has not seen and ear has not heard, and which have not entered the heart of man, all that God has prepared for those who love Him" (1 Cor. 2:9; cf. Isa. 64:4).

If these things are foolishness to human wisdom, hidden from the human eye, unheard by the human ear, and foreign to the human heart, how can anyone perceive the realities of the kingdom? "For to us God revealed them through the Spirit" (1 Cor. 2:10). God opens hearts to understand the inconceivable wealth of riches and blessing in his kingdom.

Those who do get a glimpse of the value of the kingdom will then joyfully give all they have to obtain it. Note that the man who found the treasure sold all he owned out of sheer joy (Matt. 13:44). Sacrificing his possessions for something far greater was no drudgery for him—he was rejoicing over his new-found riches, not mourning the junk he had sold. Relinquishing all his other possessions was a joyous price to pay for such immense wealth.

That is how it is with salvation. To the unregenerate mind, the thought of yielding everything to Christ is odious. But a believing heart surrenders to the Master with great joy. The glorious freedom from sin and the unending blessings of eternal life far outweigh any cost.

Paul is a prime illustration of someone who understood the joy of giving up all things to gain something of eternal value. In Philippians 3:7–8, he wrote: "Whatever things were gain to me, those things I have counted as loss for the sake of Christ. More than that, I count all things to be loss in view of the surpassing value of knowing Christ Jesus my Lord, for whom I have suffered the loss of all things, and count them but rubbish in order that I may gain Christ." In comparison to the rich treasure of knowing Christ, everything else in Paul's life he considered trash.

This man is buying treasure. He will liquidate everything to get it. His heritage, his self-righteousness, his money, his education, and all his most precious possessions are mere garbage compared to the wealth he will obtain. He is glad to give it all up for the kingdom. That is the nature of saving faith.

The Cost of Following Christ

Must we literally sell everything and take an oath of poverty in order to be saved? No. Nor do these parables teach that sinners must rid themselves of their sins before coming to Christ. They do mean that saving faith retains no privileges and makes no demands. It safeguards no cherished sins, treasures no earthly possessions more than Christ, clings to no secret self-indulgences. Instead, faith begets a heart that longs to surrender unconditionally to whatever the Lord demands.

Eternal life is indeed a free gift (Rom. 6:23). Salvation cannot be earned with good deeds or secured with money. It has already been purchased by Christ, who paid the ransom with his blood. He has secured full atonement for all who believe. There is nothing left to pay, no possibility that our own works can be meritorious. But that does not mean there is no cost in terms of salvation's impact on the sinner's life. Do not throw away this paradox just because it is difficult. Salvation is both free and costly. With eternal life comes immediate death to self: "Knowing this, that our old self was crucified with him, that our body of sin might be done away with, that we should no longer be slaves to sin" (Rom. 6:6). If Christ died in our stead, then we are counted as dead with him (2 Cor. 5:14), and we must so reckon ourselves—"dead to sin, but alive to God in Christ Jesus" (Rom. 6:11).

That is what Jesus meant when he spoke of taking up one's own cross to follow him. And that is why he demanded that we count the cost carefully. He was calling for an exchange of all that we are for all that he is. He was demanding implicit obedience—unconditional surrender to his lordship. Geerhardus Vos articulated this principle when he wrote:

> Jesus requires of his disciples the renunciation of all earthly bonds and possessions which would dispute God His supreme sway over their life, Matt. 10:39; 16:25; Luke 14:25–35. . . . The idea is that the inward attachment of the soul to them as the highest good must be in principle destroyed, that God may take the place hitherto claimed by them.[8]

"Faith" that scorns our Lord's demands for such surrender can hardly qualify as saving faith. No one can rightfully lay claim to him as Savior while refusing to own him as Lord.

Obviously, a new believer does not fully understand all the ramifications of Jesus' lordship at the moment of conversion. But

[8]Geerhardus Vos, *The Kingdom of God and the Church* (Nutley, N.J.: Presbyterian and Reformed, 1972), 94.

every genuine believer has a desire to surrender. This is what distinguishes true faith from a bogus profession: true faith produces a heart that is humble, submissive, and obedient. As spiritual understanding unfolds, that obedience grows deeper, and the genuine believer displays an eagerness to please Christ by abandoning everything to his lordship. This willingness to surrender to divine authority is a driving force in the heart of every true child of the kingdom. It is the inevitable expression of the new nature.

Counting the Cost

These parables are a clear warning to those who want to have Jesus without counting the cost. Our Lord himself counseled the frivolous multitudes to calculate the cost carefully before following him (Luke 14:28–31). Far from welcoming the positive response of the uncommitted masses, he sought only those willing to invest all they had in his kingdom.

Wise investors would not usually put all their money into a single investment. But that is exactly what both men in these parables did. The first man sold everything and bought one field, and the second man sold everything and bought one pearl. But they had counted the cost, and they knew that what they were buying was worthy of the ultimate investment. Again, that is a perfect picture of saving faith. Someone who truly believes in Christ does not hedge bets. Having counted the cost, the true believer gladly gives everything for Christ.

Moses counted the cost. Scripture tells us that he "consider[ed] the reproach of Christ greater riches than the treasures of Egypt; for he was looking to the reward" (Heb. 11:26). He gave up spectacular worldly wealth in order to suffer for Christ's sake. To the Egyptians in Pharaoh's court, it must have seemed that he was trading riches for a reproach. But Moses knew that he was really trading Egypt for a heavenly reward. He gave up incredible wealth without a second thought, because he understood the priceless value of the kingdom of heaven.

That is the kind of response the Lord Jesus called for: wholehearted commitment. A desire for him at any cost. Unconditional surrender. A full exchange of self for the Savior. It is the only response that will open the gates of the kingdom. Seen through the eyes of this world, it is as high a price as anyone can pay. But from a kingdom perspective, it is really no sacrifice at all.

13

The First and Last

At the end of *The Pilgrim's Progress,* John Bunyan notes that there is an entrance to hell even from the gates of heaven. Judas is proof of that. The night he betrayed Christ with a kiss, he stepped forever out of Jesus' presence and sealed his eternal doom. Who knows how many like him have come near enough to learn the truth and profess faith in Jesus, only to forfeit heaven completely because they have never surrendered to Jesus' lordship? In a sense, their entrance to hell is from the gates of heaven.

But there is a contrasting reality as well, illustrated often in the Lord Jesus' earthly ministry. It is that even the lowest of sinners may be ushered into heaven from the very doorstep of hell. Publicans, prostitutes, thieves, and beggars all found in Christ a Savior who gave them abundant and everlasting life in exchange for the remnants of their squandered earthly existence. He came to seek and to save the lost, and he loved plucking them as brands from the fire. No one, no matter how dissipated by sin, was beyond the reach of his redemptive power. He did what no one else could do for them. He cast legions of stubborn evil spirits out of the demon-possessed (Luke 8:26–35), and he touched and made whole the ravaged bodies of lepers (Matt. 8:1–3). He gravitated to such people, and they in turn were drawn to him for salvation.

Jesus always saved them to the uttermost (cf. Heb. 7:25). Every repentant sinner who surrendered in faith to Christ received full salvation. An influential Jewish religious leader (John 3:1–16) was not preferred over an adulterous Samaritan woman (John 4:7–29). And the Lord made disciples of both a guileless Israelite like Nathaniel (John 1:47–51) and a thieving tax collector like Matthew (Matt. 9:9).

That is the way salvation operates. All the redeemed receive the same eternal life, whether they are young or old, respectable or contemptible, Pharisees or tax-gatherers. No one who comes to Christ is either preferred or slighted because of past experience. The same eternal life is offered to all.

That is an important truth to grasp. As we have seen, saving faith is an exchange of all that we are for all that Christ is. But we need to understand that this does not mean that we barter for eternal life. We do not buy salvation by surrendering our lives. Nor is the gift of eternal life given in proportion to the quality or the length of the life we yield. Everyone who surrenders to Christ gets all Christ has to give in return. Jesus gave a parable in Matthew 20:1–16 that illustrates this truth:

> The kingdom of heaven is like a landowner who went out early in the morning to hire laborers for his vineyard. And when he had agreed with the laborers for a denarius for the day, he sent them into his vineyard. And he went out about the third hour and saw others standing idle in the market place; and to those he said, "You too go into the vineyard, and whatever is right, I will give you." And so they went. Again he went out about the sixth and the ninth hour, and did the same thing. And about the eleventh hour he went out, and found others standing; and he said to them, "Why have you been standing here idle all day long?" They said to him, "Because no one hired us." He said to them, "You too go into the vineyard." And when evening had come, the owner of the vineyard said to his foreman, "Call the laborers and pay them their wages, beginning with the last group to the first." And when those hired about the eleventh hour came, each one received a denarius. And when those hired first came, they thought that they would receive more; and they also received each one a denarius. And when they received it, they grumbled at the landowner, saying, "These last men have worked only one hour, and you have made them equal to us who have borne the burden and the scorching heat of the day." But he answered and said to one of them, "Friend, I am doing you no wrong; did you not agree with me for a denarius? Take what is yours and go your way, but I wish to give to this last man the same as to you. Is it not lawful for me to do what I wish with what is my own? Or is your eye envious because I am generous?" Thus the last shall be first, and the first last.

Like other parables we have examined, this one is about the kingdom of heaven (v. 1). Keep in mind that this is a spiritual lesson, not a lecture about fair labor practices. Jesus is describing how things operate in the sphere where God rules through grace, in the kingdom where Christ rules and reigns. The context gives an important clue to its meaning.

Going back to the final verse of Matthew 19, we find that the parable is bracketed by the same thought: "Many who are first will be last; and the last, first" (19:30). Obviously, the parable was given to illustrate that maxim.

What does it mean? It is a riddle in the form of a proverb. How can the one who finishes first be last and vice versa? That is possible only if the last and the first are the same. In a foot race we would call this a tie. No one is ahead and no one is behind; thus the last is first and the first is last. Everyone crosses the finish line in a dead heat.

That is exactly the point of the parable. This landowner went out early in the morning to hire laborers for his vineyard. He hired some men to work for a denarius a day. He came back to the marketplace four more times during the day—at 9:00 A.M., noon, 3:00 P.M., and once again at 5:00 P.M.—to hire more men. When evening came and it was time to pay the laborers for their work, every worker received the same pay, no matter how long he had worked.

The Question of Fairness

The laborers who had worked the entire day felt they had been cheated. But the landowner was not unfair with them; he was generous with those who worked the shorter part of the day. A denarius per day was a good wage—equal to a day's pay for a soldier. No one had any reason to complain; all were paid exactly what they had agreed to work for—a denarius a day (v. 2). They went to work on those terms, and it was more than fair. The problem had nothing to do with how they were treated. The problem was that these workers could not accept the good fortune of the others. They were filled with envy.

How easy it is from the human point of view to sympathize with those who had worked the full day! There is something in all of us that cannot accept the inequity of someone's getting extra pay unless we all do. We are conditioned to think that inequity is always injustice. But sometimes unequal treatment is an expression of generosity, and that was certainly the case here. The landowner rebuked the men for their jealousy: "Is your eye envious because I am generous?" (Matt. 20:15).

The landowner's liberality was not evil; but the laborers' jealousy was. They could not stand the thought that someone else could get equal pay without working as hard or as long as they did. And instead of rejoicing, they grumbled.

The Issue of Equality

What is the spiritual point of this parable? What could it possibly mean about the kingdom? It is really not difficult. God is the householder. The vineyard is the kingdom of heaven—God's dominion, the realm of salvation. The laborers are those who enter into the kingdom and into the service of the king. The day of work represents a person's life span. The evening is the entrance to eternity, and the denarius is eternal life.

What Jesus is saying is that everyone who comes into the kingdom inherits eternal life, whether he labors for God for years or comes to salvation in the final hour of earthly life. The length of service is not an issue, nor does it matter how hard or easy one's circumstances are. Everyone who enters the kingdom receives eternal life like everyone else. The kingdom of heaven is not a merit system. Eternal life is not dispensed according to how faithfully we have performed here on earth. It is a sheer gift of God's grace.

Some people serve Christ their whole lives. Others squander their lives then turn to the Lord on their deathbed. Either way, eternal life is the same. A dying convert inherits the same glories of eternal existence as an apostle. But that is not unfair. Eternal life is more than any of us deserves. The Father chooses gladly to give us all the fullness of the kingdom (cf. Luke 12:32).

I have a pastor friend who comes from a Jewish heritage. He prayed for and witnessed to his mother from the day he became a Christian, but she steadfastly rejected Jesus as Messiah right up to the end. In the last week of her life, he shared the gospel with her one more time, and she embraced Jesus as Lord and Christ. My friend now has the wonderful confidence that she will inherit the same eternal life as he. They will spend eternity together in the kingdom. Is that equitable? Maybe not, but it shows the marvelous grace of a loving God.

When Jesus turned away the rich young ruler in Matthew 19, Peter turned to Jesus and said, "Behold, we have left everything and followed You; what then will there be for us?" (Matt. 19:27). In other words, "We started work at 6:00 A.M. We were the first ones here, and we signed up as lifetime members at a great cost. What will we get in return?"

The parable of the laborers in the vineyard is an answer to that question. The disciples were not quite clear about what their ultimate reward for following Christ would be. Some of them, I believe, still thought that at any moment Christ would overthrow the evil political forces and establish a visible, earthly kingdom. Perhaps they thought they would be granted special thrones to rule over the prime real estate. Even after Jesus rose from the dead, they asked him, "Lord, is it at this time You are restoring the kingdom to Israel?" (Acts 1:6). Is now when we get our crowns and our thrones?

Just after Jesus told this parable, he predicted his death (Matt. 20:17–19). The next few verses relate how the mother of James and John came to Jesus to ask that her sons be granted special thrones on either side of Jesus in the kingdom. They still did not understand the message.

A place in the kingdom is not something to be earned. It is given by God without regard to how long one worked or how hot the day was. The kingdom will include tax collectors, harlots, beggars, and blind people. There will be apostles, martyrs, and people who served God their entire lives. But there will also be men who were converted in foxholes just before they were blown to eternity by exploding mortar shells. All these people inherit the same eternal life and blessing, not because they earned it, but because God is gracious.

The Epistles describe differing rewards and crowns for service, but that is not the point this parable makes. The issue here is the equality of eternal life. In Christ "there is neither Jew nor Greek, there is neither slave nor free man, there is neither male nor female; for you are all one in Christ Jesus" (Gal. 3:28). The last are first, and the first are last.

The Nature of Salvation

I cannot resist mentioning several obvious truths about salvation that flow through this parable. Realizing that the secondary details of a parable are not in and of themselves a definitive basis on which to build doctrine, I nevertheless see in this parable support for a number of important principles Scripture affirms elsewhere.

First, it is God who sovereignly initiates salvation. Like the householder who went out seeking laborers for his vineyard, God is the one who inaugurates salvation. He does the seeking and the saving, and it is he who brings sinners into his kingdom. Though we respond with a desire to follow Christ, even that desire is wrought in our hearts by God. Salvation is not ultimately a human decision. God is both the author and the finisher of our faith (cf. Heb. 12:2). We love him because he first loved us (cf. 1 John 4:19). Therefore, we have no right to determine what we ought to get. If he sought us early and we served him our whole lives, that was his choice. If he sought us late and we served but a brief time, that too was his choice.

Second, God establishes the terms of salvation. The landowner told those he hired in the morning that he would give them a denarius. He set the price; they agreed. Those who came late struck no bargain at all. The master said, "Whatever is right, I will give you" (Matt. 20:4). They accepted those terms. The rich young ruler would not do that. Christ set the price for eternal life, but he refused the terms. Those most in need are least likely to try bartering for their own terms.

Third, God continues to call men and women into his kingdom. The landowner went back again and again to call workers into the vineyard. In the same way, God never stops soliciting workers for the kingdom. Jesus said in John 9:4, "We must work the works of Him who sent Me, as long as it is day; night is coming, when no man can work." Although the night of judgment is fast approaching, he continues to call people to work.

Fourth, everyone God redeems is willing to work for him. The men in the parable were looking for work; that is why they went to the marketplace. Everyone who went into the vineyard worked. Some worked only the last hour, and others worked all day, but everyone worked. That is the way salvation is. Faith is shown by works (James 2:24).

A fifth principle I see here is that God is compassionate to those who recognize their need. The men waiting in the marketplace were there because they were in need. When the householder asked why they were standing idle, they said "Because no one hired us" (Matt. 20:7). They were so desperate for work that they had stayed in the marketplace all day. A similar sense of poverty and extreme desperation is one of the characteristics of saving faith (Matt. 5:3, 6). The Lord calls into his kingdom those who know their need, not the satisfied and self-sufficient.

Sixth, God keeps his promise. The landowner paid exactly what he said he would pay. No one received less than was promised.

And finally, while God inevitably gives what he promises, he also always gives more than we deserve. Salvation is pure grace. No one deserves eternal life, but God gives it equally to all who believe. God saves us, "not on the basis of deeds which we have done in righteousness, but according to His mercy" (Titus 3:5).

There is no place for jealousy in the kingdom. The only right response is abject humility. Everything we receive from God is undeserved blessing. How long or how well we work has nothing to do with our place in the kingdom, for all will receive far more from God than they deserve. We should never murmur because the fatted calf was killed for someone else or be resentful that heaven will be just as wonderful for those who enter the kingdom late. God's grace abounds to us all.

A *Picture of Grace*

In his record of the Savior's death, Luke includes a choice vignette not found in any of the other Gospels. It is the account of how Jesus, hanging in agony on the cross, bearing the sins of the world, nevertheless turned aside to rescue a single condemned criminal from eternal damnation. The thief was a career criminal, and Roman law had condemned him to die on a cross. Sovereign grace placed him on the same hill as the Savior, where he watched the Lord of glory die for his sins.

In the early hours of the Crucifixion the thieves on either side of Jesus were both arrogantly adding their taunts to those of the crowd (Matt. 27:44; Mark 15:32). But before this man died, his mocking changed to a confession of his own guilt and Jesus' innocence: "We are receiving what we deserve for our deeds; but this man has done nothing wrong" (Luke 23:41). Then, turning to the Lord, he added, "Jesus, remember me when You come to Your kingdom!" (v. 42).

Jesus' reply to the thief was as glorious a promise as a dying sinner could receive: "Truly I say to you, today you shall be with Me in Paradise" (v. 43). As far as we know, those were the only words Jesus ever spoke to the man. There was no verbal preevangelism, no four-point message, no appeal of any kind. But as the thief watched the sinless Savior die, faith was kindled in him. His conversion, even though it occurred as he was passing into eternity, was no less genuine than the apostle Paul's. The thief received the same everlasting life, even though his entire earthly life had been wasted in crime and disobedience. The moment his faith led him to repent, the Savior received him into the kingdom.[1]

There will be many in heaven who were more faithful, who worked harder and endured longer under greater stress than that thief. Still, by the grace of God, he was assured an eternal place in Jesus' presence.

---

[1]Note that although the thief was saved in the final moments of his earthly life, his faith bore all the marks of genuineness. Repentance wrought a dramatic change in his behavior, and he turned from mocking Christ to defending him. His admission of guilt, his acceptance of his own cross as just, and his acknowledgment that Christ was guiltless (v. 41) all show he had forsaken himself and surrendered to Christ. He probably knew little about the *facts* of the gospel, but he embraced Christ wholeheartedly as Lord.

When it comes to entering heaven, a thief has no advantage over a Pharisee. A fisherman will be no better or worse off than a tax-gatherer. The first finish last and the last first, and in the end all enjoy the fullness of eternal life to the maximum.

14

The Lost and Found

The salvation of a soul is not the stale transaction many people think it is. Redemption is not just a matter of divine accounting. God does more than keep books on who is in and who is out. He weeps over the lost and celebrates whenever one is saved. His pain is profoundly deep over humanity's lostness, and his joy is full when a sinner repents.

The Lord Jesus gave a series of parables in Luke 15 that portray the heavenly Father's compassion for lost sinners and his rejoicing over their salvation. Although two of these three parables do not directly confront the issues of submission to Jesus' lordship, repentance, faith, or any aspect of the human response, I have included them here because the truth they teach is such a critical element of the gospel according to Jesus. Together, all three parables give us a precious window into the heart of a loving God, who pursues lost souls and "is patient ... not wishing for any to perish but for all to come to repentance" (2 Peter 3:9).

The setting of Luke 15 is familiar: "All the tax-gatherers and the sinners were coming near Him to listen to Him. And both the Pharisees and the scribes began to grumble, saying, 'This man receives sinners and eats with them'" (vv. 1–2). The Greek verb tense in verse 1 ("were coming") signifies continual action, meaning that the tax-gatherers and sinners came to Jesus as a matter of habit. Wherever he went, a crowd of undesirables gathered around him. These were publicans, criminals, robbers, thugs, harlots, and other riffraff who made no effort at all to live by the standard of Jewish law.

As we have seen, this troubled the self-righteous Pharisees a great deal. They were so hopelessly preoccupied with the trivia of the law that they had no time to be concerned with serious sinners. Nor could they stomach a Messiah who was popular among the offscouring of society and who at the same time was critical of the rabbinical traditions.

Jesus, knowing the Pharisees' hearts, rebuked them through three parables that contrasted their self-righteous attitude with the Father's tender compassion for the lost. All three parables make the same point—that God does not sit passively by while people are going to hell. He does not delight in the destruction of the wicked. Instead, he loves them, pursues them, and longs for them to be saved. And he is jubilant at the redemption of even one lost sinner.

The Hundred Sheep

The first of the parables (Luke 15:4–6) has a pastoral theme: "What man among you, if he has a hundred sheep and has lost one of them, does not leave the ninety-nine in the open pasture, and go after the one which is lost, until he finds it? And when he has found it, he lays it on his shoulders, rejoicing. And when he comes home, he calls together his friends and his neighbors, saying to them, 'Rejoice with me, for I have found my sheep which was lost!'"

The phrase "What man among you" (v. 4) implies that the compassionate behavior Jesus describes would be expected even of a common sheep farmer. No shepherd worthy of his hire would be satisfied with ninety-nine sheep out of a hundred. He would leave the ninety-nine safe in the fold and go out to search for the one lost sheep. For many shepherds, this was not only a duty; it was also a matter of their love for the sheep. Each sheep would be known to the shepherd by name (cf. John 10:3). Every night he would count and examine them when they came back into the fold. If one was lost, he would go out into the night to find it.

When the shepherd in the parable found the lost sheep, he carried it on his shoulders, with the belly of the sheep up against his neck and the legs snugly against his chest. Then he called his friends and neighbors together for a celebration of the sheep's homecoming.

The key point of this parable is the joy of the shepherd over the salvation of the sheep. The calling of his friends in to celebrate with him shows the tremendous depth of his profound joy. This was not something he could celebrate alone. He could not just quietly rejoice in his heart. His joy was abundant and overflowing; he had to share it with others.

Jesus' point is spelled out in verse 7: "I tell you that in the same way, there will be more joy in heaven over one sinner who repents rather than over ninety-nine righteous persons who need no repentance." In other words, when one sinner repents, God calls for a celebration in heaven. He is a seeking Shepherd whose desire is to rescue lost sheep.

God is not simply recording transactions, making a mark every time someone gets saved. He so longs for the souls of the lost that he will go out and pursue them. Then when the wayward lamb is brought into the fold, heaven itself is barely big enough to contain his joy. That shows the seeking heart of God.

The Ten Coins

The second parable (Luke 15:8–10) makes the same point with a different metaphor: "What woman, if she has ten silver coins and loses one coin, does not light a lamp and sweep the house and search carefully until she finds it? And when she has found it, she calls together her friends and neighbors, saying, 'Rejoice with me, for I have found the coin which I had lost.'"

The silver coins were denarii. One denarius was a good day's wages. That is what the landowner paid his laborers in the parable of Matthew 20. This woman lost one of her ten coins. She lit a lamp, swept out her house, and searched until she found the one that was missing. When she found it, her joy was as great as the shepherd's. Like him, she called a group of friends and neighbors together to share her joy. She could not conceal the gladness in her own heart.

This parable makes the same point as the one before: "In the same way, I tell you, there is joy in the presence of the angels of God over one sinner who repents" (v. 10). What touches the heart of God most deeply is the salvation of those whom he pursues and brings to repentance.

Note that verse 10 speaks of "joy in the presence of the angels." It does not actually say the angels were joyful. Whose joy is this? It is the joy of the triune God, existing in the presence of the holy angels. Of course, the angels share in the celebration, but the emphasis in both parables is on God's joy.

Had they been careful students of Scripture, the Pharisees would have better understood this side of God's character. Even the Old Testament reveals him as a God of compassion. Ezekiel 33:11 says, "'As I live!' declares the Lord God, 'I take no pleasure in the death of the wicked.'" Isaiah 62:5 says, "As the bridegroom rejoices over the bride, so your God will rejoice over you." That is exactly the image of these parables. It is uncontained joy, pure bliss, and unrestrained celebration. That is how God views the salvation of a soul.

The Two Sons

The most magnificent of the three parables begins in verse 11 and goes to verse 32. The story of the prodigal son is surely the most familiar of all Jesus' parables:

> A certain man had two sons; and the younger of them said to his father, "Father, give me the share of the estate that falls to me." And he divided his wealth between them. And not many days later, the younger son gathered everything together and went on a journey into a distant country, where he squandered his estate with loose living. Now when he had spent everything, a severe famine occurred in that country, and he began to be in need. And he went and attached himself to one of the citizens of that country, and he sent him into his fields to feed swine. And he was longing to fill his stomach with the pods that the swine were eating, and no one was giving anything to him. But when he came to his senses, he said, "How many of my father's hired men have more than enough bread, but I am dying here with hunger! I will get up and go to my father, and will say to him, 'Father, I have sinned against heaven and in your sight; I am no more worthy to be called your son; make me as one of your hired men.'" And he got up and came to his father. But while he was still a long way off, his father saw him, and felt compassion for him, and ran and embraced him, and kissed him. And the son said to him, "Father, I have sinned against heaven and in your sight; I am no longer worthy to be called your son." But the father said to his slaves, "Quickly bring out the best robe and put it on him, and put a ring on his hand and sandals on his feet; and bring the fattened calf, kill it, and let us eat and be merry; for this son of mine was dead, and has come to life again; he was lost, and has been found. And they began to be merry.

Although this parable goes into far greater detail than the previous two, it makes exactly the same point. The loving father is God, who rejoices to see the homecoming of a son once lost.

This first half of the parable focuses on the contemptible behavior of the younger son. It was completely unheard of in the culture of that day for a son to ask his father for an early inheritance. Even in our own day this would be considered uncouth at best. For this son to demand his inheritance on the spot was tantamount to saying he wished his father were dead. It is amazing that the father did not refuse the request and punish the son. But he was gracious and gave both his sons their shares of the family wealth (v. 12). He was a loving father. Although his heart was surely broken by the son's request, he gave him what he asked. The father's great fear must have been that the impetuous boy would squander it.

That is exactly what happened. The son went to a distant country, blew the money through loose living, and wound up so poor he had to feed pigs to make a living. It wasn't much of a living. He was so hungry he wanted to eat the pig slop. Approaching starvation, reduced to eating with pigs far away from his father's home, he finally came to his senses.

It is noteworthy that what ultimately brought him to his senses was sorrow over his predicament. The sorrow itself was not repentance, but it led to deep repentance (cf. 2 Cor. 7:9–10). He began with a sense of his own need. Then he admitted he had done wrong. Looking even beyond his offended human father to the heavenly Father whose law he had broken, he freely acknowledged his own guilt before God (v. 18). He determined to ask forgiveness and take the consequences. Planning his repentance carefully, he rehearsed what he would say when he got home. He would confess that he had sinned against God and against his father, and he would ask his father to appoint him a place with his hired servants (v. 19).

Here is a perfect illustration of repentant faith. Observe the young man's unqualified compliance, his abject humility, and his unequivocal willingness to do whatever his father asked. The prodigal who began by demanding an early inheritance was now willing to serve his father as a bond-servant. He was making a complete turnaround. His demeanor was one of unconditional surrender—a complete resignation of self and absolute submission to his father.

Having resolved to go to his father, he then acted on his decision (v. 20). Unlike some who say they will do something but never do (cf. Matt. 21:28–32), the prodigal son got up and returned to his father. His repentance was a complete and total reversal. He had become poor in spirit. He was mourning over his sin. His arrogance had given way to meekness and humility. He was a different young man from the one who originally left home.

While the son was still far from home, his father saw him and came running to greet him. Why was the father so quick to recognize him? He must have been out looking for him, watching into the distance to see if indeed the lost son might be coming back. Here again is a picture of the seeking heavenly Father. When a repentant sinner turns to God, he learns that God is already looking for him to come, eager to run and meet him. Before he ever gets near to God, he discovers that God has first come to embrace him.

The young prodigal did not get to the place in his speech where he was going to ask his father to make him a slave. Before he could finish the rehearsed soliloquy, his father sent slaves to get him clothing and a ring. Instead of punishing the wayward son, the father ordered a banquet to celebrate his return! He had already forgotten the son's foolishness. The issue now was not a wasted inheritance or a life squandered with loose living. His lost son had been found (v. 23)!

All three of these parables have this common theme: a seeker finds what was lost and rejoices. In every case, the seeker pictures God, who rejoices over the salvation of a sinner.

But here the story of the prodigal son takes an ugly turn, as we meet the jealous older brother (Luke 15:25–32):

> Now his older son was in the field, and when he came and approached the house, he heard music and dancing. And he summoned one of the servants and began inquiring what these things might be. And he said to him, "Your brother has come, and your father has killed the fattened calf, because he has received him back safe and sound." But he became angry, and was not willing to go in; and his father came out and began entreating him. But he answered and said to his father, "Look! For so many years I have been serving you, and I have never neglected a command of yours; and yet you have never given me a kid, that I might be merry with my friends; but when this son of yours came, who has devoured your wealth with harlots, you killed the fattened calf for him." And he said to him, "My child, you have always been with me, and all that is mine is yours. But we had to be merry and rejoice, for this brother of yours was dead and has begun to live, and was lost and has been found."

Remember, the older son had received his inheritance, too (v. 12). Instead of squandering it, he stayed home, serving the father. In fact, he was out working in the field when the prodigal returned. When he heard the music and laughter, he asked one of the servants to explain. This older son was furious that the father would celebrate the homecoming of his wayward brother. The jealous son would not even go inside. He was not about to eat with a sinner. He totally lacked the compassion of his father and was playing the part of a Pharisee.

This son's behavior might seem more socially acceptable than his younger brother's debauchery, but it was just as outrageous—and every bit as dishonoring to the father. The older son had no real love for his father, or he would have shared his father's joy. Serving his father all those years, he had just been going through the motions. He served out of duty. His chief concern was what he could get for himself (v. 29). He had no understanding of his father's heart.

Here too was a lost son. And the father sought him as well (v. 28).

The Lord always seeks to save the lost, but they must see themselves as lost. Often the most flagrant, irreligious, repugnant sinners are quicker to understand their depravity than people steeped in religious achievement and self-righteousness. These pharisaic people cannot tolerate the forgiveness of sinners—especially flagrant ones. They do not understand repentance. Far from rejoicing, they are repulsed when a sinner confesses his or her sin. They take great pride in their own apparent righteousness, but in their hearts there is no sense of submission.

The first son in the story saw his sin, felt his father's sorrow, repented, humbled himself, received forgiveness, and entered into his father's joy. The second son was bitter, unrepentant, with no sense of the cold deadness of his own heart. He forfeited his right to rejoice with his father. He was as lost as his younger brother had been, but he was too proud to see it.

God is seeking the lost. Those who acknowledge their sin and turn from it will find him running to them with open arms. Those who think they are good enough to deserve his favor will find themselves excluded from the celebration, unable to share the eternal joy of a loving Father.

15

The Vine and the Branches

One of the recurring themes of Jesus' preaching, teaching, and miracles was his absolute equality with God. He repeatedly affirmed his deity in the clearest possible terminology: "My Father is working until now, and I Myself am working" (John 5:17). "If I glorify Myself, My glory is nothing; it is My Father who glorifies Me, of whom you say, 'He is our God'" (John 8:54). "I and the Father are one" (John 10:30). "Though you do not believe Me, believe the works, that you may know and understand that the Father is in Me, and I in the Father" (10:38).

Every time Jesus called God "My Father," he was underscoring his deity. His Jewish audiences understood quite clearly what his intention was: "For this cause therefore the Jews were seeking all the more to kill Him, because He not only was breaking the Sabbath, but also was *calling God His own Father, making Himself equal with God*" (John 5:18, emphasis added).

Some of the most powerful affirmations of Jesus' deity are a chain of expressions in John's gospel known as the "I am" statements. Each of these phrases employs the name God revealed to Moses at the burning bush—"I AM" (Ex. 3:14). Jesus applied that name to himself in a series of prominent declarations: "I am the bread of life" (John 6:35). "I am the living bread that came down out of heaven" (6:51). "I am the light of the world" (8:12; 9:5). "I am the door of the sheep" (10:7). "I am the good shepherd" (10:11). "I am the resurrection and the life" (11:25). "I am the way, and the truth, and the life; no one comes to the Father, but through Me" (14:6). And this stunning, inescapable affirmation of deity: "Truly, truly, I say to you, before Abraham was born, I am" (8:58).

Jesus' stature as the great I AM of the Old Testament was essential to his role as Savior. Those who refused to acknowledge him for who he is could not be saved: "Unless you believe that I am,[1] you shall die in your sins" (8:24). This set up an extremely difficult barrier for Pharisees who were predisposed to hate him anyway. They understood that he was claiming authority over their greatest patriarchs and prophets (cf. John 4:12; 8:53). Indeed, he was claiming equality with God, and the ramifications of that they could not accept. Therefore, Jesus warned them, they would die in their sins.

On the night before his death, alone with his disciples after Judas had departed to do his evil, turncoat, treacherous deed, the Lord revealed another aspect of his deity to the remaining disciples. And once again he used the highest name of God, I AM:

> I am the true vine, and My Father is the vinedresser. Every branch in Me that does not bear fruit, He takes away; and every branch that bears fruit, He prunes it, that it may bear more fruit. You are already clean because of the word which I have spoken to you. Abide in Me, and I in you. As the branch cannot bear fruit of itself, unless it abides in the vine, so neither can you, unless you abide in Me. I am the vine, you are the branches; he who abides in Me, and I in him, he bears much fruit; for apart from Me you can do nothing. If anyone does not abide in Me, he is thrown away as a branch, and dries up; and they gather them, and cast them into the fire, and they are burned. If you abide in Me, and My words abide in you, ask whatever you wish, and it shall be done for you. By this is My Father glorified, that you bear much fruit, and so prove to be My disciples (John 15:1–8).

The imagery Jesus used in that discourse was not a parable but a metaphor. Parables are stories whose interpretation must be supplied separately. A metaphor contains its own interpretive elements. Here Jesus explicitly says that he is the Vine, for example, and the Father is the Vinedresser.

Other elements of the imagery are not quite as clear, however. "You are the branches" (v. 5) is spoken to the disciples. Does he mean the fruit-bearing branches as well as the fruitless ones? Some interpreters say the unproductive branches represent fruitless Christians and this proves that true believers might live spiritually barren lives. At first glance that interpretation might seem to have merit. But look at verse 6. The empty branches are cut off, dried, gathered, and cast into the fire: "They are burned." Could that possibly describe a true believer?

How are we to interpret this admittedly difficult metaphor? As

---

[1]The word *He*, which appears in the *New American Standard Bible* at this point, has been added by the translators. It does not appear in the Greek texts.

always, we must consider the context. And here we find an important clue to Jesus' meaning. Remember what was happening in the Upper Room. Take note of the characters in that night's drama: "Jesus knowing that His hour had come that He should depart out of this world to the Father, having loved His own who were in the world, He loved them to the end. And during supper, the devil having already put into the heart of Judas Iscariot, the son of Simon, to betray Him" (John 13:1–2).

The Cast of Characters

Here, then, is the cast: Jesus, the Father, Jesus' disciples, and Judas the betrayer. All of them were weighing heavily on Jesus' mind that night. He was eager to affirm his great love for the Eleven. He must have also been grieving over Judas, who had utterly rejected his love and set out to betray him. Most of all, he knew that he and the Father shared an infinite love; yet he was burdened with the knowledge that tomorrow he would be the object of the Father's wrath as he bore the burden of our sin on the cross.

It is not surprising, then, that Christ, the Father, the Eleven faithful disciples, and Judas all play a part in the vine-and-branches metaphor. Christ is the True Vine. The Father is the Vinedresser. The disciples (along with all true disciples) are the fruit-bearing branches. And Judas (as well as all false disciples) represents the barren branches.

The True Vine

The metaphor of a vine and branches would have been familiar imagery for our Lord's disciples. The Old Testament often spoke of Israel as God's vine. Jehovah cared for the vine, tended it, pruned it, and loved it. Nevertheless, the vine degenerated and bore no fruit, which grieved the Vinedresser:

Let me sing now for my well-beloved
A song of my beloved concerning His vineyard.
My well-beloved had a vineyard on a fertile hill.
And He dug it all around, removed its stones,
And planted it with the choicest vine.
And He built a tower in the middle of it,
And hewed out a wine vat in it;
Then He expected it to produce good grapes,
But it produced only worthless ones.

"And now, O inhabitants of Jerusalem and men of Judah,
Judge between Me and My vineyard.
"What more was there to do for My vineyard that I have not done
   in it?
Why, when I expected it to produce good grapes did it produce
   worthless ones?
"So now let Me tell you what I am going to do to My vineyard:
I will remove its hedge and it will be consumed;
I will break down its wall and it will become trampled ground.
"And I will lay it waste;
It will not be pruned or hoed,
But briars and thorns will come up.
I will also charge the clouds to rain no rain on it."

For the vineyard of the LORD *of hosts is the house of Israel.*
                              (Isa. 5:1–7a, emphasis added)

God took away the wall of the vineyard and left it unprotected.
Gentile nations trampled it and utterly laid it to waste. Israel was cut
off, no longer God's vine. The covenant people had forfeited their
spiritual privileges.

Jesus was telling the disciples that he was the *true* Vine. Old
Testament Israel was only a pale earthly shadow. Such comparisons
are common in the New Testament. Repeatedly we are told that
many things in the Old Testament are only imperfect likenesses of
some greater heavenly reality—the "true" thing. For example, there
was an earthly tabernacle with a human high priest; now Christ is our
Great High Priest in the "true tabernacle" (Heb. 8:2). In contrast to
the created light of Genesis 1:3, Christ is the "true light" (John 1:9).
Manna fell from heaven to feed the Israelites in the wilderness; Jesus
said he is the "true bread out of heaven" (John 6:32). Likewise,
contrasting with the Old Testament picture of Israel, Jesus is the
"true" Vine.

The horticultural imagery is ideal for the point Jesus was making.
Living branches belong entirely to the central vine; fruitful branches
must depend completely on the main stem for nourishment, support,
strength, and vitality. They are offshoots of the vine. They bear its
likeness. They flow with its juices. They radiate its life and character.
In Jesus' words, they *abide* in the vine.

The Vinedresser

Remember that John 15:1–8 is one long figure of speech. As we
noted in interpreting some of the parables, figurative language must
not be made to bear more meaning than is clearly intended. The
symbolism is not meant to extend to every fine detail. For example, in

this metaphor Christ is portrayed as a plant but the Father as a person. Some who reject the deity of Christ have tried to suggest that this proves that Christ is not of the same essence as the Father. They claim that if Jesus is God, he and the Father ought to have equivalent roles in the metaphor. If Jesus is the Vine, they claim, the Father should be the root. And so they argue that the imagery here disproves Jesus' deity.

But that misses the entire point. As we noted at the outset of this chapter, in the very expression "I am" Jesus was employing the name of God. By tying the words "I am" to expressions such as "the bread of life," "the way, the truth and the life," and "the true vine," Jesus was boldly asserting his identity as Jehovah of the Old Testament. Besides, the metaphor of the vine and branches does affirm Jesus' deity by portraying him as the source and sustainer of life.

Still, the vine/branches metaphor is not primarily a lesson about Jesus' deity. Our Lord was using this imagery to underscore the reality of every believer's union with him. As the Father cares for the Son, so he cares for those joined to the Son by faith. That glorious truth is the central point Jesus was making here. It is one of the most sublime truths in all Scripture! Believers are united by faith to the beloved Son of God.

Vinedressers had two chief means of maximizing the fruit that grew on the vine. One was to cut off the barren limbs. The other was to prune new shoots from the fruit-bearing branches. This all insured that the vine would produce more fruit, not just leafy growth. Verse 2 describes both chores: "Every branch in Me that does not bear fruit, He takes away; and every branch that bears fruit, He prunes it, that it may bear more fruit." Barren branches grow rapidly, and new ones sprout quickly. They must be carefully and regularly pruned. It is the only way to insure maximum quantities of fruit.

The Fruitful Branches

The identity of the healthy, fruit-bearing branches seems clear—they represent genuine Christians. It is the nature of the Christian to produce fruit. "We are His workmanship, created in Christ Jesus for good works, which God prepared beforehand, that we should walk in them" (Eph. 2:10). The inevitable result of genuine salvation is good works. We are not saved by works, but works are the only proof that faith is genuine, vibrant, and alive (James 2:17). Fruit is the only possible validation that a branch is abiding in the True Vine: "You will know them by their fruits. Grapes are not gathered from thorn bushes, nor figs from thistles, are they? Even so, *every* good tree bears good fruit; but the bad tree bears bad fruit" (Matt. 7:16–17, emphasis added). If someone's faith is genuine, that person's life will bear good fruit.

The Vinedresser prunes these fruitful branches *so that they will bear more fruit.* The pruning represents God's loving discipline. The Father "disciplines us for our good, that we may share His holiness" (Heb. 12:10). And God is glorified in the process. As John 15:8 says, "By this is My Father glorified, that you bear much fruit."

The vinedresser might remove extraneous shoots in several ways. Sometimes the tip was simply pinched off. Other times a knife would be used to make a clean cut, neatly excising the useless growth. Large, heavy branches had to be topped to prevent them from becoming so long and weak that their own weight tore them from the vine. And grape clusters were thinned out while they were still flowering so that the healthiest fruit would grow even larger and more abundantly.

Spiritual pruning is the necessary process whereby the Father removes everything that limits our fruitfulness. He cuts out sins and other distractions that sap our spiritual strength.

The pruning knife he uses so skillfully is the Word of God. Note verse 3: "You are already clean because of the word which I have spoken to you." The word translated "clean" is the same Greek word Jesus uses in verse 2 to describe the pruning process. God's Word prunes the sin out of our lives. Charles Spurgeon said, "The Word is often the knife with which the great Husbandman prunes the vine; and, brothers and sisters, if we were more willing to feel the edge of the Word, and to let it cut away even something that may be very dear to us, we should not need so much pruning by affliction."[2]

Sometimes the pruning process is painful. We might even see other branches that we think need pruning more than we do. But the Vinedresser always knows what he is doing. He only wants us to bear much fruit.

And he prunes us only because he loves us. Using a different metaphor, Hebrews 12:6–7 says, "Those whom the Lord loves He disciplines, and He scourges every son whom He receives. It is for discipline that you endure; God deals with you as with sons; for what son is there whom his father does not discipline?" Likewise the Vinedresser gives the closest scrutiny to the branches he cares most about. He spends no time dressing the fruitless branches or pruning

[2]C. H. Spurgeon, *Expository Encyclopedia*, vol. 4 (Grand Rapids: Baker, 1977), 337.

small shoots off them, because those branches are fit only to be taken away and burned.

The Judas Branches

The fruitless branches are only superficially attached to the vine. To the external eye there is a connection. There is even leafy growth and other tokens of life. But something is missing. They are not adequately tied into to the vine's vascular system. They are incapable of bearing fruit. They are fit only to be cut off and destroyed.

Every gardener understands this principle. Fruitless branches are detrimental to the vine. They take sap away from the fruit-bearing branches. Wasted sap means less fruit. Even after careful pruning these branches will remain barren. There is no way to make them bear fruit. Moreover, after you cut them off they are still worthless; they cannot even be used for fuel. So they are thrown into heaps and burned like garbage. Verse 2 says they are "taken away." The vinedresser does not recycle or rehabilitate them; he removes them and destroys them.

Spiritually, the equivalent of a fruitless branch is a phony Christian—someone who professes faith in Christ but does not really know him. These are branches that only appear to be connected to the True Vine. Their relationship to him is entirely superficial. They do not have his life flowing through them, so they cannot bear spiritual fruit by any means. These are the branches Jesus threatens with removal. We might call them Judas branches.

In fact, the classic example of a fruitless branch is Judas. Only a short time before Jesus spoke the words in John 15, Judas had walked out into the night, a doomed branch, cut off from the Vine.

Jesus, of course, had never been fooled by Judas's duplicity. He knew Judas's heart, and he never counted Judas as a true disciple. Earlier that same evening, the Lord had girded himself with a towel and humbly knelt before the Twelve to wash their feet. Afterward, he said this: "You are clean, but not all of you" (John 13:10). The apostle John adds this commentary: "He knew the one who was betraying Him; for this reason He said, 'Not all of you are clean' " (v. 11). Judas was not clean; he had never undergone "the washing of regeneration and renewing by the Holy Spirit" (Titus 3:5). Although Judas appeared to the other disciples as if he were truly one of them, Jesus knew better. Judas was a fruitless branch fit only to be removed from the Vine and burned.

It was not that Judas had salvation but then lost it. Our Lord said of the true sheep: "I give eternal life to them, and they shall never perish; and no one shall snatch them out of My hand" (John 10:28). True believers are secure in Him: "All that the Father gives Me shall come to Me, and the one who comes to Me I will certainly not cast out" (John 6:37). Branches that abide in the True Vine will never be removed.

But wait. In verse 2 our Lord says "Every branch *in Me* that does not bear fruit, He takes away" (emphasis added). Doesn't that suggest that these barren branches are true believers? No, that pushes the symbolism too far. Other passages in Scripture use this same imagery of parasitic, unfruitful branches. Romans 11:17–24, for example, represents Israel as an olive tree from which God has removed branches. Those branches were cut off because of unbelief (Rom. 11:20). In Romans 9:6, Paul wrote, "They are not all Israel who are descended from Israel." A person can be in the family tree but not be a true Israelite. Likewise, one can be a branch on the True Vine without really abiding in Christ.

Throughout Scripture we read warnings to those who associate themselves with Jesus but whose faith is a facade. Such people appear to be in Christ but do not truly abide in him. The Vinedresser will remove them from the Vine. This cutting off is precisely the process the apostle John was describing in 1 John 2:19: "They went out from us, but they were not really of us; for if they had been of us, they would have remained with us; but they went out, in order that it might be shown that they all are not of us."

And so the fruitless branches represent counterfeit disciples— people who were never truly saved. They do not abide in Christ, the True Vine; they are not truly united with him by faith. They are Judas branches. They can bear no genuine fruit. In the end the Father removes them to preserve the life and fruitfulness of the other branches.

The imagery of burning suggests that these fruitless branches are doomed to hell. Like Judas, they are hopeless apostates. They may be eminent church members. They may have acquired much spiritual knowledge. They may be teachers of doctrine, even scholars. They may have gone through all the rituals. But they are not genuine believers, and God will remove them.

Tragically, multitudes fit this category. Paul wrote, "*Many* walk, of whom I often told you, and now tell you even weeping, that they are enemies of the cross of Christ, *whose end is destruction*" (Phil. 3:18– 19, emphasis added). These are the branches that will be cut off and burned.

Do not misunderstand or miss Jesus' stark warning in this passage. Far from painting a scenario that can be used to defend the carnal-

Christian fallacy, our Lord was teaching his disciples a truth that would help them to understand Judas's treachery. Judas's faith was a sham. His commitment to Jesus was superficial. He was a fruitless branch. "It would have been good for that man if he had not been born" (Mark 14:21).

John 15:1–8 is a sobering passage, reminding us that it is a terrifying thing to fall into the hands of the living God (cf. Heb. 10:31). Barren branches have nothing to look forward to except awful, fiery judgment. Yet the corresponding truth is equally blessed. Fruitful branches, those actually abiding in the True Vine, are in the hands of a loving and gracious Vinedresser. As he carefully prunes and tends us, there may be some pain in the cutting. But we can be certain that he is doing it for our own good so that we will bear much fruit for his glory.

PART FOUR

JESUS EXPLAINS
HIS GOSPEL

16

The Call to Repentance

Having examined how Jesus dealt with individuals and having studied the parables and figures he used to illuminate truth for his disciples, we now turn our focus to the rich doctrinal content of the message he proclaimed to the multitudes. Here we will explore the principal themes that flavored Jesus' discourses and weigh the popularized gospel of today against the Savior's own teaching. In the process, we will attempt to gain a clearer understanding of the terminology Jesus employed. Most of the current controversy regarding the gospel hinges on the definitions of a few key words, including *repentance, faith, discipleship,* and *Lord.* In this final section, we will study these terms and see how Jesus himself used them.

We begin with a chapter on repentance, because that is where the Savior began. Matthew 4:17 records the dawning of Christ's public ministry: "From that time [the imprisonment of John the Baptist] Jesus began to preach and say, 'Repent, for the kingdom of heaven is at hand.'" I noted in chapter 4 that the opening word of that first sermon characterized the theme of Jesus' entire earthly ministry. We have further observed that he described his own objective thus: "calling sinners to repentance" (Luke 5:31). Repentance was a recurring motif in all his public sermons. He stood boldly before the stiff-necked multitudes and proclaimed, "Unless you repent, you will all likewise perish" (Luke 13:3, 5).

The Missing Note

When was the last time you heard the gospel presented in those terms? It is not fashionable in the twentieth century to preach a gospel that demands repentance. How did the message of today

175

become so different from the gospel according to Jesus? As early as 1937, Dr. H. A. Ironside noted that the biblical doctrine of repentance was being diluted by those who wished to exclude it from the gospel message. He wrote, "The doctrine of repentance is the missing note in many otherwise orthodox and fundamentally sound circles today."[1] He spoke of "professed preachers of grace who, like the antinomians of old, decry the necessity of repentance lest it seem to invalidate the freedom of grace."[2] Dr. Ironside, himself a dispensationalist, denounced the teaching of extreme dispensationalists who taught that repentance was for another age. "Our Lord's solemn words, 'Except ye repent, ye shall all likewise perish,' are as important today as when first uttered," Ironside wrote. "No dispensational distinctions, important as these are in understanding and interpreting God's ways with man, can alter this truth."[3]

Even in his day Ironside recognized the dangers of an incipient easy-believism. He wrote:

> Shallow preaching that does not grapple with the terrible fact of man's sinfulness and guilt, calling on "all men everywhere to repent," results in shallow conversions; and so we have myriads of glib-tongued professors today who give no evidence of regeneration whatever. Prating of salvation by grace, they manifest no grace in their lives. Loudly declaring they are justified by faith alone, they fail to remember that "faith without works is dead"; and that justification by works before men is not to be ignored as though it were in contradiction to justification by faith before God.[4]

Nevertheless, many prominent dispensationalists continued to advance the notion that preaching repentance to the unsaved violates the spirit and content of the gospel message. Dr. Lewis Sperry Chafer's *Systematic Theology* listed repentance as one of "the more common features of human responsibility which are too often erroneously added to the one requirement of *faith* or *belief*."[5] Chafer noted that the word *repentance* is not found in the gospel of John and occurs only once in Romans. He pointed out also that in Acts 16:31 Paul did not tell the Philippian jailer to repent. Chafer viewed that silence as an "overwhelming mass of irrefutable evidence [making it]

[1]H. A. Ironside, *Except Ye Repent* (Grand Rapids: Zondervan, 1937), 7.
[2]Ibid., 11.
[3]Ibid., 10.
[4]Ibid., 11.
[5]Lewis Sperry Chafer, *Systematic Theology* (Dallas: Dallas Seminary, 1948), 3:372.

clear that the New Testament does not impose repentance upon the unsaved as a condition of salvation."[6]

The Discarding of Repentance

Voices today continue to promulgate the same ideas. *The Ryrie Study Bible* includes a synopsis of doctrine that lists repentance as "a false addition to faith" when made a condition for salvation, except "when [repentance is] understood as a synonym for faith."[7] Another influential teacher says essentially the same thing: "The Bible requires repentance for salvation, but repentance does not mean to turn from sin, nor a change in one's conduct. . . . Biblical repentance is a change of mind or attitude concerning either God, Christ, dead works or sin."[8] Even a seminary professor writes, "Repentance means to change one's mind; it does not mean to change one's life."[9] These writers and others have thus redefined repentance in a way that evacuates its moral ramifications. They write it off as simply a change of mind about who Christ is.[10] This kind of repentance has nothing to do with turning from sin or abandoning self. It is utterly devoid of any recognition of personal guilt, any intent to obey God, or any desire for true righteousness.

That is not the kind of repentance Jesus preached. As we have seen repeatedly, the gospel according to Jesus is as much a call to forsake sin as it is a summons to faith. From his first message to his last, the Savior's theme was calling sinners to repentance—and this meant not only that they gained a new perspective on who he was, but also that

[6]Ibid., 376. This was a curious conclusion to a section Chafer began by affirming "as dogmatically . . . as language can declare, that repentance is essential to salvation and that none could be saved apart from repentance" (p. 373). Chafer's apparent self-contradiction turns on his definition of repentance: he saw it as simply a change of mind (p. 372), a turning from unbelief to faith. Repentance as he defined it has no reference to sin and contrition. He declared that repentance in the context of salvation is nothing more than "a synonym for the word *belief*" (p. 377). Thus in Chafer's system, calling people to faith in Christ is the same as preaching repentance. One concludes that Chafer would have preferred to eliminate the word *repentance* from the gospel presentation altogether, and thus avoid the risk of confusing "the glories of grace" in the minds of those who understood repentance as something more than simple faith (p. 378).

[7]Charles C. Ryrie, *The Ryrie Study Bible* (Chicago: Moody Press, 1976), 1950.

[8]G. Michael Cocoris, *Lordship Salvation—Is It Biblical?* (Dallas: Redención Viva, 1983), 12.

[9]Thomas L. Constable, "The Gospel Message," *Walvoord: A Tribute* (Chicago: Moody Press, 1982), 207.

[10]Charles C. Ryrie, *Balancing the Christian Life* (Chicago: Moody Press, 1969), 176.

they turned from sin and self to follow him. The message he commands us to preach is the same: "repentance for forgiveness of sins" (Luke 24:47).[11]

What Is Repentance?

Repentance *is* a critical element of conversion,[12] but do not dismiss it as simply another word for believing. The Greek word for "repentance" is *metanoia*, from *meta*, "after" and *noeō*, "to understand." Literally it means "afterthought" or "change of mind," but biblically its meaning does not stop there.[13] As *metanoia* is used in the New Testament, it *always* speaks of a change of purpose, and specifically a turning from sin.[14] In the sense Jesus used it, repentance calls for a repudiation of the old life and a turning to God for salvation.[15]

Such a change of purpose is what Paul had in mind when he described the repentance of the Thessalonians: "You turned to God

[11]Note that this is Luke's record of our Lord's Great Commission. Luke is the only one of the evangelists to record Jesus' words about the content of the message he was commissioning the disciples to preach. Repentance is clearly the heart of the gospel call he was commissioning his disciples to take into all the world.

[12]Berkhof writes: "True repentance never exists except in conjunction with faith, while, on the other hand, wherever there is true faith, there is also real repentance. . . . The two cannot be separated; they are simply complementary parts of the same process" (Louis Berkhof, *Systematic Theology* [Grand Rapids: Eerdmans, 1939], 487).

[13]"The predominantly intellectual understanding of *metanoia* as a change of mind plays very little part in the NT. Rather the decision by the whole man to turn around is stressed. It is clear that we are concerned neither with a purely outward turning nor with a merely intellectual change of ideas" (J. Goetzman, "Conversion," in Colin Brown, gen. ed., *New International Dictionary of New Testament Theology* [Grand Rapids: Zondervan, 1986], 1:358).

[14]W. E. Vine, *Vine's Expository Dictionary of Old and New Testament Words* (Old Tappan, N.J.: Revell, 1981), 3:280.

[15]"It demands radical conversion, a transformation of nature, a definitive turning from evil, a resolute turning to God in total obedience (Mk. 1:15; Mt. 4:17; 18:3). . . . This conversion is once-for-all. There can be no going back, only advance in responsible movement along the way now taken. It affects the whole man, first and basically the centre of personal life, then logically his conduct at all times and in all situations, his thoughts, words and acts (Mt. 12:33ff. par.; 23:26; Mk. 7:15 par.). The whole proclamation of Jesus . . . is a proclamation of unconditional turning to God, of unconditional turning from all that is against God, not merely that which is downright evil, but that which in a given case makes total turning to God impossible (Mt. 5:29f., 44; 6:19f.; 7:13f. par.; 10:32–39 par.; Mk. 3:31ff. par.; Lk. 14:33, cf. Mk. 10:21 par.)" (J. Behm, "*Metanoia*" in Gerhard Kittel, ed., *Theological Dictionary of the New Testament* [Grand Rapids: Eerdmans, 1967], 4:1002).

from idols to serve a living and true God" (1 Thess. 1:9). Note three elements of repentance: a turning to God; a turning from evil; and the intent to serve God. No change of mind can be called true repentance if it does not include all three elements. The simple but all too often overlooked fact is that a true change of mind will necessarily result in a change of behavior.

Repentance is not merely shame or sorrow for sin, although genuine repentance always involves an element of remorse.[16] It is a redirection of the human will, a purposeful decision to forsake all unrighteousness and pursue righteousness instead.

Nor is repentance merely a human work. It is, like every element of redemption, a sovereignly bestowed gift of God. The early church, recognizing the authenticity of Cornelius's conversion, concluded, "Well then, God has granted to the Gentiles also the repentance that leads to life" (Acts 11:18; cf. 5:31). Paul wrote to Timothy that he should gently correct those who oppose the truth, "if perhaps God may grant them repentance leading to the knowledge of the truth" (2 Tim. 2:25). If God is the one who grants repentance, it cannot be viewed as a human work.

Above all, repentance is not a presalvation attempt to set one's life in order. The call to repentance is not a command to make sin right before turning to Christ in faith. Rather it is a command to recognize one's lawlessness and hate it, to turn one's back on it and flee to Christ, embracing him with wholehearted devotion. As J. I. Packer has written, "The repentance that Christ requires of His people consists in a settled refusal to set any limit to the claims which He may make on their lives."[17]

Repentance is not simply a mental activity; genuine repentance involves the intellect, emotions, and will.[18] Geerhardus Vos wrote:

Our Lord's idea of repentance is as profound and comprehensive as his conception of righteousness. Of the three words that are used in the Greek Gospels to describe the process, one emphasizes the emotional element of regret, sorrow over the past evil course of life, *metamélomai;* Matt. 21:29–32; a second expresses reversal of the entire mental

[16]Thayer's Greek lexicon defines *metanoia* as "the change of mind of those who have begun to abhor their errors and misdeeds, and have determined to enter upon a better course of life, so that it embraces both a recognition of sin and sorrow for it and hearty amendment, the tokens and effects of which are good deeds" (Joseph Henry Thayer, trans., *Greek-English Lexicon of the New Testament* [Grand Rapids: Zondervan, 1962], 406).

[17]J. I. Packer, *Evangelism and the Sovereignty of God* (Downers Grove, Ill.: InterVarsity, 1961), 72.

[18]Cf. Berkhof, *Systematic Theology,* 486.

attitude, *metanoéō*, Matt. 12:41; Luke 11:32; 15:7, 10; the third denotes a change in the direction of life, one goal being substituted for another, *epistréphomai*; Matt. 13:15 (and parallels); Luke 17:4; 22:32. Repentance is not limited to any single faculty of the mind: it engages the entire man, intellect, will and affections. . . . Again, in the new life which follows repentance the absolute supremacy of God is the controlling principle. He who repents turns away from the service of mammon and self to the service of God.[19]

Intellectually, repentance begins with a recognition of sin—the understanding that we are sinners, that our sin is an affront to a holy God, and more precisely, that we are personally responsible for our own guilt. The repentance that leads to salvation must also include a recognition of who Christ is along with some understanding of his right to govern people's lives.

Emotionally, genuine repentance often accompanies an overwhelming sense of sorrow. This sorrow in and of itself is not repentance; one can be sorry or ashamed without being truly repentant. Judas, for example, felt remorse (Matt. 27:3), but he was not repentant. The rich young ruler went away sorrowful (Matt. 19:22), but he was not repentant. Nevertheless, sorrow can lead to genuine repentance. Second Corinthians 7:10 says, "The sorrow that is according to the will of God produces a repentance without regret." It is difficult to imagine a true repentance that does not include at least an element of contrition—not sorrow for getting caught; not sadness because of the consequences; but a sense of anguish at having sinned against God. In the Old Testament, repentance was often shown with sackcloth and ashes, the symbols of mourning (cf. Job 42:6; Jonah 3:5–6).

Volitionally, repentance involves a change of direction, a transformation of the will. Far from being only a change of mind, it constitutes a willingness—more accurately, a determination—to abandon stubborn disobedience and surrender the will to Christ. As such, genuine repentance will inevitably result in a change of behavior. The behavior change is not itself repentance, but it is the fruit repentance will certainly bear. Where there is no observable difference in conduct, there can be no confidence that repentance has taken place (Matt. 3:8; cf. 1 John 2:3–6; 3:17).

Real repentance alters the character of the whole person. As D. Martyn Lloyd-Jones said:

[19]Geerhardus Vos, *The Kingdom of God and the Church* (Nutley, N.J.: Presbyterian and Reformed, 1972), 92–93.

Repentance means that you realize that you are a guilty, vile sinner in the presence of God, that you deserve the wrath and punishment of God, that you are hell-bound. It means that you begin to realize that this thing called sin is in you, that you long to get rid of it, and that you turn your back on it in every shape and form. You renounce the world whatever the cost, the world in its mind and outlook as well as its practice, and you deny yourself, and take up the cross and go after Christ. Your nearest and dearest, and the whole world, may call you a fool, or say you have religious mania. You may have to suffer financially, but it makes no difference. That is repentance.[20]

Repentance is not a one-time act. The repentance that takes place at conversion begins a progressive, lifelong process of confession (1 John 1:9). This active, continuous attitude of repentance produces the poverty of spirit, mourning, and meekness Jesus spoke of in the Beatitudes (Matt. 5:3–6). It is a mark of every true believer.

The Fruits of Repentance

When Jesus preached, "Repent, for the kingdom of heaven is at hand" (Matt. 4:17), those who heard him understood the message. With their rich heritage in Old Testament and rabbinical teaching, his hearers would not have been confused about the meaning of repentance. They knew he was calling for far more than simply a change of mind or a new perspective on who he was. Repentance to them meant a complete surrender of their will and an inevitable change of behavior—a new way of life, not just a different opinion. They realized he was calling them to admit their sin and turn from it, to be converted, to turn around, to forsake their sin and selfishness and follow him instead.

After all, the Jewish concept of repentance was well developed. The rabbis held that Isaiah 1:16–17 described nine activities related to repentance: "Wash yourselves, make yourselves clean; remove the evil of your deeds from My sight. Cease to do evil, learn to do good; seek justice, reprove the ruthless; defend the orphan, plead for the widow." Note carefully the progression: beginning internally with a cleansing, repentance then manifests itself in attitudes and actions.

The Old Testament was filled with rich truth about repentance. Ezekiel 33:18–19, for example, says, "When the righteous turns from his righteousness and commits iniquity, then he shall die in it. But when the wicked turns from his wickedness and practices justice and righteousness, he will live by them." Second Chronicles 7:14 is a

[20]D. Martyn Lloyd-Jones, *Studies in the Sermon on the Mount* (Grand Rapids: Eerdmans, 1959), 2:248.

familiar prescription for repentance "[If] My people who are called by My name humble themselves and pray, and seek My face and turn from their wicked ways, then I will hear from heaven, will forgive their sin, and will heal their land." Isaiah 55:6–7 gives the Old Testament invitation to salvation, and repentance is a key element: "Seek the LORD while He may be found; call upon Him while He is near. Let the wicked forsake his way, and the unrighteous man his thoughts; and let him return to the LORD, and He will have compassion on him; and to our God, for He will abundantly pardon." Jonah 3:10 says, "When God saw their deeds, that they turned from their wicked way, then God relented concerning the calamity which He had declared He would bring upon them. And He did not do it."

Look carefully at that verse from Jonah. How did God evaluate the Ninevites' repentance? By their *deeds*. It was not that he read their thoughts or heard their prayers, though an omniscient God certainly could have seen the reality of their repentance that way. But he looked for righteous works.

John the Baptist also demanded to see good deeds as proof of repentance. He preached the message of repentance even before Jesus began his ministry (cf. Matt. 3:1–2). Scripture records that when the religious hypocrites came to John for baptism, "He said to them, 'You brood of vipers, who warned you to flee from the wrath to come? Therefore bring forth fruit in keeping with repentance'" (Matt. 3:7–8).

What a greeting! It was a far cry from saying, "Ladies and gentlemen, here are our esteemed leaders." We don't know why they had come for baptism, but obviously their motives were wrong. Perhaps they were trying to gain favor with the people or be associated with John's popularity. Whatever their reasons, they had not really repented, and John refused their overture. He condemned them instead as religious phonies.

Why was John so harsh? Because these hypocrites were poisoning a whole nation with their fatal deception. Nothing about their behavior indicated that they had truly repented. There is a critical lesson here: If repentance is genuine, we can expect it to produce observable results.

What are the fruits of repentance? That is the question the tax-gatherers asked John the Baptist (Luke 3:10). His answer to them was, "Collect no more than what you have been ordered to" (v. 13). To some soldiers who asked the same question, his response was, "Do not take money from anyone by force, or accuse anyone falsely, and be content with your wages" (v. 14).

In other words, there must be a sincere change in one's lifestyle. A person who has genuinely repented will stop doing evil and begin to live righteously. Along with a change of mind and attitude, true repentance will begin to produce a change in conduct.

Radical change was also what the apostle Paul considered proof of repentance. Note how he described his ministry to King Agrippa: "I did not prove disobedient to the heavenly vision, but kept declaring . . . to the Gentiles, that they should repent and turn to God, *performing deeds appropriate to repentance*" (Acts 26:19–20, emphasis added). That true believers will show their repentance with righteous behavior was obviously a crucial element of Paul's message.[21]

The Gospel and Repentance

Repentance has always been the foundation of the New Testament call to salvation. When Peter gave the gospel invitation at Pentecost, in the first public evangelism of the post-Resurrection era, repentance was at the heart of it: "Repent, and let each of you be baptized in the name of Jesus Christ for the forgiveness of your sins" (Acts 2:38).

No message that eliminates repentance can properly be called the gospel, for sinners cannot come to Jesus Christ apart from a radical change of heart, mind, and will. That demands a spiritual crisis leading to a complete turnaround and ultimately a wholesale transformation. It is the only kind of conversion Scripture recognizes.[22]

In Matthew 21:28–31 Jesus used a parable to illustrate the hypocrisy of a profession of faith without repentance:

> "But what do you think? A man had two sons, and he came to the first and said, 'Son, go work today in the vineyard.' And he answered and said, 'I will, sir'; and he did not go. And he came to the second and said the same thing. But he answered and said, 'I will not'; yet he afterward regretted it and went. Which of the two did the will of his father?"

You may wonder why Jesus did not include a third son who said, "I will" and kept his word. Perhaps it is because this story characterizes humanity, and we all fall short (cf. Rom. 3:23). Thus Jesus could describe only two kinds of religious people: those who pretend to be

[21]See appendix 1.

[22]"Conversion as Jesus understands it . . . is more than a break with the old nature. . . . It embraces the whole walk of the man who is claimed by the divine lordship. . . . 'To be converted,' embraces all that the dawn of God's kingdom demands of man" (J. Behm, "*Metanoia*," 4:1003).

obedient but are actually rebels, and those who begin as rebels but repent.

Jesus told the parable for the benefit of the Pharisees, who did not view themselves as sinful and disobedient. When he asked them which son did the will of his father, they correctly answered, "The latter" (Matt. 21:31). In admitting that, they condemned themselves for their own hypocrisy.

How Jesus' rebuke must have stung them! "Truly I say to you that the tax-gatherers and harlots will get into the kingdom of God before you" (Matt. 21:31). The Pharisees lived under the delusion that God approved of them because they made a great show of their religion. The problem was that it was only a show. They were like the son who said he would obey but did not. Their claim that they loved God and kept his law amounted to nothing. Those Pharisees were like many today who say they believe in Jesus but refuse to obey him. Their profession of faith is hollow. Unless they repent, they will perish.

Tax-gatherers and harlots have an easier time than Pharisees getting into the kingdom because they are more likely to recognize their sin and repent of it. Even the worst of sins will not keep a sinner out of heaven if he or she repents. On the other hand, even the most impressive Pharisee who shelters his sin and refuses to acknowledge or repent of it will find himself shut out of the kingdom. There is no salvation apart from the repentance that renounces sin.

Many today hear the truth of Christ and immediately respond as did the son who said he would obey but did not. Their positive response to Jesus will not save them. The fruit of their lives shows that they have never truly repented.

On the other hand, many turn their backs on sin, unbelief, and disobedience and embrace Christ with a faith that obeys. Theirs is true repentance, manifested by the righteousness it produces. They are the truly righteous (1 Peter 4:18). And that is the ultimate aim of the gospel according to Jesus.

17

The Nature of True Faith

Just as I am, without one plea
But that Thy blood was shed for me,
And that Thou bidd'st me come to Thee,
O Lamb of God, I come! I come!

That stanza, penned by Charlotte Elliot in the nineteenth century, has probably been used as background for the evangelistic invitation more than any other hymn in history. The thought those words convey is a glorious biblical reality: sinners may come to Christ just as they are—solely on the basis of repentant faith—and he will save them. The Lord's own wonderful promise is in John 3:16: "God so loved the world, that He gave His only begotten Son, that *whoever* believes in Him should not perish, but have eternal life" (emphasis added). Later he added, "The one who comes to Me I will certainly not cast out" (John 6:37).

The erosion of the gospel in our day has given this truth an insidious twist. The language of the modern message sounds vaguely similar to "Just as I Am," but the difference in meaning is profound. Sinners today hear not only that Christ will receive them as they are, but also that he will let them stay that way! Many erroneously believe they can come to Christ, receive absolution and immortality, then walk away to continue living life as they please, even choosing "to leave God out and live according to the old nature."[1]

A few years ago leaders of an international Christian youth organization asked me to preview a training film they produced. The subject was evangelism, and the film instructed youth workers *not to*

[1]Charles C. Ryrie, *Balancing the Christian Life* (Chicago: Moody Press, 1969), 35.

tell unsaved young people they must obey Christ, give him their hearts, surrender their lives, repent of their sins, submit to his lordship, or follow him. Telling the unsaved they must do those things confuses the gospel message, the film said. It advocated giving only the objective facts about Jesus' death (making no mention of the Resurrection), and pressing on them the need to believe. The film concluded that the sum total of saving faith is understanding and accepting the facts of the gospel.

I once spoke at a Bible conference where a well-known Bible teacher brought a message on salvation. He suggested that telling unsaved people they must surrender to Christ is the same as preaching works. He defined salvation as the unconditional gift of everlasting life given to people who believe the facts about Christ, *whether they choose to obey him or not.* One of his main points was that salvation may or may not alter a person's behavior. Transformed conduct is certainly desirable, he said, but even if no change in lifestyle occurs, the one who has believed the facts of the gospel can rest in the certainty of heaven.

Multitudes approach Christ on those terms. Thinking he will not confront their sin, they respond eagerly—but with no sense of the severity of their guilt before God, and with no desire to be freed from sin's bondage. They have been deceived by a corrupted gospel. They have been told that faith alone will save them, but they neither understand nor possess real faith. The "faith" they are relying on is only intellectual acquiescence to a set of facts. It will not save.

Eternal Life from Dead Faith?

Not all faith is redemptive. James 2:14–16 says faith without works is dead and cannot save.[2] James describes spurious faith as pure hypocrisy (v. 16), mere cognitive assent (v. 19), devoid of any verifying works (vv. 17–18)—no different from the demons' belief (v. 19). Obviously there is more to saving faith than merely conceding a set of facts. Faith without works is useless (v. 20).

Yet some in contemporary evangelicalism refuse to allow for any kind of relationship between faith and works. With this limitation, they are forced to receive virtually any profession of faith as the real

[2]The question of James 2:14, introduced by the Greek participle *me*, grammatically presumes a negative answer: "Can that faith save him? Of course not!" Cf. A. T. Robertson, *Word Pictures in the New Testament* (Nashville: Broadman, 1933), 6:34.

thing.[3] At least one writer explicitly stated that dead faith *can* save.[4] Amazingly, one popular interpretation of James 2 teaches that dead faith is actually *proof* of salvation.[5]

Others admit the inefficacy of "faith" that is no more than a barren, academic recognition of the truth, but balk at defining faith in terms that imply submission or commitment of one's life.[6] In fact, it is commonly believed that faith and commitment are innately disconnected.[7] The typical idea of faith relegates it to a momentary act that takes place in the mind, a decision to believe the facts of the gospel— "nothing more than a response to a divine initiative."[8]

Herein lies the fallacy of today's popular approach to evangelism. The gospel appeal is tacked on to a wholly inadequate explanation of

[3]"One gets the impression that [they see] no distinction" (Johnny V. Miller, review of *The Gospel Under Siege, Trinity Journal* 4 [Spring 1983], 93–94).

[4]A. Ray Stanford, *Handbook of Personal Evangelism* (Hollywood, Fla.: Florida Bible College, n.d.), 102–3.

[5]Zane C. Hodges, *The Gospel Under Siege* (Dallas: Redención Viva, 1981), 19. Hodges postulates that in order for faith to be dead, it must have been alive at one time (p. 20). He theorizes that the salvation spoken of in James 2:14 means deliverance from the temporal consequences of sin, not eternal salvation (p. 23). Thus he concludes that James is talking to redeemed people beset by dead orthodoxy—in Hodges' words, their faith has become "little more than a creedal corpse" (p. 33). Though their faith has lapsed, Hodges believes their eternal salvation is secure. The fact that their faith is dead, he says, simply proves it was once alive—and therefore they must be saved. But that is skewed logic. "Dead faith" does not necessitate faith that was once alive, any more than Ephesians 2:1 ("You were dead in your trespasses and sins") implies that individual sinners were once spiritually alive.

[6]Cf. Livingston Blauvelt, Jr., "Does the Bible Teach Lordship Salvation?" *Bibliotheca Sacra* (January–March 1986), 37–45. Blauvelt begins his article with a recognition that intellectual assent is not saving faith: "Many people 'say' they have faith (James 2:14) but have no genuine conversion. Mere verbal assent or mental acquiescence to the fact of Christ's death, without any conviction of personal sin, is inadequate" (p. 37). But Blauvelt's entire discussion of the true nature of faith consists of only four paragraphs arguing that saving faith has nothing to do with commitment, after which he writes, "The term faith in the New Testament sense involves believing that Jesus of Nazareth is Christ the Son of God and that he died for one's sins and rose from the dead (John 20:31; 1 Corinthians 15:3–4). Faith is trusting Christ for everlasting life" (p. 43). It is difficult to see how such faith apart from any kind of commitment to Christ differs from "mere verbal assent or mental acquiescence."

[7]Ryrie, *Balancing the Christian Life,* 170. Here Ryrie writes, "The message of faith plus commitment of life . . . cannot be the gospel."

[8]Hodges, *Gospel Under Siege,* 21. Although *The Gospel Under Siege* is labeled "a study on faith and works," this brief statement is as close as Hodges comes in the book to giving a definition of faith: "Faith, as we have perceived it in the simple, direct statements of the Bible about the saving transaction, is nothing more than a response to a divine initiative. It is the means by which the gift of life is received."

what it means to believe. The modern definition of faith eliminates repentance, erases the moral significance of believing, obviates the work of God in the sinner's heart, and makes an ongoing trust in the Lord optional. Far from championing the truth that human works have no place in salvation, modern easy-believism has made faith itself a wholly human work, a fragile, temporary attribute that may or may not endure.[9]

But it is not a biblical view of faith to say one may have it at the moment of salvation and never experience its fruit. Paul's words in 2 Timothy 2:12 speak powerfully to this issue: "If we endure, we shall also reign with Him, if we deny Him, He also will deny us." Endurance is the mark of those who will reign with Christ in his kingdom. Clearly, enduring is a characteristic of true believers, while disloyalty and defection reveal a heart of unbelief. Those who deny Christ, he will deny. Paul goes on to say, "If we are faithless, He remains faithful; for He cannot deny Himself" (v. 13). Thus God's faithfulness is a blessed comfort to loyal, abiding believers, but a frightening warning to false professors (cf. John 3:17–18).

Faith As Scripture Describes It

We have seen already that repentance is granted by God; it is not a human work (Acts 11:18; 2 Tim. 2:25). Likewise, faith is a supernatural gift of God. Ephesians 2:8–9 is a familiar passage: "By grace you have been saved through faith; and that not of yourselves, it is the gift of God; not as a result of works, that no one should boast." What is "the gift of God" Paul speaks of? Westcott calls it "the saving energy of faith."[10] However, the phrase "that not of yourselves" has no clear antecedent. The Greek pronoun translated "that" is neuter and the word for "faith" is feminine. The antecedent of *that*, it would seem, cannot be the word *faith*. The problem is, there is no clear

---

[9]Shockingly, Hodges writes, "It is widely held in modern Christendom that the faith of a genuine Christian cannot fail. But this is not an assertion that can be verified from the New Testament" (ibid., 68); and "There is nothing to support the view that perseverance in the faith is an inevitable outcome of true salvation" (p. 83). Contrast that statement with Paul's inspired words in Colossians 1:22–23: "He has now reconciled you in His fleshly body through death, in order to present you before Him holy and blameless and beyond reproach—*if indeed you continue in the faith firmly established and steadfast, and not moved away from the hope of the gospel*" (emphasis added). What is that but a guarantee that if faith is genuine, it will endure to the end? Cf. also 1 Corinthians 15:1–2; 2 Timothy 2:12; Hebrews 2:1–3; 3:14; 4:14; 6:11–12; 12:14; James 1:2; 1 John 2:19.

[10]B. F. Westcott, *St. Paul's Epistle to the Ephesians* (Minneapolis: Klock and Klock, n.d., reprint of 1906 volume), 32.

antecedent in this passage. "That" might refer to the act of believing, employing an antecedent that is not stated but understood. It is also possible that Paul had in mind the entire process—grace, faith, and salvation—as the gift of God. Both possibilities certainly are in keeping with the context: "Even when we were dead in our transgressions, [God] made us alive together with Christ (by grace you have been saved)" (v. 5). Spiritually dead, we were helpless until God intervened to quicken us. Faith is an integral part of the "gift" his grace bestowed on us.

Consistently the Scriptures teach that faith is not conjured up by the human will but is a sovereignly granted gift of God. Jesus said, "No one can come to Me, unless the Father who sent Me draws him" (John 6:44). And "No one can come to Me, unless it has been granted him from the Father" (v. 65). Acts 3:16 speaks of "the faith which comes through Him." Philippians 1:29 says, "To you it has been granted for Christ's sake . . . to believe in Him." And Peter wrote to fellow believers as "those who have received a faith of the same kind as ours" (2 Peter 1:1). How do we know that faith is God's gift? Left to ourselves, no one would ever believe: "There is none who understands, there is none who seeks for God" (Rom. 3:11). "So then it does not depend on the man who wills or the man who runs, but on God who has mercy" (Rom. 9:16). God draws the sinner to Christ and gives the ability to believe. Without that divinely generated faith, one cannot understand and approach the Savior. "A natural man does not accept the things of the Spirit of God; for they are foolishness to him, and he cannot understand them, because they are spiritually appraised" (1 Cor. 2:14). That is precisely why when Peter affirmed his faith in Christ as the Son of God, Jesus told him, "Blessed are you, Simon Barjona, because flesh and blood did not reveal this to you, but My Father who is in heaven" (Matt. 16:17). Faith is graciously given to believers by God himself.

As a divine gift, faith is neither transient nor impotent. It has an abiding quality that guarantees that it will endure to the end. The familiar words of Habakkuk 2:4, "The righteous will live by his faith" (cf. Rom. 1:17; Gal. 3:11; Heb. 10:38), speak not of a momentary act of believing, but of a living, enduring trust in God. Hebrews 3:14 emphasizes the permanence of genuine faith. Its very durability is proof of its reality: "We have become partakers of Christ, if we hold fast the beginning of our assurance firm until the end." The faith God gives can never evaporate. And the work of salvation cannot ultimately be thwarted. In Philippians 1:6 Paul wrote, "I am confident of this very thing, that He who began a good work in you will perfect it until the day of Christ Jesus" (cf. also 1 Cor. 1:8; Col. 1:22–23).

The faith God graciously supplies produces both the volition and the ability to comply with his will (cf. Phil. 2:13: "God . . . is at work in you, both to will and to work for His good pleasure"). Thus faith is inseparable from obedience. Berkhof sees three elements to genuine faith: An intellectual element (*notitia*), which is "a positive recognition of the truth"; an emotional element (*assensus*), which includes "a deep conviction [and affirmation] of the truth"; and a volitional element (*fiducia*), which involves "a personal trust in Christ as Savior and Lord, including a surrender . . . to Christ."[11] Modern popular theology tends to recognize *notitia* and often *assensus* but eliminate *fiducia*. Yet faith is not true faith if it lacks this attitude of surrender to Christ's authority.

Writing about the verb "to obey" (*peithō*), W. E. Vine says:

> *Peithō* and *pisteuō*, "to trust," are closely related etymologically; the difference in meaning is that the former implies the obedience that is produced by the latter, cp. Heb. 3:18, 19, where the disobedience of the Israelites is said to be the evidence of their unbelief. . . . When a man obeys God he gives the only possible evidence that in his heart he believes God. . . . *Peithō* in N.T. suggests an actual and outward result of the inward persuasion and consequent faith.[12]

So the person who has believed will *yearn* to obey. Because we retain the vestiges of sinful flesh, no one will obey perfectly (cf. 2 Cor. 7:1; 1 Thess. 3:10), but the desire to do the will of God will be ever present in true believers (cf. Rom. 7:18).[13] That is why faith and obedience are so closely linked throughout Scripture.

[11]Louis Berkhof, *Systematic Theology* (Grand Rapids: Eerdmans, 1939), 503–5. Berkhof seems to borrow heavily here from Augustus Strong, *Systematic Theology* (Philadelphia: Godson, 1907), 837–38. Strong is as explicit as Berkhof in defining the volitional element of faith, *fiducia*. He says it involves "surrender of the soul, as guilty and defiled, to Christ's governance." Thus we find "lordship salvation" at the very heart of the definition of faith.

[12]W. E. Vine, *Vine's Expository Dictionary of Old and New Testament Words* (Old Tappan, N.J.: Revell, 1981), 3:124.

[13]Romans 7 is the classic text describing the believer's struggle with his sinful flesh. Note that while Paul acknowledged his own disobedience, he wrote that the desire to do good was his consuming passion: "I am not practicing what I would like to do, but I am doing the very thing I hate" (v. 15); "The wishing [to do good] is present in me" (v. 18); "I joyfully concur with the law of God in the inner man" (v. 22); and "I myself with my mind am serving the law of God" (v. 25). Though the apostle Paul described himself as the chief of sinners (1 Tim. 1:15), those who love reveling in debauchery will not find a kindred spirit in him.

A concept of faith not producing surrender of the will corrupts the message of salvation. Paul spoke of the gospel as something to be obeyed (Rom. 10:16 KJV; 2 Thess. 1:8). Here is how he characterized conversion: "Though you were the slaves of sin, you became obedient from the heart" (Rom. 6:17). The result he sought in his ministry of evangelism was "obedience . . . by word and deed" (Rom. 15:18). And he wrote repeatedly of "the obedience of faith" (Rom. 1:5; 16:26).

Clearly, the biblical concept of faith must lead to obedience. "Believe" is treated as if it were synonymous with "obey" in John 3:36: "He who believes in the Son has eternal life; but he who does not obey the Son shall not see life." Acts 6:7 shows how salvation was understood in the early church: "A great many . . . were becoming obedient to the faith." Obedience is so closely related to saving faith that Hebrews 5:9 uses it as a synonym: "Having been made perfect, He became to all those who obey Him the source of eternal salvation." Hebrews 11, the great treatise on faith, presents obedience as a by-product of faith: "By faith . . . Abraham obeyed" (v. 8)—and not just Abraham. All the heroes of faith listed in Hebrews 11 showed their faith by obedience.

Obedience is the inevitable manifestation of true faith. Paul recognized this when he wrote to Titus about "those who are defiled and unbelieving. . . . They profess to know God but by their deeds they deny Him" (Titus 1:15–16).[14] To Paul, their perpetual disobedience proved their disbelief. Their actions denied God more loudly than their words proclaimed him. This is characteristic of unbelief, not faith, for true faith always produces righteous works. As the Reformers were fond of saying, we are justified by faith alone, but justifying faith is never alone. Spurgeon said, "Although we are sure that men are not saved for the sake of their works, yet we are equally

[14]Incredibly, Zane Hodges asserts that Paul was describing true believers when he wrote those words to Titus (*Gospel Under Siege,* 96). He writes, "The people Paul has in mind in Titus 1:16 are evidently the same as those of whom he says in verse 13: 'Therefore rebuke them sharply, that they may be sound in the faith.' The Greek word for 'sound' means to be healthy. Hence, the persons he thinks of are not individuals who are not 'in the faith' at all. Rather, they are people whom he regards as spiritually 'sick' and who need a rebuke designed to restore them to good health." That completely ignores the fact that Paul referred to these people as "defiled and unbelieving, [with] both their mind and their conscience . . . defiled" (v. 15) and "detestable and disobedient . . . worthless for any good deed" (v. 16). That cannot be a description of the children of God.

sure that no man will be saved without them."[15] True faith is manifest only in obedience.

Faith and faithfulness were not substantially different concepts to the first-century Christian. In fact, the same word is translated both ways in our English Bibles.[16] Writing on "faith" in his commentary on Galatians, Lightfoot writes:

> The Greek *pistis* . . . and the English "faith" hover between two meanings; *trustfulness,* the frame of mind which relies on another; and *trustworthiness,* the frame of mind which can be relied upon. Not only are the two connected together grammatically, as active and passive sense of the same word, or logically, as subject and object of the same act; but there is a close moral affinity between them. Fidelity, constancy, firmness, confidence, reliance, trust, belief—these are the links which connect the two extremes, the passive with the active meaning of "faith." Owing to these combined causes, the two senses will at times be so blended together that they can only be separated by some arbitrary distinction. . . . In all such cases it is better to accept the latitude, and even the vagueness, of a word or phrase, than to attempt a rigid definition. . . . And indeed the loss in grammatical precision is often more than compensated by the gain in theological depth. In the case of "the faithful" for instance, does not the one quality of heart carry the other with it, so that they who are trustful are trusty also; they who have faith in God are steadfast and unmovable in the path of duty?[17]

And so the faithful (believing) are also faithful (obedient). "Fidelity, constancy, firmness, confidence, reliance, trust, [and] belief" are all indivisibly wrapped up in the idea of believing. Righteous living is an inevitable by-product of real faith (Rom. 10:10).

Of course, that is not to say that faith results in anything like sinless perfection. All true believers understand the plea of the demon-possessed boy's father, "I do believe; help my unbelief" (Mark 9:24). Those who believe will desire to obey, however imperfectly they may follow through at times. So-called faith in God that does not produce this yearning to submit to his will is not faith at all. The state of mind that refuses obedience is pure and simple unbelief.

[15]Charles H. Spurgeon, *The New Park Street Pulpit* (Grand Rapids: Zondervan, 1962 reprint of 1858 volume), 4:265.

[16]Cf. Galatians 5:22, where *pistis* as a fruit of the Spirit is rendered "faithfulness." This is the same word translated "faith" in Ephesians 2:8: "By grace you have been saved through faith."

[17]J. B. Lightfoot, *The Epistle of St. Paul to the Galatians* (Grand Rapids: Zondervan, n.d.), 154–55.

Faith As Jesus Presented It

The Beatitudes (Matt. 5:3–12) reveal the character of true faith as well as any passage of Scripture I know.[18] These traits—poverty of spirit, hunger and thirst for righteousness, purity of heart, and so on—are not just an unobtainable legal standard. These are characteristics common to all who believe. The first of the Beatitudes leaves no doubt about whom the Lord is speaking: "Blessed are the poor in spirit, *for theirs is the kingdom of heaven*" (Matt. 5:3, emphasis added). He is describing redeemed people, those who have believed, those who are part of the kingdom. Here is what their faith is like.

Its foundational characteristic is humility—a poverty of spirit, a brokenness that acknowledges spiritual bankruptcy. Genuine believers see themselves as sinners; they know they have nothing to offer God that will buy his favor. That is why they mourn (v. 4), with the sorrow that accompanies true repentance. It crushes the believer into meekness (v. 5). He hungers and thirsts for righteousness (v. 6). As the Lord satisfies that hunger, he makes the believing one merciful (v. 6), pure in heart (v. 7), and a peacemaker (v. 9). The believer is ultimately persecuted and reviled for righteousness' sake (v. 10).

That is Jesus' description of the genuine believer. Each of the characteristics he names—starting with humility and reaching fruition in obedience—is a consequence of true faith. And note that the obedience of faith is more than external; it issues from the heart. That is one reason their righteousness is greater than the righteousness of the scribes and Pharisees (v. 20). Jesus goes on to characterize true righteousness—the righteousness that is born of faith (cf. Rom. 10:6)—as obedience not just to the letter of the law, but to the spirit of the law as well (vv. 21–48). This kind of righteousness does not merely avoid acts of adultery; it goes so far as to avoid adulterous thoughts. It eschews hatred the same as murder.

If you see that God's standard is higher than you can possibly attain, you are on the road to the blessedness Jesus spoke of in the Beatitudes. It begins with the humility that grows out of a sense of utter spiritual poverty, the knowledge that we are poor in spirit. And it consummates inevitably in righteous obedience. Those are characteristics of a supernatural life. They are impossible apart from faith, and it is impossible that someone with true faith might be utterly

[18]For my complete commentary on the Beatitudes, see John MacArthur, *The MacArthur New Testament Commentary: Matthew 1–7* (Chicago: Moody Press, 1985), 131–233. For a popular treatment of the same passage, see John MacArthur, *Kingdom Living Here and Now* (Chicago: Moody Press, 1980).

lacking these characteristics that are common to everyone in the kingdom (Matt. 5:3).

When Jesus wanted to illustrate the character of saving faith, he took a little child, stood him in the midst of the disciples, and said, "Truly I say to you, unless you are converted and become like children, you shall not enter the kingdom of heaven" (Matt. 18:3). A child was the perfect picture of obedient humility,[19] an object lesson about saving faith.

Jesus used this illustration to teach that if we insist on retaining the privileges of adulthood—if we want to be our own boss, do our own thing, govern our own lives—we cannot enter into the kingdom of heaven. But if we are willing to come on the basis of childlike faith and receive salvation with the humility of a child, with a willingness to surrender to Christ's authority, then we are coming with the right attitude.

Jesus said, "My sheep hear My voice, and I know them, and they *follow* Me; and I give them eternal life; and they shall never perish" (John 10:27–28, emphasis added). Who are the true sheep? The ones who follow. Who are the ones who follow? The ones who are given eternal life.

Faith obeys. Unbelief rebels. The direction of one's life should reveal whether that person is a believer or an unbeliever. There is no middle ground.[20] Merely knowing and affirming facts apart from obedience to the truth is not believing in the biblical sense. Those who cling to the memory of a one-time decision of "faith" but lack any evidence of the outworking of faith had better heed the clear and solemn warning of Scripture: "He who does not obey the Son shall not see life, but the wrath of God abides on him" (John 3:36).

[19]Children, of course, do not always obey. But they are under the authority of another, and when they disobey, they are chastened.

[20]Again, this is not to deny the obvious truth that Christians can and do fall into sin. But even in the case of a sinning believer, the Spirit will operate by producing conviction, hatred for one's sin, and some kind of desire for obedience. The idea that a true believer can continue in unbroken disobedience from the moment of conversion, without ever producing any righteous fruit whatsoever, is foreign to Scripture.

18

The Promise of Justification

Without a doubt, the most unsettling aspect of Jesus' Sermon on the Mount is this shocking statement: "Therefore you are to be perfect, as your heavenly Father is perfect" (Matt. 5:48).

If the gauge of righteousness is absolute perfection, what hope is there for anyone?

The people listening to Jesus that day believed that the scribes and Pharisees were the embodiment of the highest human righteousness. And in a sense they were—they held to the strictest imaginable legalistic standards. Here is how the apostle Paul chronicled his life as a Pharisee: "Circumcised the eighth day, of the nation of Israel, of the tribe of Benjamin, a Hebrew of Hebrews; as to the Law, a Pharisee; as to zeal, a persecutor of the church; as to the righteousness which is in the Law, found blameless" (Phil. 3:5–6). The Pharisees fasted, prayed, abstained from questionable practices, paid tithes, gave alms, memorized Scripture—and even devised their own rigid laws that went beyond what God had commanded in Scripture.

Yet Jesus said, "Unless your righteousness *surpasses* that of the scribes and Pharisees, you shall not enter the kingdom of heaven" (Matt. 5:20, emphasis added). If you believe that establishes an impossible standard, you have understood the message.

Remember the rich young ruler? He was a Pharisee who evidently believed he had kept the law as completely as humanly possible. After he walked away unbelieving, Jesus told his disciples, "It is hard for a rich man to enter the kingdom of heaven" (Matt. 19:23). What was their response? Astonished, they asked him, "Then who can be saved?" (v. 25).

Jesus' reply was, "With men this is impossible, but with God all things are possible."

Salvation is impossible for sinful humanity. We have no redeeming resources of our own. We cannot atone for our sins. We cannot even believe without God's sovereign enablement (John 6:44, 65); we cannot conjure up faith out of the human will. And we certainly cannot live up to God's standard of perfect righteousness.

In the sixteenth century, a German monk named Martin Luther sat in the tower of the Black Cloister in Wittenberg, meditating on the perfect righteousness of God. Although he was the most scrupulous of monks, attending confession for hours each day, seeking forgiveness for the minutest of sins, he realized that the standard of perfect righteousness was absolutely unattainable. He thought of divine righteousness as an unrelenting, unforgiving, avenging wrath and believed his state was hopeless. Recounting the experience that transformed his life, he later said:

> That expression "righteousness of God" was like a thunderbolt in my heart. . . . I hated Paul with all my heart when I read that the righteousness of God is revealed in the gospel [Rom. 1:16–17]. Only afterward, when I saw the words that follow—namely, that it's written that the righteous shall live through faith [1:17]—and in addition consulted Augustine, I was cheered. When I learned that the righteousness of God is his mercy, and that he makes us righteous through it, a remedy was offered to me in my affliction.[1]

The remedy Luther found was the doctrine of justification by faith. His discovery launched the Reformation and put an end to the Dark Ages. What Luther came to realize is that God's righteousness, revealed in the gospel, is reckoned in full to the account of everyone who turns to Christ in repentant faith. God's own righteousness thus becomes the ground on which believers stand before him.

This doctrine of justification is most fully expounded by the apostle Paul. The book of Romans in particular includes a lengthy treatise on justification, in which Paul demonstrates that as far back as Genesis, God graciously saved people by reckoning his righteousness to them because of their faith. No one has ever been saved through the merit system—salvation has been available only by grace through faith ever since our first parents fell. Abraham is the prime example of this: "Abraham believed God, and it was reckoned to him as righteousness" (Rom. 4:3).

[1]Martin Luther, *Table Talk*, Theodore G. Tappert, ed., in Helmut T. Lehmann, gen. ed., *Luther's Works*, 55 vols. (Philadelphia: Fortress, 1967), 54:308–9.

What Is Justification?

During his earthly ministry, Jesus rarely used the word *justification*. Nevertheless, justification by faith was the underlying theme of the message he preached. Look again at the parable of the Pharisee and the publican:

> He also told this parable to certain ones who trusted in themselves that they were righteous, and viewed others with contempt: "Two men went up into the temple to pray, one a Pharisee, and the other a tax-gatherer. The Pharisee stood and was praying thus to himself, 'God, I thank Thee that I am not like other people: swindlers, unjust, adulterers, or even like this tax-gatherer. I fast twice a week; I pay tithes of all that I get.' But the tax-gatherer, standing some distance away, was even unwilling to lift up his eyes to heaven, but was beating his breast, saying, 'God, be merciful to me, the sinner!'" (Luke 18:9–13).

Jesus must have drawn gasps from the Pharisees when he punctuated his story with this pronouncement: "I tell you, this man [the tax-gatherer] went down to his house *justified* rather than the other [the Pharisee]; for everyone who exalts himself shall be humbled, but he who humbles himself shall be exalted" (v. 14, emphasis added).

The parable reveals that justification is instantaneous. The repentant tax-collector "went down to his house justified"; that is, there was no time lapse—no works of penance, no ritual, no sacrament, no confessional exercise, no meritorious deeds he needed to do before he could be whole in God's eyes. Everything had already been done on his behalf. He was justified by faith on the spot.

Here our Lord simply states the *fact* of justification; he does not explain the *theology* of it. Still, the parable is an ideal portrait of justification by faith, in perfect harmony with the doctrine that Paul would later articulate so clearly in Romans 3–5.

Justification may be defined as an act of God whereby he imputes to a believing sinner the full and perfect righteousness of Christ, forgiving the sinner of all *un*righteousness, declaring him or her perfectly righteous in God's sight, thus delivering the believer from all condemnation. That definition contains several elements: imputed righteousness, forgiveness of sins, a new standing before God, and a reversal of God's wrath. Those all indicate that justification is a legal verdict. It is a *forensic* reality that takes place in the court of God, not in the heart of the sinner. In other words, justification is an instantaneous change of one's standing before God, not a gradual transformation that takes place within the one who is justified.

There are two serious errors to avoid in the matter of justification. First, do not confuse justification with sanctification. Roman Catholic

theology makes this error. *Sanctification* is the work of God whereby
he sets the believer apart from sin. Sanctification is a practical reality,
not simply a legal declaration. Sanctification involves a change in the
sinner's character, not just a new standing before God. By including
sanctification as an aspect of justification, Catholic theology renders
instantaneous justification impossible. Worse, this view substitutes
the believer's own imperfect righteousness in place of Christ's
unblemished righteousness, as the basis of justification.

There is a second, equally dangerous error: Do not separate
justification and sanctification so radically that you allow for one
without the other. This is the error of *antinomianism*. God will not
justify those he does not sanctify. God does not offer justification as a
stand-alone means of salvation. Election, regeneration, faith, justification, sanctification, and even glorification are all integral facets of
God's saving work: "Whom He foreknew, He also predestined to
become conformed to the image of His Son [sanctification], . . . and
whom He predestined, these He also called; and whom He called,
these He also justified; and whom He justified, these He also
glorified" (Rom. 8:29–30). Justification cannot be isolated and made
to represent the sum of God's saving work. Yet that is exactly the
error that is rampant in contemporary theology.

Imputed Righteousness

The cornerstone of justification is the reckoning of righteousness to
the believer's account. This is the truth that sets Christian doctrine
apart from every form of false religion. We call it "imputed
righteousness." Apart from it, salvation is utterly impossible.

Theologian James Buchanan wrote, "[Guilt] cannot be extin-
guished by repentance or even by regeneration; for while these may
improve or even renew our character, a divine sentence of condemnation can only be reversed by a divine act of remission."[2] Sin defiles
us. The apostle James wrote, "Whoever keeps the whole law and yet
stumbles in one point, he has become guilty of all" (James 2:10). No
amount of doing good can make up for even one sin. The person who
has sinned owes an impossible debt.

Moreover, a righteous God cannot simply overlook sin or act as if it
never occurred. There must be atonement for sin. Law demands a
penalty for sin, and it is a penalty that must be paid: "The wages of
sin is death" (Rom. 6:23).

---

[2]Cited in John Murray, *Collected Writings*, 4 vols. (Edinburgh: Banner of
Truth, 1977), 2:202.

Yet atonement alone does not fully solve the problem. If it were somehow possible for sinners to atone for their sins and obtain forgiveness, they would still stand before God without merit. Although their guilt would be erased, they would still lack the perfect righteousness God requires (Matt. 5:20, 48).

Imputed righteousness solves the dilemma. Christ made atonement by shedding his own blood on the cross. That provides forgiveness. And just as our sins were put to his account when he bore them on the cross, so now his righteousness is reckoned as our own. His perfect righteousness thus becomes the ground on which we stand before God.

This is a crucial point on which Protestants have historically been in full agreement: sinners are not justified because of some good thing in them; God can declare them righteous because he first imputes to them the perfect righteousness of Christ. We stand before God as if we were perfectly just. Judicially, the Father views us as if our righteousness were on the same lofty plane as his Son's!

Again, this is owing to no good thing in us—not even God's sanctifying or regenerating work in our hearts. Justification is possible exclusively through the imputed righteousness of Christ: "To the one who does not work, but believes in him who justifies the ungodly, *his faith is reckoned as righteousness*" (Rom. 4:5, emphasis added). "Those who receive the abundance of grace and of *the gift of righteousness* will reign in life through the One, Jesus Christ" (5:17, emphasis added). "Through the obedience of the One the many will be made [declared] righteous" (v. 19). "Now apart from the Law the righteousness of God has been manifested, being witnessed by the Law and the Prophets, even *the righteousness of God through faith in Jesus Christ for all those who believe*" (3:22, emphasis added). "He made Him who knew no sin to be sin on our behalf, that we might become the righteousness of God in Him" (2 Cor. 5:21). "Not having a righteousness of my own derived from the Law, but that which is through faith in Christ, *the righteousness which comes from God on the basis of faith*" (Phil. 3:9, emphasis added).

Forgiveness of Sins

Justification also guarantees the forgiveness and remission of sins. That may seem obvious from the meaning of the word. Yet it is not the kind of forgiveness that merely excuses or disregards wrongdoing. As noted, if God simply ignored sins, he would compromise his own holiness. Instead, the penalty sin demands was fully paid in the death of Christ. We are therefore "justified as a gift by his grace through the redemption which is in Christ Jesus; whom God displayed publicly as a propitiation in His blood through faith. This was to demonstrate His righteousness . . . *that He might be just and the justifier of the one who has faith in Jesus"* (Rom. 3:24–26, emphasis added).

God can justify without besmirching his own righteousness because Christ made *propitiation*. That is a technical term describing the reconciliation of God to the sinner. Christ atoned for our sins; God is therefore propitiated. In other words, he is kindly disposed to us and eager to forgive. The enmity has been removed. The full price was paid, so God can receive believing sinners with no taint on his own righteousness.

A New Standing

"This man went down to his house justified" (Luke 18:14) describes the tax-gatherer's standing before God. It is not difficult to imagine the Pharisees' anger when Jesus related this story. In essence he was telling them that a pathetic publican in abject repentance was more acceptable to God than they were.

The reason for this is quite simple: They "trusted *in themselves* that they were righteous" (Luke 18:9, emphasis added). Likewise, the Pharisee in the parable was seeking justification on the basis of his own righteousness: "I am not like other people: swindlers, unjust, adulterers, or even like this tax-gatherer. I fast twice a week; I pay tithes of all that I get" (vv. 11–12). We commonly call such people self-righteous. Have you ever considered why? It is because they assume they have ample righteousness of their own and do not see the need for imputed righteousness.

But the tax-gatherer was under no such delusion. All he could do was repent and plead for mercy. And so perfect righteousness was imputed to his account. Forever thereafter he stood before God fully justified.

Reversal of God's Wrath

Justification is the polar opposite of condemnation. One of the most blessed of all biblical truths is found in Romans 8:1: "There is therefore now no condemnation for those who are in Christ Jesus." Justification by faith is what makes that possible. If God's demeanor toward us were determined by our own behavior, no one could escape his wrath; for all of us are wretched sinners—even the most mature saint in Christ (cf. Rom. 7:24). But we who are in Christ need not fear condemnation; we have been justified.

What do you suppose would have become of the tax-gatherer in Jesus' parable? Do you think he would have continued praying in fear and anguish week after week? Certainly not. Like Matthew and Zaccheus, two real-life tax-gatherers we have already met, this man would have discovered that justification offers the only possible relief from the guilt of sin. We can be certain that his life would not have continued as before.

Justification and the Life of the Believer

We noted above that antinomianism is the notion of justification apart from sanctification. Luther himself coined the term, for already in his lifetime, some were beginning to corrupt the doctrine he had rediscovered, claiming that justification by faith rendered unnecessary the preaching of the law, obedience to the law, or sanctification as evidence of justification. Luther said of them: "But our antinomian friends wish in their folly to flatter secure men and to make them good by reminding them of [imputed] righteousness, though such an age as ours is incapable of being terrified by the lightning of the law. On account of the great sense of [false] security it's necessary to thunder and lightning with the law."[3]

Luther's remedy for antinomianism was preaching the law of God, because he rightly understood that those who comfort themselves with the promise of justification while living in wanton unrighteousness are thereby shown that theirs is a false security.

Does justification by faith make way for licentious living? Not if the doctrine is properly understood. Paul anticipated the antinomian argument: "What shall we say then? Are we to continue in sin that grace might increase?" (Rom. 6:1). "What then? Shall we sin because we are not under law but under grace? May it never be" (v. 15). Romans 6 is Paul's rebuttal to antinomianism. He argues that our union with Christ guarantees we shall no longer be slaves of sin: "Our old self was crucified with Him, that our body of sin might be done away with, that we should no longer be slaves to sin; for he who has died is freed from sin" (vv. 6–7).

Those who argue against lordship salvation often base their theology on the faulty assumption that the work of God in salvation stops with justification. The rest, many believe, is purely the believer's own effort. Sanctification, obedience, surrender, and all

[3]Luther, *Table Talk*, 55:308–9.

aspects of discipleship are left up to believers to do or not do as they choose. Thus while touting salvation by grace apart from works, they have actually established a system that is almost wholly dependent on human works for any measure of practical righteousness.

Thankfully, the gospel according to Jesus does not abandon believers to their own energies. The glorious justification our Lord spoke of is only the beginning of the abundant life he promised (cf. John 10:10). "He who believes in Me, as the Scripture said, 'From his innermost being shall flow rivers of living water'" (John 7:38). The salvation he promised brings not only justification, but also sanctification, union with him, the indwelling Holy Spirit, and an eternity of blessing. It is not merely a one-time legal transaction.

But a one-time legal transaction—justification—is the turning point. It is what moves us into a new relationship with God so that we can walk in the light as he is in the light (cf. 1 John 1:7). It is what brings peace with God in place of enmity (Rom. 5:1). It is what makes us heirs according to the hope of eternal life (Titus 3:7). It is the heart of all God's work on our behalf, beginning with his foreknowledge before the foundation of the world and carrying on to our final glorification with him (Rom. 8:29–30). And thus it is the very heart of the gospel according to Jesus.

——— *19* ———

The Way of Salvation

No passage in all of Scripture attacks modern-day easy-believism with more force than Matthew 7:13–14. It is the conclusion of the Sermon on the Mount, and it amounts to the Savior's own presentation of the way of salvation. How different it is from the trend of modern evangelism! There is no encouragement in these words for those who think they can be saved by a casual acceptance of the facts about Jesus Christ: "Enter by the narrow gate; for the gate is wide, and the way is broad that leads to destruction, and many are those who enter by it. For the gate is small, and the way is narrow that leads to life, and few are those who find it." Here our Lord brings the Sermon on the Mount to its evangelistic climax.

This passage crushes the claim of those who say the Sermon on the Mount is not gospel but law.[1] In fact, these closing verses are pure gospel,[2] with as pointed an invitation as has ever been issued. This closing lesson also debunks the opinion that the Sermon on the Mount is merely a discourse on ethics for us to stand back and admire. Jesus is clearly not interested in bouquets for his moral teachings. And his challenge here erases any possibility that the Sermon on the Mount is truth for some prophetic tomorrow; Jesus is preaching to people in the here and now, and his message is urgent.

Each person inevitably must make a choice. Scripture presents that choice in several ways. Through Moses, God confronted the Israelites, saying, "I have set before you life and death, the blessing and

[1]E.g., Charles C. Ryrie, *Dispensationalism Today* (Chicago: Moody Press, 1965), 108. Ryrie writes, "Where can one find a statement of the gospel in the sermon? . . . A plain statement of the gospel [cannot be found] in the Sermon."

[2]Cf. R. C. H. Lenski, *The Interpretation of Matthew's Gospel* (Columbus, Ohio: Wartburg, 1943), 180.

the curse. So choose life in order that you may live" (Deut. 30:19). Joshua challenged the Israelites as they entered the Promised Land, "Choose for yourselves today whom you will serve: whether the gods which your fathers served which were beyond the River, or the gods of the Amorites in whose land you are living; but as for me and my house, we will serve the LORD" (Josh. 24:15). Elijah called for a decision on Mount Carmel: "How long will you hesitate between two opinions? If the LORD is God, follow Him; but if Baal, follow him" (1 Kings 18:21). God told Jeremiah, "You shall also say to this people, 'Thus says the LORD, "Behold, I set before you the way of life and the way of death"'" (Jer. 21:8).

What to do with Jesus Christ is a choice each person must make, but it is not just a momentary decision. It is a once-for-all verdict with ongoing implications and eternal consequences—the ultimate decision. Jesus himself stands at the crux of each person's destiny and demands a deliberate choice of life or death, heaven or hell. Here, in the culmination of all he has said in the Sermon on the Mount, the Lord requires that each person choose between following the world on the easy, well-traveled road or following him on the difficult road. You will not find a plainer statement of the gospel according to Jesus anywhere in Scripture.

Here are two gates, the great and the small; two roads, the broad and the narrow; two destinations, life and destruction; and two crowds, the few and the many. The Lord also identifies two kinds of trees and their fruit, good and bad; two kinds of builders, wise and foolish; and two kinds of foundations, rock and sand (Matt. 7:13–27). The choices are clear-cut. He demands a decision. We all are at the crossroads, and each individual must choose which way he or she will go.

Two Gates

"Enter by the narrow gate," Christ says, using an imperative verb that conveys a sense of urgency, a demand for action now. It is not enough to stand and appreciate the gate—one must enter.

It is also important to go through the *right* gate. There is only one gate that opens to the narrow way. Jesus said, "I am the door; if anyone enters through Me, he shall be saved" (John 10:9) and, "He who does not enter by the door . . . he is a thief and a robber" (John 10:1). "I am the way, and the truth, and the life; no one comes to the Father, but through Me," he said in John 14:6. "There is salvation in no one else; for there is no other name under heaven that has been given among men, by which we must be saved" (Acts 4:12). "There is one mediator also between God and men, the man Christ Jesus" (1 Tim. 2:5). Christ is the gate. He is the way. There is no other avenue to heaven.

Every other choice is wrong. There is no in between, no third alternative, no other gate. The options are simple and straightforward. There is no room for the kind of broad ecumenical tolerance our humanistic culture fancies. As John Stott says, "Jesus cuts across our easy-going syncretism."[3] There are not many good religions; there is only one. And so the options are only two—the true and the false, the right and the wrong, God's way and humankind's way.

All this world's religions are based on human achievement. Biblical Christianity alone recognizes divine accomplishment—the work of Christ on humankind's behalf—as the sole basis of salvation. Christ's death on the cross paid the price of our sin (1 Cor. 15:3), and his resurrection revealed that he had conquered death (v. 20). Salvation is not a merit system, in which people can earn favor with God. No one could ever do enough good works to gain acceptance by God (Rom. 3:10–18). Even the Law of Moses did not make people righteous; it was given to show how sinful and disobedient we really are (v. 20). As we noted in chapter 18, God through his grace imputes to believers the righteousness of Christ (vv. 21–24). On that basis alone they can stand before him.

And so the only choice is between the plethora of religions based on human achievement and the one religion of divine accomplishment. Scripture says, "Now to the one who works [whoever chooses a religion of human achievement], his wage is not reckoned as a favor but as what is due.[4] But to the one who does not work, but believes in him who justifies the ungodly [whoever submits to the religion of divine accomplishment], his faith is reckoned as righteousness" (Rom. 4:4–5).

The narrow way and the broad way do not contrast religion with paganism. Jesus is not setting the higher religions against the lower ones, or even Christianity against open immorality. The choice is between divine accomplishment and human achievement. Both systems claim to be the way to God. The wide gate is not marked "This Way to Hell"; it is labeled "Heaven," the same as the narrow gate. It just does not go there.

Satan is a master at religious deception. He disguises himself as an angel of light (2 Cor. 11:14). He paints his gate so that it looks like

[3]John R. W. Stott, *Christian Counter-Culture* (Downers Grove, Ill.: InterVarsity, 1978), 193.
[4]The wage that is due is death (Rom. 6:23).

the door to heaven, and *"many* are those who enter by it" (Matt. 7:13, emphasis added). But our Lord describes the right gate as narrow. In fact, many commentators say that the best contemporary expression of the narrow gate is a turnstile.[5] Only one person can pass through at a time. No one comes into the kingdom of Christ as part of a group. Many Jews in Jesus' day based their hope of heaven on their national lineage. And many contemporary churchgoers base their hope on their denominational affiliation or their church membership. Here Jesus refutes all those ideas. The gate admits only one at a time, for salvation is intensely personal. It is not enough to be born in a Christian family or to ride the coattails of a believing spouse. Believing is an individual act.

Entering the narrow gate is not easy. Luke 13 records that while Jesus was teaching in the villages, someone asked him, "Lord, are there just a few who are being saved?" (v. 23). His answer annihilates modern easy-believism: *"Strive* to enter by the narrow door; for many, I tell you, will seek to enter and will not be able" (emphasis added). The Greek word for "strive" is *agōnizomai,* implying an agonizing, intense, purposeful struggle. It is the same word used in 1 Corinthians 9:25 of an athlete battling to win a victory. It is also used in Colossians 4:12 of Epaphras laboring fervently, and in 1 Timothy 6:12 of the Christian who "fights the good fight of faith." It is a struggle, a battle, an extreme effort. There is almost a violence implied. And appropriately so, because entering the kingdom is like going into battle. In Matthew 11:12 Jesus said, "The kingdom of heaven suffers violence, and violent men take it by force." Luke 16:16 says, "The gospel of the kingdom is preached, and everyone is forcing his way into it" (cf. Acts 14:22). Peter wrote, "If it is with difficulty that the righteous is saved, what will become of the godless man and the sinner?" (1 Peter 4:18).

How does that fit the modern notion that salvation is easy? What does it do to the popular teaching that becoming a Christian is only a matter of believing some facts, signing on the dotted line, walking an aisle, raising your hand, or praying some prefabricated prayer? Could it be that many of our "converts" are on the wrong road because they took the easy way through the wrong gate?

Salvation is *not* easy. "The gate is small . . . and few are those who find it" (Matt. 7:14). The implication is that unless a person is looking diligently for the gate, he or she is not likely to know it is there. In

---

[5]D. Martyn Lloyd-Jones, *Studies in the Sermon on the Mount* (Grand Rapids: Eerdmans, 1959), 2:221.

Jeremiah 29:13 God says, "You will seek Me and find Me, when you search for Me with all your heart."

The message of Jesus cannot be made to accommodate any kind of cheap grace or easy-believism. The kingdom is not for people who want Jesus without any change in their lives. It is only for those who seek it with all their hearts.

In fact, many who approach the gate turn away when they discover how narrow it is. Did you ever try to get through a turnstile with an armload of suitcases? That is the imagery Jesus' words evoke. The narrow gate is not wide enough for superstars who want to enter with all their valuables. The rich young ruler searched until he found the gate. But when he saw that entering meant that he had to leave his baggage behind, he turned away. Whoever we are, whatever we treasure, when we reach the narrow gate, we can expect to have to drop everything. Extra baggage—such as self-righteousness, selfishness, sin, and materialism—will not make it through intact. The good news is that although the gate is narrow, it is wide enough to accommodate the chief of sinners (cf. 1 Tim. 1:15).

For those who insist on taking luggage, the broad gate may be more appealing. It is marked "Heaven"—it may even be marked "Jesus"—but it is not going to heaven and it has nothing to do with Jesus. It is the gate for the religion of the masses, a wide-open gate through which anyone can pass without jettisoning self-righteousness, pride, material possessions, or even sin. But there is no salvation for those who choose this gate.

Receiving Christ does not mean that we can merely add Jesus to the refuse of our lives. Salvation is a total transformation: "If any man is in Christ, he is a new creature; the old things passed away; behold, new things have come" (2 Cor. 5:17). What could be clearer than that? Old things pass away. Sin and selfishness and worldly pleasure are replaced by new things. This is the whole point of salvation: it produces a changed life.

Two Ways

The two ways are closely identified with the two gates. One is broad and open, and the other is hard and narrow (Matt. 7:14). Psalm 1 also speaks of these two ways: "The Lord knows the way of the righteous, but the way of the wicked will perish." The choice is the same as it has always been: either the broad and crowded way of the ungodly, or the narrow way of the godly.

The broad way is certainly easier. There is no precipice. There is plenty of latitude for those who want to sample the moral smorgasbord offered by the crowd on this road. You can just stroll and roam. There are hardly any limitations, no curbs, no boundaries. There is tolerance of every conceivable sin—just as long as you say you love Jesus. Or as long as you are religious. Or whatever else you want to be.

This road requires no character. You can be like a fish floating downstream, carried by the current. This, in the language of Ephesians 2:2, is "the course of this world." It is the "way which seems right to a man, but its end is the way of death" (Prov. 16:25).

God's way is a constricted road, a narrow path that leads to life. Here there is no space for any deviation. Then again, there is no room for the self-governed multitudes.

But Jesus does not seek multitudes; he seeks and saves only those who know they are lost. As we have noted, our Lord did not prompt people to make snap decisions to follow him without counting the cost. Nor did he necessarily invite eager inquirers to jump on his bandwagon. In fact, he often seemed to encourage potential followers to turn away.

In John 6:64, for example, Jesus challenged the faith of those who called themselves disciples: "There are some of you who do not believe." Verse 66 says, "As a result of this, many of His disciples withdrew, and were not walking with Him any more." Jesus turned to the Twelve, and said, "Will ye also go away?" (v. 67 KJV). He did not want casual followers, but people willing to give their lives for him.

Luke 14 describes how Jesus handled the fawning masses that followed him everywhere: "Now great multitudes were going along with Him; and He turned and said to them, 'If anyone comes to Me, and does not hate his own father and mother and wife and children and brothers and sisters, yes, and even his own life, he cannot be My disciple. Whoever does not carry his own cross and come after Me cannot be My disciple. . . . So therefore, no one of you can be My disciple who does not give up all his own possessions'" (vv. 25–27, 33). The Lord makes the narrow path as hard as he possibly can, by demanding that those who really want to follow him step out of the crowd and pick up a cross—an instrument of torture and death.

Try preaching that at the next "revival" meeting and see how many come down the aisle! But perhaps the people who *would* come might understand the commitment that is required.

Those on the narrow way should also expect persecution. "An hour is coming for everyone who kills you to think that he is offering service to God" (John 16:2). It is hard to walk this narrow way with bare feet. It is not a luscious meadow. The road is hard. But Jesus never presented Christianity as a soft option for weak-kneed, feeble souls. When a person becomes a Christian, that person is then and there declaring war on hell. And hell fights back. Following Christ can cost your very life—it certainly costs your life in a spiritual sense. The fainthearted and compromisers need not apply.

Does that sound like a horrible road to travel? It isn't. Christ himself leads the way and supplies the strength needed to finish the course (cf. Phil. 4:12–13). His yoke is easy and his load is light (Matt. 11:30).

Two Destinations

The choice between the two gates and the two ways is a choice for eternity. The broad road that starts out so easy gets curiously hard at the very end; it ends up in hell. What looks so inviting from this end only leads to destruction.

The narrow gate and the constricted path may not look very appealing, but they point the way to eternal life. This way that starts out hard opens up into the eternal bliss of heaven.

Two Crowds

Finally, there are two groups of people traveling the different roads. Matthew 7:13 speaks of the crowds passing through the wide gate: "Many are those who enter by it." As for the narrow gate, "Few are those who find it" (v. 14). It is a tragic fact that multitudes of religious people are headed for hell, not heaven. Even in the Old Testament, true believers were only a remnant, never the majority. In Matthew 22:14 Jesus said, "Many are called, but few are chosen." In Luke 12:32 Jesus looked at his disciples and said, "Do not be afraid, little flock." The word translated "little" in that verse is *micron*, from which we get the prefix *micro*, meaning something very small. It is the same word used in Matthew 13:32 of the mustard seed, one of the smallest seeds. The believing remnant has always been a little flock, a few souls who labor in the power of God, knowing their own human inability, but willing to pay the price. The rest of humankind takes the broad road. But the majority is seldom right.

The broad way is the natural choice, from a human point of view. People prefer sin to righteousness. Jesus said, "Men loved the darkness rather than the light; for their deeds were evil" (John 3:19). It is easy to fall in step with the crowd. You can even add Jesus to all your treasured sins and possessions so you can feel religious. You can go to church and be as active or as passive as you desire. You never have to deny yourself or take up a cross. The only problem is that the natural way ends in disaster.

Someone sent me a clipping from a daily newspaper in Melbourne, Australia. It is a letter to the editor written just after a Billy Graham Crusade:

> After hearing Dr. Billy Graham on the air, viewing him on television, and reading reports and letters concerning him and his mission, I am heartily sick of the type of religion that insists my soul (and everyone else's) needs saving—whatever that means. I have never felt that I was lost. Nor do I feel that I daily wallow in the mire of sin, although repetitive preaching insists that I do.
>
> Give me a practical religion that teaches gentleness and tolerance, that acknowledges no barriers of color or creed, that remembers the aged and teaches children of goodness and not sin.
>
> If in order to save my soul I must accept such a philosophy as I have recently heard preached, I prefer to remain forever damned.

A sad letter. But the truth is, that man understood the stark choices and made the wrong one. The great tragedy is that there are multitudes on the road with him—and most of them think they are heading for heaven. Instead they will end in destruction and damnation, victims of satanic delusion.

I am convinced that the popular evangelistic message of our age actually lures people into this deception. It promises a wonderful, comfortable plan for everyone's life. It obliterates the offense of the cross (cf. 1 Cor. 1:23; Gal. 5:11). Though it presents Christ as the Way, the Truth, and the Life, it says nothing of the small gate or the narrow way. Its subject is the love of God, but there is no mention of God's wrath. It sees people as deprived, not depraved. It is full of love and understanding, but there is no mention of a holy God who hates sin. There is no summons to repentance, no warning of judgment, no call for brokenness, no expectation of a contrite heart, and no reason for deep sorrow over sin. It is a message of easy salvation, a call for a hasty decision, often accompanied by false promises of health, happiness, and material blessing. This is not the gospel according to Jesus.

"The gate is small, and the way is narrow that leads to life, and few are those who find it." How could Jesus be any clearer? This is the only path his gospel points to. It is not an easy or popular road, but it is the only one that leads to eternal glory.

20

The Certainty of Judgment

When the Reformers rediscovered the great truth of justification by faith and began to articulate it in their writings, Rome's response was to argue that this doctrine rendered holy living superfluous. If the perfect righteousness of Christ is imputed to sinners solely on the basis of faith, then those who have been justified can simply live any way they please yet be guaranteed of heaven. Being perfectly righteous in God's eyes, they have no need of practical righteousness.

The Reformers answered that charge by showing that sanctification is inevitable in the experience of every true believer. John Calvin wrote:

> By faith we apprehend the righteousness of Christ, which alone reconciles us to God. This faith, however, you cannot apprehend without at the same time apprehending sanctification; for Christ "is made unto us wisdom, and righteousness, and sanctification, and redemption" (1 Cor. i.30). *Christ, therefore, justifies no man without also sanctifying him.*[1]

Contemporary Protestantism tends to forget those theological roots. In fact, those who decry lordship salvation as heresy have fallen into precisely the error Rome tried to pin on the early Reformers. Many of them explicitly teach that justification by faith makes holiness nonessential. They see practical sanctification as desirable, even pivotal, but nonetheless unrelated to the matter of justification and unnecessary for eternal salvation. As we noted in a previous chapter, they tend to view the forensic element of justification as the sum total of God's saving work. Practical sanctification may or may not occur,

[1]John Calvin, *Institutes of the Christian Religion*, 2 vols. (Grand Rapids: Zondervan, 1972), 2:99, emphasis added.

they say, depending on the person's willingness to obey. While acknowledging that every believer is justified, they want to make room for believers who might not be sanctified.

But that view completely subverts Reformation theology. While justification and sanctification are distinct theological concepts, both are essential elements of salvation. God will not declare a person righteous without also making him or her righteous. Salvation includes all God's work on our behalf, from his foreknowledge of us before the foundation of the world to our ultimate glorification in eternity future (Rom. 8:29–30). One cannot pick and choose, accepting eternal life while rejecting holiness and obedience. When God justifies people he also sanctifies them.[2]

D. Martyn Lloyd-Jones wrote:

> Do we realize that if we truly understand the doctrine of justification by faith we have already grasped the essence and the nerve of the New Testament teaching about holiness and sanctification? Have we realized that to be justified by faith guarantees our sanctification, and that therefore *we must never think of sanctification as a separate and subsequent experience?* (emphasis added).[3]

Scripture challenges those who define salvation as a purely judicial act with no practical consequences. Hebrews 12:14 speaks of "the sanctification without which no one will see the Lord." The King James Version renders Hebrews 12:14: "Follow . . . holiness, without which no man shall see the Lord."

That verse does not make holiness a prerequisite for justification, but it recognizes it as the sure result. In other words, sanctification is a *characteristic* of all who are redeemed, not a *condition* for their receiving salvation. Those whose faith is authentic are certain to become holy, and those who lack true faith can never be holy. They have no hope of seeing God, except to stand before him in judgment.

Many who think they are saved but live unholy lives will be shocked to discover in the final judgment that heaven is not their destiny. It is hard to picture a more horrifying scene than that described by Jesus in Matthew 7:21–23:

> "Not everyone who says to Me, 'Lord, Lord,' will enter the kingdom of heaven; but he who does the will of My Father who is in heaven. Many will say to Me on that day, 'Lord, Lord, did we not prophesy in Your name, and in Your name cast out demons, and in Your name perform

---

[2]In 1 Corinthians 1:2 and 6:11, for example, all believers are said to be sanctified.

[3]D. Martyn Lloyd-Jones, *Romans: The New Man* (Grand Rapids: Zondervan, 1974), 190.

many miracles?' And then will I declare to them, 'I never knew you; depart from Me, you who practice lawlessness.'"

Those who think of salvation as merely a legal transaction, a reckoning apart from practical righteousness, will have a difficult time with this warning of Jesus. It puts salvation in very practical terms. It reiterates the key statement of the Sermon on the Mount: "I say to you, that unless your righteousness surpasses that of the scribes and Pharisees, you shall not enter the kingdom of heaven" (Matt. 5:20).

Here in Matthew 7, the Lord gives us a glimpse of the coming judgment and the tragedy of those who will stand before the throne with high expectations but only a verbal profession or mere intellectual knowledge. They will protest that they did things for the Lord, but their words and their hearts are empty. Tragically, Christ will turn them away from heaven.

Notice the key phrase in verse 21, identifying the kind of person who will inhabit heaven. It is "he who does the will of My Father." It is not the one who says he knows Jesus or who believes certain facts about him. It is the one who *does* the Father's will. The one who practices lawlessness will be excluded (v. 23). The lesson here is that if a person lives a life of disobedience, it does not matter what he says or what good things that person has done. He or she is an unbeliever in danger of eternal damnation.

This is a very strong admonition, but it is an indispensable part of the gospel according to Jesus. These brief verses and those that follow immediately condemn two wrong responses to Christ: the first, professing belief but refusing to do what faith calls for (Matt. 7:22–23); and the second, hearing without obeying (vv. 24–27).

Saying Without Doing: The Sin of Empty Words

Note that the "many" who will be turned away in judgment are not pagans. They are religious people who have chosen the road of human achievement. They are the same "many" we met in Matthew 7:13, who took the wide gate and broad way. Their plea will be the religious deeds they have done (v. 22). Paul said people like this hold "to a form of godliness, although they have denied its power" (2 Tim. 3:5). They are much like the Pharisees, obsessed with religious activity, not necessarily apostates, heretics, anti-Christs, atheists, or agnostics—just people trying to earn God's favor through external works rather than living out the righteousness that is based on faith (cf. Rom. 10:5–10).

The works they do are *only* external. They are hypocrites who say

The Gospel According to Jesus

the right things but do not do them from the heart. In fact, despite all the good things they will claim to have done, the reason they will be turned away is that they do not do the will of the Father (Matt. 7:21). They live lawlessly (v. 23). They know the right words and might appear good on the outside, but their character does not match. They are like many in the church today who affirm sound doctrine but are not saved.

These people even say, "Lord, Lord," (Matt. 7:21–22). Again, this reveals their basic orthodoxy. They know about Jesus' lordship and even give verbal assent to it, but they do not submit to him as Lord. They are like those to whom Jesus spoke in Luke 6:46: "Why do you call me 'Lord, Lord,' and do not do what I say?" They are fervent, pious, and respectful. Three times they repeat, "in Your name . . . in Your name . . . in Your name" (v. 22). They have been busy doing things in the Lord's name—even wondrous things, all the while thinking they are serving him with zeal. But their words are empty.

To say "Lord, Lord" and then disobey is the moral equivalent of a Judas kiss. One who has been given real faith is as concerned with doing the will of God as with affirming the facts of true doctrine.

Jesus spoke the words of Matthew 7:21–23 as a warning to people who think they are saved but do not live in obedience to God. Unlike preachers today who go to excessive lengths to avoid upsetting anyone's assurance, our Lord was determined to destroy the false hope of all who falsely thought they were redeemed. He often challenged such people. He never encouraged someone who was unsure of salvation to ignore the doubts. His message stands in stark contrast to the gospel of today, which seems designed specifically to prop up false assurance. The pattern of modern evangelism is to give people a pleasing and easy message; take them through a simple formula; get them to pray a prayer, sign a card, or whatever; then tell them they are saved and should never doubt it. Such an approach to witnessing actually fights against the Holy Spirit, whose ministry is to bring both assurance to those who are truly saved (Rom. 8:16) and conviction to those who are not (John 16:8–9). God knows the difference; we do not. It is not our job to certify people's salvation.

Periodic doubts about one's salvation are not necessarily wrong. Such doubts must be confronted and dealt with honestly and biblically. Scripture encourages spiritual self-examination. In 2 Corinthians 13:5 Paul wrote, "Test yourselves to see if you are in the faith; examine yourselves! Or do you not recognize this about yourselves, that Jesus Christ is in you—unless indeed you fail the test?" That admonition is largely ignored—and often explained away[4]—in the contemporary church.

It has become quite popular to teach professing Christians that they can enjoy assurance of salvation no matter what their lives are like. After all, some argue, if salvation is a gift to people who simply believe the gospel facts, what does practical living have to do with assurance? That teaching is nothing but practical antinomianism. It encourages people living in hypocrisy, disobedience, and sin by offering them a false assurance. It discourages self-examination. And that clearly violates Scripture. We are *commanded* to examine ourselves at least as often as we celebrate the Lord's Supper (1 Cor. 11:28).

Self-examination is especially important in an age like ours. When statistics tell us that more than a billion people in the world are Christians, one must wonder who established the criteria. Such figures certainly do not square with what Jesus said about many on the broad road and few on the narrow. Checking a box on a survey to indicate that you are a born-again Christian does not guarantee your eternal destiny. Even those who belong to the right church can be deceived and utterly devoid of the righteousness of God through Christ.

There are several categories of deceived people in the church. Obviously there are hypocrites, those who merely try to appear religious. Others are nominal, superficial people who call themselves Christians because they have gone to Sunday school since childhood or "made a decision" for Christ but have no ongoing interest in living out the implications of faith. Still others are heavily involved in church or religious activities; they know the facts of the gospel but are not obedient to the Word of God. Perhaps they go to church

---

[4]Cf. Zane C. Hodges, *The Gospel Under Siege* (Dallas: Redención Viva, 1981), 95. Hodges writes, "Often Paul's statements are treated in a very one-dimensional way. Even though every epistle he wrote is addressed to those who have already come to saving faith, his assertions are too frequently taken as though he was constantly concerned about the eternal destiny of his readers. But there was no reason why he should have been. . . . There is not even a single place in the Pauline letters where he expresses doubt that his audience is composed of true Christians . . . That they could conceivably be unregenerate is the farthest thought from the apostle's mind." Hodges does not mention 2 Corinthians 13:5 or attempt to explain what possible second dimension it might have. As a pastor, I take issue with Hodges' assertion that Paul was unconcerned about the destiny of members of the flocks he pastored. I have never known a pastor who would say he is certain about the salvation of every one of his church members. Paul had every reason to encourage these church members—especially in licentious Corinth—to test the reality of their profession of faith.

because they are looking for good feelings, blessings, experiences, healings, miracles, or ecstatic gifts. Maybe they are committed to the denomination, the church, the organization, but not the Word of God. They may love theology purely as an academic interest. Whatever the reasons, *many* (Matt. 7:22) who have identified themselves with Christ and Christianity will be turned away at the Judgment.

Note carefully that preaching, prophesying, casting out demons, and doing miracles—even under the guise of orthodoxy—are not proofs of true salvation. God can, and often does, work through unsaved people. He used unregenerate Balaam (Num. 23:5)—he even used Balaam's donkey! Caiaphas, the vile high priest, prophesied Christ's death for the nation of Israel (John 11:51–52). Mighty works may also be done by Satan's power, or they can be falsified. The magicians of Egypt were able to duplicate some of the miracles Moses performed. The evil sons of Sceva in Acts 19 cast out demons. Matthew 24:24 prophesies that false christs and false prophets will come and do signs and wonders. Satan can do some amazing things, and he will do almost anything to deceive an unbeliever into thinking he or she is saved.

Miracles and prophecies and mighty wonders are not the same as a holy life, and without true holiness, no one will see God (Heb. 12:14). God wants us to reflect his character: "Like the Holy One who called you, be holy yourselves also in all your behavior; because it is written, 'You shall be holy, for I am holy'" (1 Peter 1:15–16). "You are to be perfect, as your heavenly Father is perfect" (Matt. 5:48). Because God is holy, those in whom he dwells will progress more and more toward holiness. Because God is perfect, those who are truly his children will move on in the direction of his perfect standard. If you are stalled, or if you are slipping in the opposite direction, it is right that you examine yourself.

Pursuing the standard of perfection does not mean we can never fail. It means that when we fail we deal with it. Those with true faith will fail—and in some cases, fail pathetically and frequently—but a genuine believer will, as a pattern of life, be confessing sin and coming to the Father for forgiveness (1 John 1:9). *Perfection* is the standard; *direction* is the test. If your life does not reveal growth in grace and righteousness and holiness, you need to examine the reality of your faith—even if you believe you have done great things in the name of Christ.

Hearing Without Obeying: The Sin of Empty Hearts

Our Lord now expands on the danger of the coming judgment with a brief illustration. This is the conclusion of the Sermon on the

Mount. The illustration brings together all he has had to say regarding faith, righteousness, and the need to live according to the divine standard. It is a final appeal to people in danger of judgment:

> Therefore everyone who hears these words of Mine, and acts upon them, may be compared to a wise man, who built his house upon the rock. And the rain descended, and the floods came, and the winds blew, and burst against that house; and yet it did not fall, for it had been founded upon the rock. And everyone who hears these words of mine, and does not act upon them, will be like a foolish man, who built his house upon the sand. And the rain descended, and the floods came, and the winds blew, and burst against that house; and it fell, and great was its fall (Matt. 7:24–27).

What seems at first glance to be a very simple story is in fact a powerful commentary on people who have heads full of knowledge but hearts empty of faith. It contrasts those who obey and those who do not. Some people hear and act on the message, while some hear but do not act. Our Lord's obvious lesson is that the difference between the two is a matter of eternal consequence.

This is a final reiteration of the central theme of the Sermon on the Mount—that those without genuine righteousness will not enter the kingdom of heaven (Matt. 5:20). The words again are aimed at those who profess to know God, who think of themselves as part of the kingdom, but whose lives do not reveal the character of the King.

Two men are described in Matthew 7:24–27, picturing different kinds of hearers. Both built houses. Apparently they built them in the same area, because the same storm and flood hit them. The houses probably even looked much the same. The only difference Jesus mentions is the foundations on which they were built. One man built on rock, and the other built on sand.

This was another powerful rebuke to the religion of the Pharisees. They had no regard for spirituality of the soul, for purity of heart, or for integrity of behavior. They were hypocrites, concerned only with appearances, not with obedience to God. Their whole religion was like a structure built on sand. It looked good at first sight, but in the end it was only a waste of effort, doomed to sure destruction.

The Pharisees prayed, fasted, and gave their alms, but only to parade their piety and enhance their reputations. Much of Jesus' message in the Sermon on the Mount had been directed at them and the people who were poisoned by their teaching. Jesus began his message with a call for humility, repentance, meekness, righteous hunger, mercy, and purity (Matt. 5:1–8). The Pharisees had only contempt for those qualities. They favored pride, spiritual arrogance, self-righteousness, and showy religious works. Then Jesus called for righteousness that surpassed the Pharisees' righteousness (v. 20), implying that something was lacking in their religion. He debunked their practice of religious hair-splitting, which permitted them to obey the letter of the law but ignore its real aim (vv. 21–47). He followed that with a rebuke of their ostentatious style (6:1–18). He chided them for their judgmental attitude (7:1–5) and called their teaching into question (vv. 15–20).

Now Jesus challenges them to *act* on his sayings (v. 24). Whether they do or not will be the test of whether they are wise or foolish. Ultimately, their response will determine whether they hear those awful words, "Depart from Me, you who practice lawlessness" (Matt. 7:23).

Interpreters have proposed several interpretations of what it means to build on the rock. Some have pointed out that in the Old Testament, God is called a rock (Ps. 18:2). Others note that Paul referred to Christ as the only foundation (1 Cor. 3:11). But let the passage speak for itself: "Everyone who hears these words of Mine, *and acts upon them,* may be compared to a wise man, who built his house upon the rock" (v. 24, emphasis added). Obeying the words of Christ is equivalent to building on solid rock.

Colossians 1:21–23 says, "Although you were formerly alienated and hostile in mind, engaged in evil deeds, yet He has now reconciled you . . . if indeed you continue in the faith firmly established and steadfast." James 1:22, a familiar verse, says, "Prove yourselves doers of the word, and not merely hearers who delude themselves." First John 2:3–4 says, "By this we know that we have come to know Him, if we keep His commandments." Titus 1:15–16 says, "Those who are defiled and unbelieving . . . profess to know God but by their deeds they deny Him, being detestable and disobedient, and worthless for any good deed."

All those passages teach that genuine believers receive Christ *and* continue in him. They hear his Word *and* do it. They know his commandments, *and* they keep them. They do not claim to know God yet deny him with their deeds. The validation of salvation is a life of obedience. It is the only possible proof that a person really knows Jesus Christ. If one does not obey Christ as a pattern of life, then professing to know him is an empty verbal exercise.

Think for a moment about this: One man built his house the quick and easy way, while the other built the hard way. Building on sand requires no preparation. You do not have to dig. You do not have to prepare. You just slap it up. It is a short-cut, bringing quick results but not lasting ones.

Much of modern evangelism is building on the sand. It allows no time for conviction of sin; no opportunity for deep repentance; no chance to understand *why* we must come to grips with the reality of our lostness; and no occasion for the Holy Spirit to work. The bandwagon is moving, and if you want to jump on, you'd better do it. Arthur Pink wrote, "There are some who say they are saved before they have any feeling sense that they are lost."[5] Multitudes who name the name of Jesus have foolishly built on the shallow, shifting sand of hearing but not obeying (cf. Matt. 7:26). The contemporary brand of Christianity has become superficial, tolerant of people who have not dug deep and put in the right foundation.

Jesus said that a wise man does not build a tower without counting the cost (Luke 14:28). He is willing to dig deep, he has thought out the responsibility, he understands what he is committing to, and he wants to do it right. This is the man who hears and obeys (Matt. 7:24).

The day of judgment is coming. That is what the wind, rain, and flood (Matt. 7:25, 27) speak of. God is sending the storm of judgment. Some will stand and some will fall. Those who stand are true believers; those who fall are those who never really believed at all. The difference will be seen in whether obedience followed the hearing, whether a life of righteousness followed the profession of faith.

This illustration is marvelously consistent with the warning of Matthew 7:21–23. In both cases, the test of true faith is whether or not it produces obedience.

Thus Jesus' Sermon on the Mount ends with a devastating warning of judgment: "and great was its fall." It is a warning of doom, characteristic of Jesus' preaching, but again, markedly different from the trend of contemporary evangelism. The gospel according to Jesus clearly calls for a radical difference—not merely a new opinion, but a response of full commitment.

What was the result of the sermon? A great revival? Thousands of conversions? No. If anyone repented, it is not mentioned. Matthew 7:28–29 tells us, "The result was that when Jesus had finished these words, the multitudes were amazed at His teaching; for He was teaching them as one having authority, and not as their scribes."

All they did was analyze Jesus' style! This was exactly what he had counseled them not to do. They were "amazed." The Greek word literally means they were "struck out of their senses." In the vernacular of today, we would say the sermon blew their minds. This was not a negative reaction; in fact, many today might interpret it as a

---

[5]Arthur W. Pink, *An Exposition of the Sermon on the Mount* (Grand Rapids: Baker, 1953), 424.

saving response. After all, these people admitted they had never heard such wisdom, never seen such depth, never understood such rich truth. No one had ever issued such fearful warnings about hell. And certainly no one had ever confronted the religious leaders like that! Jesus spoke with such boldness! He did not quote other rabbis, but he stood on his own authority. He touched every dimension of human life in a breathtaking economy of words. Never had such profound insight been expressed in a single, powerful message. The crowds thought he was wonderful.

But it was not a saving response; they had already started building on the sand. There was no repentance, no expression of obedience— only analysis.

And that is where it ends.

But it cannot end here for a true believer. One with genuine faith cannot hear the Lord's words and walk away without acting on them. The faithful will be more than shocked, more than amazed, more than admiring—they will be obedient. They are building a structure on solid rock.

21

The Cost of Discipleship

In previous chapters we have touched on Jesus' call to discipleship. Here we will examine it more closely. Let me say again unequivocally that Jesus' summons to deny self and follow him was an invitation to salvation, not an offer of a "higher life," or a second step of faith following salvation. The contemporary teaching that separates discipleship from salvation springs from ideas that are foreign to Scripture.[1]

Every Christian is a disciple.[2] In fact, the Lord's Great Commission was to go into all the world and "make disciples . . . teaching them to observe all that I have commanded you" (Matt. 28:19–20). That means that the mission of the church and the goal of evangelism is to make disciples. Disciples are people who believe, those whose faith motivates them to obey all Jesus commanded. The word *disciple* is used consistently as a synonym for *believer* throughout the book of Acts (6:1–2, 7; 11:26; 14:20, 22; 15:10). Any distinction between the two words is purely artificial. Though introduced by sincere and well-meaning men, it has given birth to a theology of easy-believism that disposes of the hard demands of Jesus.

[1]Cf. Zane C. Hodges, *The Hungry Inherit* (Portland: Multnomah, 1980), 83–84, where Hodges writes, "How fortunate that one's entrance into the kingdom of God [does] not depend on his discipleship. If it did, how few would ever enter that kingdom!" Yet didn't Jesus himself explicitly teach that "few" would enter? Wasn't that the whole point of his warning about the small gate and the narrow road? "Few are those who find it" (Matt. 7:14).

[2]It is also apparent, however, that not every disciple is necessarily a true Christian (cf. John 6:66). The term *disciple* is sometimes used in Scripture in a general sense, to describe those who, like Judas, outwardly followed Christ. It certainly is not restricted to some higher level of believers. The disciple in Matthew 8:21–22, for example, was anything but committed.

When Jesus called disciples, he carefully instructed them about the cost of following him. Halfhearted people who were not willing to make the commitment did not respond. Thus he turned away anyone who was reluctant to pay the price—such as the rich young ruler. He warned all who thought of becoming disciples to count the cost carefully. "Which one of you, when he wants to build a tower, does not first sit down and calculate the cost, to see if he has enough to complete it? Otherwise, when he has laid a foundation, and is not able to finish, all who observe it begin to ridicule him, saying, 'This man began to build and was not able to finish'" (Luke 14:28–30). About those verses, John Stott has written penetratingly:

> The Christian landscape is strewn with the wreckage of derelict, half-built towers—the ruins of those who began to build and were unable to finish. For thousands of people still ignore Christ's warning and undertake to follow him without first pausing to reflect on the cost of doing so. The result is the great scandal of Christendom today, so-called "nominal Christianity." In countries to which Christian civilization has spread, large numbers of people have covered themselves with a decent, but thin, veneer of Christianity. They have allowed themselves to become somewhat involved; enough to be respectable but not enough to be uncomfortable. Their religion is a great, soft cushion. It protects them from the hard unpleasantness of life, while changing its place and shape to suit their convenience. No wonder the cynics speak of hypocrites in the church and dismiss religion as escapism.[3]

A Christian is not one who simply buys "fire\insurance," who "accepts Christ" just to escape hell. As we have seen repeatedly, true believers' faith expresses itself in submission and obedience. Christians follow Christ. They are committed unquestionably to Christ as Lord and Savior. They desire to please God. They are humble, meek learners (*mathētēs* in the Greek text). When they fail, they seek forgiveness and move forward. That is their spirit and their direction.

The call to Christian discipleship explicitly demands just that kind of total dedication. It is full commitment, with nothing knowingly or deliberately held back. No one can come to Christ on any other terms. Those who think they can simply affirm a list of gospel facts and continue to live any way they please should examine themselves to see if they are really in the faith (2 Cor. 13:5).

In Matthew 10:32–39, Jesus challenged his disciples, saying:

> "Everyone therefore who shall confess Me before men, I will also confess him before My father who is in heaven. But whoever shall deny

[3]John R. W. Stott, *Basic Christianity* (London: Inter-Varsity, 1958), 108.

Me before men, I will also deny him before My Father who is in heaven. . . .

"He who loves father or mother more than Me is not worthy of Me; and he who loves son or daughter more than Me is not worthy of Me. And he who does not take his cross and follow after Me is not worthy of Me. He who has found his life shall lose it, and he who has lost his life for My sake shall find it."

Our Lord gave no more definitive statement on discipleship than that. There he spells out in the clearest possible language the cost of discipleship. The words are addressed to the Twelve in particular (Matt. 10:5), but they are principles of discipleship applicable to us all. Verse 24 says, "A disciple is not above his teacher." "A disciple" here means any disciple, and the words that follow, to the end of the chapter, apply to discipleship in general.

Those who see disciples as a separate class of more dedicated believers will point out that the Twelve—or at least eleven of them— were already believers in Christ and thus did not need instruction on what it means to come to Christ with saving faith. It is true that most of the disciples were undoubtedly already born again, but that does not negate the impact of these words for them. The fact is, these men were already called *disciples*, too (10:1). This was not an invitation to a higher kind of relationship, but a reminder of what had already been established when they believed. Our Lord was continuing to teach them the meaning of faith and salvation, and constantly reminding them of the commitment they had made when they chose to follow him.

These words apply to you and me as well. Luke 14:25–35 contains similar words—in even stronger language—which Jesus spoke not just to the Twelve but to the multitudes that came to hear him.

Matthew 10:2 refers to the Twelve as "apostles." That means "sent ones." Their basic training being complete, Jesus sent them out to preach. In this parting charge to them, however, he uses the word *disciple*, not *apostle*. His words apply to every disciple, serving as a signpost to every potential follower of Jesus.

Confessing Christ Before Others

Verses 32–33 are reminiscent of the awesome judgment scene in Matthew 7:21–23: "Everyone therefore who shall confess Me before men, I will also confess him before My father who is in heaven. But whoever shall deny Me before men, I will also deny him before My Father who is in heaven." Does that mean confession before others is a condition of becoming a true Christian? No, but it means that a characteristic of every genuine believer is that he or she will profess faith in Christ unreservedly. Paul wrote, "I am not ashamed of the gospel, for it is the power of God for salvation" (Rom. 1:16).

The heart of real discipleship is a commitment to be like Jesus Christ. That means both acting as he did and being willing to accept the same treatment. It means facing a world that is hostile to him and doing it fearlessly. It means confessing before others that Jesus is Lord and being confident that he will also speak on our behalf before the Father.

"Confess" means to affirm, to acknowledge, to agree. It is a statement of identification, faith, confidence, and trust. One can confess Christ with the mouth, as Romans 10:9 says, and also confess him through righteous behavior, as Titus 1:16 implies. We are to confess Christ "before men." This emphasizes the public character of the confession, and its meaning cannot be avoided. In Romans 10:10 we read, "With the heart man believes, resulting in righteousness, and with the mouth he confesses, resulting in salvation." If the heart truly believes, the mouth will be eager to confess. Confession is not merely a human work, it is prompted and energized by God, subsequent to the act of believing but inseparable from it. Again, confession is characteristic of true faith; it is not an additional condition of salvation.

First John 4:15 says, "Whoever confesses that Jesus is the Son of God, God abides in him, and he in God." What is the mark of true Christians? They confess Jesus as the Son of God.

This does not mean that a disciple will always stand up for the Lord. Peter denied the Lord three times on the night he was betrayed. Then there was Timothy, perhaps the finest of Paul's disciples, pastor of the church at Ephesus. This dedicated young man with such marvelous pastoral gifts was a model disciple. But he may have experienced a temporary spiritual malfunction, or perhaps he was susceptible to fear. Paul had to write to him, "Do not be ashamed of the testimony of our Lord" (2 Tim. 1:8).

A moment of failure does not invalidate a disciple's credentials. We have all failed to confess Christ before others more often than we would like to admit. But if we are true disciples, we will not purposely and in a calculated way keep our faith hidden from everyone all the time. Even Joseph of Arimathea, whom the apostle John called a "secret disciple," had the boldness to go to Governor Pilate after the Crucifixion and ask for the body of Jesus (John 19:38).

Christ says that he will confess us before the Father in heaven (Matt. 10:32). What does that mean? Christ will say on the day of judgment, "This one belongs to Me." He will affirm his loyalty to those who have affirmed their loyalty to him. The other side of it is also stated: "But whoever shall deny Me before men, I will also deny him before My Father who is in heaven" (v. 33). This does not speak primarily of open rejecters—people who would deny Christ flagrantly, have nothing to do with him, despise him, speak against him, or blaspheme his name. The truth certainly applies to people like that, but our Lord is talking specifically about false disciples, people who claim to be Christians but are not.

When put to the test, false disciples consistently deny the Lord, either by their silence, by their actions, or by their words. In fact, the idea here encompasses all these things. It speaks of someone whose entire life is a denial of Christ. He may claim to believe, but everything about his way of living exudes denial (cf. Titus 1:16). Churches are filled with such people, masquerading as disciples but denying the Lord in some very disturbing ways. Christ will deny them before God (v. 33).

Matthew 25:31–46 details what will happen in the Judgment. Specifically, this passage describes the separation of the sheep and goats at the end of the Tribulation, at the judgment of the nations (v. 32). But its principle applies to individuals in every phase of God's judgment. Here the Lord puts the sheep (those who have confessed him) on his right hand, and the goats (those who have denied him) on his left (v. 33), and ushers the sheep into the kingdom. These are the righteous people who have confessed him. How do we know? He says, "I was hungry, and you gave Me something to eat; I was thirsty, and you gave Me drink; I was a stranger, and you invited Me in; naked, and you clothed Me; I was sick, and you visited Me; I was in prison, and you came to Me" (vv. 35–36). Once again, we see that the pattern of their lives reveals the reality of their claim to know Christ. Those who fail to live in a way that is consistent with faith in Christ are sent to eternal punishment (v. 46).

Getting the Priorities Straight

A second hallmark of a true disciple is loving Christ even more than one's own family (Matt. 10:34–37). Verse 37 in particular is very strong: "He who loves father or mother more than Me is not worthy of Me; and he who loves son or daughter more than Me is not worthy of Me."

If you think that is forceful, look at the parallel passage in Luke 14:26–27: "If anyone comes to Me, and does not hate his own father and mother and wife and children and brothers and sisters, yes, and even his own life, he cannot be My disciple."

To be a disciple, must we literally hate our families? Obviously this does not call for hatred in any sense that would violate the clear commandments of God, such as, "Honor your father and your mother" (Ex. 20:12) and "Husbands, love your wives" (Eph. 5:25). The key to this passage is the phrase "yes, and even his own life" (Luke 14:26). The Lord is saying we must be unquestioningly loyal to him, even above our families—and especially above ourselves. Scripture teaches that we are to deny self (Matt. 16:24), consider ourselves dead (Rom. 6:11), lay the old self aside (Eph. 4:22)—to treat the selfish aspect of our beings with the utmost contempt (cf. 1 Cor. 9:27). That is the same attitude we are to have toward our earthly possessions and even toward our families.

Why is this language so severe? Why does Christ use such offensive terms? Because he is as eager to drive the uncommitted away as he is to draw true disciples to himself. He does not want halfhearted people to be deceived into thinking they are in the kingdom. Unless he is the number-one priority, he has not been given his rightful place.

Taking up the Cross

Those who are not willing to lose their lives for Christ are not worthy of him (Matt. 10:38). They cannot be his disciples (Luke 14:27). These statements cannot be made to accommodate the casual approach to conversion that is in vogue in our generation. Jesus is not asking people to add him to the milieu of their lives. He wants disciples willing to forsake *everything*. This calls for full-scale self-denial—even willingness to die for his sake if necessary.

When Matthew 10:38 says, "He who does not take his cross and follow after Me is not worthy of Me," it does not mean bearing the "cross" of a difficult situation, a chronic disease, or a nagging spouse. I have heard devotional sermons spiritualizing the cross to mean everything from a cranky mother-in-law to a leaky roof to a 1957 Chevy! But that is not what the word *cross* meant to Jesus' first-century audience. It did not call to their minds the idea of long-term difficulties or troublesome burdens. It did not even evoke thoughts of Calvary—the Lord had not gone to the cross yet, and they did not understand that he would.

When Jesus said "take up your cross" to them, they thought of a cruel instrument of torture and death. They thought of dying in the most agonizing method known to man. They thought of poor, condemned criminals hanging on crosses by the roadside. Doubtless they had seen men executed in that fashion.

Jesus' listeners understood that he was calling them to die for him. They knew he was asking them to make the ultimate sacrifice, to surrender to him as Lord in every sense.

Jesus adds a final paradoxical thought on the meaning of discipleship: "He who has found his life shall lose it, and he who has lost his life for My sake shall find it" (Matt. 10:39). "He who has found his life" seems to refer to a person who has guarded his physical safety by denying Christ under pressure or to someone who clings to his life rather than taking up the cross. Because his first concern is securing his physical life, that person loses his eternal soul. Conversely, one who is willing to forfeit his life for Christ's sake will receive eternal life.

The Bible does not teach salvation by martyrdom. The Lord was not advising the disciples to try to get themselves killed for him. Again he was referring to a pattern, a direction. He was simply saying that genuine Christians do not shrink back, even in the face of death. To express it another way, when confronted with a decision between serving self and serving the Lord, the true disciple is the one who chooses to serve the Lord, even at great personal expense.

Again, this teaching is not absolute in the sense that it disallows temporary failures like that of Peter. But even Peter did ultimately prove himself to be a true disciple, didn't he? The time came when he willingly gave his life for Jesus' sake.

Luke 9:23 records similar words of Jesus: "If anyone wishes to come after Me, let him deny himself, and take up his cross daily, and follow Me." Notice the addition of the one word: "daily." The life of a disciple invites persecution and therefore must be a life of daily self-denial. Paul wrote to the Corinthians, "I protest, brethren, by the boasting in you, which I have in Christ Jesus our Lord, I die daily" (1 Cor. 15:31).

The idea of daily self-denial does not jibe with the contemporary supposition that believing in Jesus is a momentary decision. A true believer is one who signs up for life. The bumper-sticker sentiment "Try Jesus" is a mentality foreign to real discipleship—faith is not an experiment, but a lifelong commitment. It means taking up the cross daily, giving all for Christ each day. It means no reservations, no uncertainty, no hesitation (Luke 9:59–61). It means nothing is knowingly held back, nothing purposely shielded from his lordship, nothing stubbornly kept from his control. It calls for painful severing of ties with the world, sealing the escape hatches, and ridding oneself of any kind of security to fall back on in case of failure. Genuine believers know they are going ahead with Christ until death. Having put their hand to the plow, they will not look back (Luke 9:62).[4]

That is how it must be for all who would follow Jesus Christ. It is the stuff of true discipleship.

[4]Notice that in this same verse our Lord says that the one who *does* look back is unfit for the kingdom of God.

22

The Lordship of Christ

A magazine article inveighing against lordship salvation began with the question "Must a person make Christ Lord as a condition for salvation?" No less than ten times in the brief two-page piece the author spoke of "making Christ Lord" of one's life.[1] That terminology has become so familiar in our generation that some Christians are tempted to think of it as biblical. It is not.

Scripture never speaks of anyone "making" Christ Lord, except God himself, who "has made Him both Lord and Christ" (Acts 2:36). He *is* Lord of all (Rom. 14:9; Phil. 2:11), and the biblical mandate is not to "make" Christ Lord, but rather to bow to his lordship. Those who reject his lordship or give mere lip service to his sovereignty are not saved (cf. 1 Cor. 12:3; Luke 6:46–49). We observed from Jesus' words in Matthew 7:22 that many who verbally or intellectually admit the lordship of Christ will be turned away from heaven because they do not do the will of the Father in heaven.

All who believe the Word of God will agree that Jesus is Lord. He is ever and always Lord, whether or not anyone acknowledges his lordship or surrenders to his authority.

Nevertheless, some contemporary evangelical writers have questioned the place of Christ's lordship in the gospel message. While not denying that Christ is Lord, they suggest that it is a truth best kept out of the good news we proclaim to unbelievers. The article I referred to earlier says this:

> It is imperative to trust Christ as personal Savior and be born again. But this is only the first decision. Acknowledging Jesus as Lord is made by

[1]Rich Wager, "This So-Called 'Lordship Salvation,'" *Confident Living* (July–August 1987), 54–55.

229

believers [*sic*]. . . . The decision to trust Christ as Savior and then make Him Lord are two separate, distinct decisions [*sic*]. The first is made by nonbelievers, the second only by believers. The two decisions may be close or distant in time. But salvation must always precede lordship. It is possible, but miserable, to be saved without ever making Christ Lord of your life.[2]

Does that sound like the gospel according to Jesus? It certainly is not. We have seen that Jesus frequently made his lordship the central issue with unbelievers. Everything he said to the rich young ruler in Matthew 19, for example, demanded recognition of his lordship. And in Matthew 7:21–22 and Luke 6:46–49 he challenged the bogus profession of those who called him Lord but did not really know him, and he made it clear that obedience to divine authority is a prerequisite of entry into the kingdom. Clearly, his lordship is an integral part of the message of salvation.

Scripture reveals a number of eternal attributes encompassed in the name *Lord*. Salvation has no meaning or efficacy apart from them.

Jesus Is God

To say that Jesus is Lord is first of all to acknowledge that he is Almighty God, the Creator and Sustainer of all things (Col. 1:16–17). This is a profound declaration of truth. There is little question that the Bible teaches that Jesus is God. Only cultists and unbelievers dispute this truth. Scripture declares him to be God (John 1:1; cf. v. 14). God the Father addresses him as God (Heb. 1:8). He displays the attributes of deity—he is omnipresent (Matt. 18:20), omnipotent (Phil. 3:21), and unchanging (Heb. 13:8). He forgives sins (Matt. 9:2–7), receives worship (Matt. 28:17), and has absolute authority over all things (v. 18). Christ encompasses the fullness of God in human flesh (Col. 2:9). He is one with the Father. In John 10:30 he said plainly, "I and the Father are one." Jesus' critics clearly understood he was claiming to be God on this (v. 33) and many other occasions (e.g., John 5:18; 8:58–59; Mark 14:61–64).

We are seeing God in action when we read of the works of Christ. When we hear his words as recorded in the New Testament, we are hearing the words of God. When we hear Christ express emotion, we are listening to the heart of God. And when he gives a directive, it is the commandment of God. There is nothing he does not know, nothing he cannot do, and no way he can fail. Jesus is God in the fullest possible sense.

[2]Ibid., 55.

Jesus Is Sovereign

As God, Jesus is our sovereign Lord. He claimed, for example, to be Lord of the Sabbath (Matt. 12:8), meaning that his authority as Lawgiver superseded even the authority of the law. In John 5:17 Jesus defended his right to violate the Pharisees' man-made Sabbath laws: "My Father is working until now, and I Myself am working." He thus claimed equal authority with God, and the Jewish leaders were so incensed at him for it that they tried to kill him (5:18). When Jesus encountered opposition like that, he never engaged obstinate unbelievers in dialogue. He did not bother to try to argue theology with them. He simply appealed again to his own inherent authority as God (vv. 19–47; cf. John 10:22–42).

The fact that the Jewish leaders could not kill Jesus before his time was further proof of his sovereignty: "I lay down My life that I may take it again. No one has taken it away from Me, but I lay it down on My own initiative. I have authority to lay it down, and I have authority to take it up again" (John 10:17–18). The influence of Jesus' authority extends to every person. In fact, all judgment has been committed to him: "For not even the Father judges anyone, but he has given all judgment to the Son" (John 5:22). Notice the reason for this: "in order that *all* may honor the Son, even as they honor the Father" (v. 23, emphasis added). Likewise, those who dishonor the Son by rejecting his right to be sovereign also dishonor the Father.

In the final judgment, every knee will bow and every tongue will confess Christ as Lord, to the glory of God the Father (Phil. 2:11–12). That does not mean, of course, that all will be saved, but that even those who die in unbelief will be forced to confess the lordship of Jesus. His sovereignty is limitless. Marc Mueller has expressed the breadth of Jesus' sovereignty with these words: "He is the Almighty God, the Matchless Cosmic Sovereign, who as Creator and Redeemer (Jn. 1:9–13) has the right and power to demand compliance and submission to His imperial, veracious authority."[3]

Jesus Is Savior

Although he is sovereign God, Jesus took on himself the limitations of human flesh and dwelt personally among sinful men and women (John 1:14). While on earth, he experienced all the sorrows and tribulations of humanity—except that he never sinned (Heb. 4:15). He walked on earth, showed his love, demonstrated his power, and revealed in his behavior the righteousness of God. Yet his demeanor

[3]Marc Mueller, "Jesus Is Lord," *Grace Today* (August 1981), 6.

was that of a servant. Scripture says he "emptied Himself, taking the form of a bond-servant, and being made in the likeness of men. And being found in appearance as a man, He humbled Himself by becoming obedient to the point of death, even death on a cross" (Phil. 2:7–8).

In other words, though he is sovereign Lord of all, he surrendered everything, even to the point where he willingly died the most painful, humiliating death known to humankind. He did it on our behalf. Though he was sinless, and therefore not worthy of death (cf. Rom. 6:23), he suffered the guilt of our sin: "He Himself bore our sins in His body on the cross, that we might die to sin and live to righteousness" (1 Peter 2:24).

The death of Christ for us was the ultimate sacrifice. It paid the penalty of our sin in full, and opened the way for us to have peace with God. Romans 5:8 says, "While we were yet sinners, Christ died for us. . . . Having now been justified by His blood, we shall be saved from the wrath of God through Him."

Even in death Christ was Lord. His resurrection was proof of that. Paul writes that Christ "was declared to be the Son of God with power by the resurrection from the dead" (Rom. 1:4). Philippians 2:9–11 describes the Father's response to Jesus' humility and death: "Therefore also God highly exalted Him, and bestowed on Him the name which is above every name, that at the name of Jesus every knee should bow, of those who are in heaven, and on earth, and under the earth, and that every tongue should confess that Jesus Christ is Lord, to the glory of God the Father."

Therefore, when we invite people to receive Christ as Savior, we ask them to embrace One who is Lord and was declared to be so by God the Father, who also demands that every knee bow to his sovereignty. Salvation belongs to those who receive him (John 1:12), but they must receive him for all that he is—"the blessed and only Sovereign, the King of kings and Lord of lords" (1 Tim. 6:15).

Jesus Is Lord

Jesus *is* Lord. Consistently Scripture affirms the lordship of Christ in every way. He is Lord in judgment. He is Lord over the Sabbath. He is Lord over all (Acts 10:36). He is called Lord (*kurios* in the Greek text) no less than 747 times in the New Testament.[4] The book

[4]For an excellent lexical analysis of the New Testament usage of *kurios*, see Kenneth L. Gentry, "The Great Option: A Study of the Lordship Controversy," *Baptist Reformation Review* 5 (Spring 1976), 63–69.

of Acts alone refers to him as Lord 92 times, while calling him Savior only twice. Clearly in the early church's preaching, the lordship of Christ was the heart of the Christian message.

The centrality of Jesus' lordship to the gospel message is clear from the way Scripture presents the terms of salvation. Those who dichotomize between believing in Christ as Savior and yielding to him as Lord have a difficult time with many of the biblical invitations to faith, such as Acts 2:21: "Everyone who calls on the name of the *Lord* shall be saved"; or Acts 2:36: "Let all the house of Israel know for certain that God has made Him *both Lord and Christ*—this Jesus whom you crucified"; or Acts 16:31: "Believe in the *Lord* Jesus, and you shall be saved"; and particularly Romans 10:9–10: "If you confess with your mouth *Jesus as Lord,* and believe in your heart that God raised Him from the dead, you shall be saved" (emphasis added).

All those passages indisputably include the lordship of Christ as part of the gospel according to Jesus. We have seen that Jesus' lordship includes the ideas of dominion, authority, sovereignty, and the right to govern. If those ideas are implicit in the phrase "confess . . . Jesus as Lord" (Rom. 10:9), then it is clear that people who come to Christ for salvation must do so in obedience to him—that is, with a willingness to surrender to him as Lord.

Not surprisingly, the opponents of lordship salvation have made Romans 10 a focus of their attack. Much has been written in recent years attempting to explain how one can confess Jesus as Lord yet continue to rebel against his authority. Some take the position that the term *Lord,* when used by Scripture in connection with the gospel, does not mean "sovereign master," but rather "deity." Charles Ryrie is the most articulate of those who have used this argument. He writes:

> To be sure, Lord does [often] mean Master, but in the New Testament it also means God (Acts 3:22), owner (Luke 19:33), sir (John 4:11), man-made idols (I Cor. 8:5), and even one's husband (I Peter 3:6). . . .
>
> . . . In I Corinthians 12:3 Paul said, "No man can say that Jesus is the Lord [literally, Lord Jesus], but by the Holy Ghost." Lord in this sense must mean Jehovah-God for the simple reason that unsaved people can and do say Lord, meaning Sir, in reference to Christ, before they even have the Spirit of God. . . .
>
> Why is Lord Jesus (meaning God-Man) such a significant statement that it can only be said by the Spirit of God guiding a person? It is because this is the essence of our salvation since it focuses on the uniqueness of the Savior. Almost all "saviours" claim mastery over the lives of their followers. . . . But what religion, other than Christianity,

has a savior who claimed to be both God and man in the same person? *If Lord in the phrase means Master, then the claim to uniqueness is absent.* If Lord in the phrase means Jehovah-God, then Jesus is unique, and this is the very heart of the message of salvation in Christianity. . . .

. . . This same emphasis is seen in Romans 10:9: "That if thou shalt confess with thy mouth the Lord Jesus . . . thou shalt be saved." It is the confession of Jesus as God and thus faith in the God-Man that saves from sin (emphasis added).[5]

In other words, Dr. Ryrie claims those who argue that "Lord" means "sovereign master" divest the call to faith of its significance with regard to the deity of Christ.

But that is a straw argument. It is not necessary to eliminate the concept of deity from the word *Lord* to understand that it means "master." Ryrie is most certainly correct to say that "Lord" means God. But if anything, that only strengthens the view that absolute rulership is inherent in the word. Certainly when Thomas said to Jesus, "My Lord and my God" (John 20:28), he was using "Lord" as more than an expression of deity. He was not saying, "My God and my God"; he was affirming that Jesus is both God and Master. What kind of god would he be if he were not sovereign?

Look, for example, at the context of Romans 10:9. Verse 12 uses the phrase "Lord of all" to describe the Savior. It means he is Lord over all, Jews and Gentiles, believers and nonbelievers alike. Any interpretation that attempts to rid the term of its meaning of sovereign dominion makes no sense at all. Reading that truth into verse 9 results in an even stronger statement: "If you confess with your mouth Jesus as Lord [of all] . . . you shall be saved."[6]

Certainly the word *Lord* includes the idea of deity in every context where Scripture calls Jesus "Lord" in connection with the gospel message. That Christ is God is a fundamental component of the gospel message. No one who denies the deity of Christ could be saved (cf. 1 John 4:2–3). But inherent in the idea of deity is authority, dominion, and the right to command.[7] A person living in rebellion against Christ's authority does not acknowledge him as Lord in any sense (cf. Titus 1:16).

[5]Charles C. Ryrie, *Balancing the Christian Life* (Chicago: Moody Press, 1969), 173–75.

[6]This calls into question Darrell Bock's declaration that Romans 10 "provides no clear definition of Paul's understanding of the term 'Lord.'" Darrell L. Bock, "Jesus as Lord in Acts and in the Gospel Message," *Bibliotheca Sacra* 143 (April–June 1986), 147. On the contrary, it is clear from Romans 10:12 that Paul placed no limits on the extent of Christ's authority as Lord.

[7]See n. 21, p. 35.

The signature of saving faith is surrender to the lordship of Jesus Christ. The definitive test of whether a person belongs to Christ is a willingness to bow to his divine authority. In 1 Corinthians 12:3 Paul made it clear that "no one speaking by the Spirit of God says, 'Jesus is accursed'; and no one can say, 'Jesus is Lord,' except by the Holy Spirit."

That does not mean that it is impossible for unsaved people to utter the words "Jesus is Lord," for obviously they can and do. Jesus himself pointed out the paradox of those who called him Lord but did not really believe it (Luke 6:46). Even the demons know and admit who he is (cf. James 2:19). Mark 1:24 records that as Jesus was teaching in the synagogue, a demon-possessed man stood and cried out, "What do we have to do with You, Jesus of Nazareth? Have you come to destroy us? I know who you are—the Holy One of God!" Mark 3:11 says that "whenever the unclean spirits beheld Him, they would fall down before Him and cry out, saying, 'You are the Son of God.'" One demon inside a man possessed by legions of unclean spirits called out, "What do I have to do with You, Jesus, Son of the Most High God?" (Mark 5:7).

First Corinthians 12:3 cannot refer to just saying the words "Jesus is Lord." It must mean more. It includes acknowledging him as Lord by obeying Him, by surrendering one's will to his lordship, by affirming him with one's deeds as well as one's words (cf. Titus 1:16).

This in no way establishes a gospel of human works.[8] Notice that it is the Holy Spirit who enables a person to confess Jesus as Lord: "No one can say, 'Jesus is Lord,' except by the Holy Spirit." Surrender to Jesus as Lord is no more a meritorious human work than believing he is Savior. Neither act is a good deed done to earn favor with God. Both are the sovereign work of God in the heart of everyone who believes. And one is impossible without the other. Jesus could not be Savior if he were not Lord. Furthermore, if he were not Lord, he could not be King or Messiah or our great High Priest. Apart from his lordship, every aspect of his saving work is impossible.

When we come to Jesus for salvation, we come to the One who is Lord over all. Any message that omits this truth cannot be called the gospel. It is a defective message that presents a savior who is not Lord, a redeemer who does not demonstrate authority over sin, a weakened, sickly messiah who cannot command those he rescues.

---

[8]Cf. Wager, "This So-Called 'Lordship Salvation,'" 54: "But the lordship of Christ as a prerequisite for salvation places the emphasis on works rather than on grace. God does not need anything from man. His salvation is an unconditional gift. Man's role can be no more than that of a recipient who believes the gift to be sufficient payment for his sins."

The gospel according to Jesus is nothing like that. It represents Jesus Christ as Lord and Savior and demands that those who would receive him take him for who he is. In the words of Puritan John Flavel, "The gospel offer of Christ includes all his offices, and gospel faith just so receives him; to submit to him, as well as to be redeemed by him; to imitate him in the holiness of his life, as well as to reap the purchases and fruits of his death. It must be an entire receiving of the Lord Jesus Christ."[9]

A. W. Tozer wrote in the same vein, "To urge men and women to believe in a divided Christ is bad teaching for no one can receive half of Christ, or a third of Christ, or a quarter of the Person of Christ! We are not saved by believing in an office nor in a work."[10]

He is Lord, and those who refuse him as Lord cannot use him as Savior. Everyone who receives him must surrender to his authority, for to say we receive Christ when in fact we reject his right to reign over us is utter absurdity. It is a futile attempt to hold onto sin with one hand and take Jesus with the other. What kind of salvation is it if we are left in bondage to sin?

[9]John Flavel, *The Works of John Flavel* (London: Banner of Truth, reprint, n.d.), 2:111.
[10]A. W. Tozer, *I Call It Heresy!* (Harrisburg, Pa.: Christian Publications, 1974), 10–11.

PART FIVE

———

JESUS FULFILLS
HIS GOSPEL

23

Tetelestai!: The Triumph Is Complete

An obscure Hindu holy man named Rao flirted with worldwide fame in 1966. An eccentric, pompous mystic, Rao became convinced he could walk on water. He was so confident in his own spiritual power that he announced he would perform the feat before a live audience. He sold tickets at a hundred dollars apiece. Bombay's elite turned out en masse to behold the spectacle.

The event was held in a large garden with a deep pool. A crowd of more than six hundred believers and curiosity-seekers assembled. The white-bearded yogi appeared in flowing robes and stepped confidently to the edge of the pool. He paused to pray silently. A reverent hush fell on the crowd. Rao opened his eyes, looked heavenward, and boldly stepped forward.

With an awkward splash he disappeared beneath the water.

Sputtering and red-faced, the holy man struggled to pull himself out of the water. Trembling with rage, he shook his finger at the silent, embarrassed crowd. "One of you," Rao bellowed indignantly, "is an unbeliever!"

A Show of Strength in Dying

All this world's so-called holy men contrast sharply with the one who really did walk on water. Jesus Christ performed many miracles, but he never staged them just for show. On the contrary, his greatest display of spiritual authority was when he died on a cross.

That is hard to comprehend but nevertheless true. Jesus did not fall victim to anyone or anything. He had come for the specific purpose of dying to atone for sin (Luke 19:10; John 1:29). His crucifixion was a vivid display of his authority over circumstances,

239

people, and even death. Far from being a tragic end to his earthly ministry, it was the culmination of all he had set out to do.

That biblical truth, unfortunately, is often overlooked. People have for centuries argued about who was to blame for killing Jesus. Sadly, some have even used the issue to justify anti-Semitism, blaming the entire Jewish race for Jesus' death.

Certainly the Jewish leaders who condemned him were culpable. They plotted, concocted false charges against Him, and blackmailed the Roman governor Pontius Pilate into carrying out their will. They were by no means innocent.

And the Roman government must share the guilt. Those who represented Rome in Jerusalem set aside justice to appease an angry crowd. They executed an innocent man.

But Jesus was not ultimately a victim of either Rome or the Jewish leaders. The apostle Peter says in Acts 2:23 that Jesus was "delivered up by the predetermined plan and foreknowledge of God." The Jewish leaders and the Roman officials who carried out his crucifixion undeniably bear guilt for the sin of what they did, but God himself had foreordained how Jesus would die.

Thus Jesus' death was an act of the Son's submissive obedience to the Father's will. And Jesus himself was in absolute control. He said, "I lay down My life that I may take it again. No one has taken it away from Me, but I lay it down on My own initiative. I have authority to lay it down, and I have authority to take it up again. This commandment I received from My Father" (John 10:17–18).

Do not think for a moment that anyone could kill Jesus against his will. The divine plan could never be short-circuited by human or satanic plots. Jesus even told Pilate, "You would have no authority over Me, unless it had been given you from above" (John 19:11). Mobs tried to murder Jesus. They once sought to hurl him off a cliff (Luke 4:29–30) and repeatedly attempted to stone him (John 8:59; 10:31). Again and again he simply passed through their midst because his time had not yet come (cf. John 7:30; 8:20).

When the hour of Jesus' death finally did come, he knew it (Matt. 26:18). Fully comprehending all it would entail in terms of the pain and agony of bearing the sin of the world, he nevertheless submitted himself willingly. John 18:4 tells us that when the soldiers came to arrest him in the Garden of Gethsemane, "Jesus therefore, *knowing all the things that were coming upon Him,* went forth, and said to them, 'Whom do you seek?'" (emphasis added). He willingly surrendered himself to them. It was his hour now, the time foreordained by God.

Control over Every Detail

No passage of Scripture speaks with more force about Jesus' omnipotence in the midst of his agony on the cross than John 19:28–30:

> Jesus, knowing that all things had already been accomplished, in order that the Scripture might be fulfilled, said, "I am thirsty." A jar full of sour wine was standing there; so they put a sponge full of the sour wine upon a branch of hyssop, and brought it up to His mouth. When Jesus therefore had received the sour wine, He said, "It is finished!" And He bowed His head, and gave up His spirit.

Throughout the Crucifixion, Jesus Christ was on a divine timetable. God was sovereignly directing every incident. Step by step, each detail of Old Testament prophecy was fulfilled. Psalm 22 and Isaiah 53 in particular outlined prophetically the specific features of his death. All of them were carried out precisely.

As he hung on the cross, Jesus knew that "all things had already been accomplished" (John 19:28)—all, that is, but one final prophecy. Psalm 69:21, where Christ speaks prophetically of his own death, says, "For my thirst they gave me vinegar to drink." And so "in order that the Scripture might be fulfilled, [He] said, 'I am thirsty'" (John 19:28). The soldiers responded. They were under divine impetus; God was moving to fulfill the prophecy.

Some have maintained that Jesus was simply a man who purposely engineered details of his life and death to coincide with selected Old Testament prophecies. A well-known book of the 1960s made precisely that argument.[1] The author pointed to phrases like "in order that the Scripture might be fulfilled" (John 19:28) as proof that Jesus manipulated circumstances to give the appearance of fulfilling Scripture.

But a mere man trying to mislead people could not have had the kind of sovereign control over events Jesus repeatedly displayed. This verse proves why. It was not Jesus alone, but everyone around him—his enemies included—who fulfilled precisely the details of Old Testament prophecy: "A jar full of sour wine [vinegar] was standing there; so they put a sponge full of the sour wine upon a branch of hyssop, and brought it up to His mouth" (John 19:29). Exactly as the prophecy had predicted.

Note that the sponge was lifted to Jesus' mouth on a branch of hyssop. Hyssop, a long reed with a bushy end, had a history of significance in the Jewish sacrificial system. Exodus 12:22 prescribed

[1]Hugh Schoenfield, *The Passover Plot* (New York: Bantam, 1965).

hyssop as the tool by which lamb's blood was to be applied to the doorposts and lintel during the first Passover. Hyssop was used in many of the Levitical sacrifices (Lev. 14:4, 6, 49–52; Num. 19:6, 18). It was so closely tied to sacrifices for sin that when David wrote his great psalm of penitence, he said, "Purify me with hyssop, and I shall be clean" (Ps. 51:7).

How fitting, then, that hyssop should be the tool at the sacrifice of the true Passover Lamb! Do you think the Roman soldiers understood the relevance of what they were doing? I am certain they did not. But Jesus sovereignly saw to it that they carried out every detail, although they surely thought *they* were displaying their power over *him!*

It Is Finished!

John 19:30 says, "When Jesus therefore had received the sour wine, He said, 'It is finished!'" The Greek expression is only one word—*tetelestai*. It was not the groan or curse of a victim; it was the proclamation of a victor. It was a shout of triumph: "IT IS FINISHED!'

The wealth of meaning in that phrase is surely impossible for the human mind to fathom. What was finished? Jesus' earthly life? Yes, but far more. Every detail of redemptive prophecy? Certainly, but not that alone.

The work of redemption was done. All that the law of God required, full atonement for sins, everything the symbolism of ceremonial law foreshadowed—the work that the Father had given Jesus to do—everything was done. Nothing was left. The ransom was paid. The wages of sin were settled. Divine justice was satisfied. The work of Christ was thus accomplished in toto. The Lamb of God had taken away the sins of the world (John 1:29). There was nothing more on earth for him to do except die so that he might rise again.

Here it is appropriate to add a crucial footnote: When Jesus said, "It is finished," he meant it. Nothing can be added to what he did. Many people believe they must supplement his work with good deeds of their own. They believe they must facilitate their own redemption through baptism, other sacraments and religious rituals, benevolent deeds, or whatever else they can accomplish through their own efforts. But no works of human righteousness can expand on what Jesus accomplished for us. "He saved us, not on the basis of deeds which we have done in righteousness, but according to His mercy" (Titus 3:5). The beginning and the end of our salvation was consummated by Jesus Christ, and we can contribute nothing.

What would you think if I took a felt-tipped pen and tried to add more features to the Mona Lisa? What if I got a hammer and chisel and offered to refine Michelangelo's Moses? That would be a travesty. They are masterpieces! No one needs to add to them.

In an infinitely greater way, that is true of Jesus' atoning work. He has paid the full price of our sins. He has purchased our redemption. He offers a salvation from sin that is complete in every sense. "It is finished!" Nothing we can do would in any way add to what he accomplished on our behalf. Nor does "lordship salvation" suggest otherwise.

Having finished his work, our Lord "bowed His head, and gave up His spirit" (John 19:30). There was no jerk, no sudden slump. He bowed his head. The Greek word evokes the picture of gently placing one's head on a pillow. In the truest sense, no man took Jesus' life from him. He laid it down of his own accord (cf. John 10:17–18). He simply and quietly yielded up his spirit, commending himself into the Father's hands (Luke 23:46).

Only the omnipotent God who is Lord of all could do that. Death could not claim Jesus apart from his own will. He died in complete control of all that was happening to him. Even in his death he was Lord.

To the human eye Jesus looked like a pathetic casualty, powerless in the hands of mighty men. But the opposite was true. He was in charge. He proved it a few days later by forever bursting the bonds of death when he rose from the grave (1 Cor. 15:20–57).

And Jesus is still in charge. "For to this end Christ died and lived again, that He might be Lord both of the dead and of the living" (Rom. 14:9).

This, then, is the gospel our Lord sends us forth to proclaim: That Jesus Christ, who is God incarnate, humbled himself to die on our behalf. Thus he became the sinless sacrifice to pay the penalty of our guilt. He rose from the dead to declare with power that he is Lord over all, and he offers eternal life freely to sinners who will surrender to him in humble, repentant faith. This gospel promises nothing to the haughty rebel, but for broken, penitent sinners, it graciously offers everything that pertains to life and godliness (2 Peter 1:3).

PART SIX

APPENDIXES

Appendix 1
The Gospel
According to the Apostles

A few years ago a well-known conference speaker wrote to ask my thoughts on the proper presentation of the gospel. I think he expected me to affirm the notion that saving faith is only a matter of believing the facts of the gospel. Instead, I gave him a distillation of what I have written in this book.

He wrote back saying that he had read my material but felt it was not a sound argument because I based my view of the gospel on Jesus' message, not on apostolic teaching. "I would have appreciated receiving a cassette tape from you on your teaching of Romans 3 and 4," he wrote. "Certainly it is wisest for us to teach the way of salvation in this day of grace for obvious reasons from these chapters, written by Paul on *precisely* this non-negotiable subject."

He added this comment, which sparked my curiosity: "Therefore, we see the wisdom of Machen (the best, perhaps, of this century) when he said, 'Nothing before the cross can properly be called the gospel.'" Dr. J. Gresham Machen was a Presbyterian from the Reformed tradition, a scholar, and most certainly a defender of the faith. It seemed to me that whatever he meant by that statement, it was not likely that he was discarding the teaching of Christ as the basis of the gospel appeal for today.

In searching for the source and context of that quotation, I encountered these words by Machen:

I know that some people hold—by a veritable delirium of folly, as it seems to me—that the words of Jesus belong to a dispensation of law that was brought to a close by his death and resurrection and that therefore the teaching of the Sermon on the Mount, for example, is not intended for the dispensation of grace in which we are now living.

Well, let them turn to the apostle Paul, the Apostle who has told us that we are not under the law but under grace. What does he say about the matter? Does he represent the law of God as a thing without validity in this dispensation of divine grace?

247

Not at all. In the second chapter of Romans, as well as (by implication) everywhere else in his Epistles, he insists upon the universality of the law of God. Even the Gentiles, though they do not know that clear manifestation of God's law which was found in the Old Testament, have God's law written upon their hearts and are without excuse when they disobey. Christians, in particular, Paul insists, are far indeed from being emancipated from the duty of obedience to God's commands. The Apostle regards any such notion as the deadliest of errors. "Now the works of the flesh," says Paul, "are manifest, which are these: Adultery, fornication, uncleanness, lasciviousness, idolatry, witchcraft, hatred, variance, emulations, wrath, strife, seditions, heresies, envyings, murders, drunkenness, revellings, and such like: of the which I tell you before, as I have also told you in time past, that they which do such things shall not inherit the kingdom of God."[1]

It is a mistake of the worst sort to set the teachings of Paul and the apostles over against the words of our Lord and imagine that they contradict one another or speak to different dispensations. The Gospels are the foundation on which the Epistles build. The entire book of James, for example, reads like a commentary on the Sermon on the Mount. Those who want to consign the sermon to another age must still deal with the fact that all its principles are repeated and expanded upon by later New Testament writers.

Those who wish to do away with "lordship salvation" gain no ground by trying to limit discussion of the gospel message to the Epistles. While Jesus' gospel was not yet fully completed until his death and resurrection, the elements of it were all clear in his teaching. Each of the apostles who wrote under inspiration underscored and amplified the truth of the gospel according to Jesus.

Paul

The apostle Paul in particular was a champion of the great doctrine of justification by faith. Yet he recognized the lordship of Christ (Rom. 10:9–10) and the place of works in a believer's life (Eph. 2:10). For him, faith was not a dormant quality that might fail to produce righteous fruit. He saw practical righteousness as the necessary and inevitable result of true faith.

It has often been imagined that Paul's view of justification differed from James', because Paul wrote, "For we maintain that a man is justified by faith apart from the works of the Law" (Rom. 3:28); while James wrote, "You see that a man is justified by works, and not by

---

[1]J. Gresham Machen, *The Christian View of Man* (Edinburgh: Banner of Truth, 1937), 186–87.

faith alone" (James 2:24). But there is no contradiction. Paul was saying that human works cannot earn favor with God, and James was saying that true faith must always result in good works. Paul was denouncing the notion that the unregenerate can buy merit with God through works. James was condemning the idea that the true believer might fail to produce good works.

The saving faith described by the apostle Paul is a dynamic force that inevitably produces practical righteousness. He did not accept dead, lifeless "faith" entirely devoid of good works. After his discourse on justification by faith in Romans 3–5, he wrote, "What shall we say then? Are we to continue in sin that grace might increase? May it never be! How shall we who died to sin still live in it?" (Rom. 6:1–2).

Paul viewed the believer as dead to sin and alive to God (6:11). He saw it as a contradiction in terms for a Christian to yield to sin's control: "Do you not know that when you present yourselves to someone as slaves for obedience, you are slaves of the one whom you obey, either of sin resulting in death, or of obedience resulting in righteousness?" (v. 16). He saw all believers as essentially obedient—not free from sin or sinless, but free from the tyranny of sin and servants of righteousness. He wrote, "Though you were slaves of sin, you became obedient from the heart to that form of teaching to which you were committed, and having been freed from sin, you became slaves of righteousness" (vv. 17–18).

Paul himself struggled greatly with sin in his life. Romans 7:7–25 chronicles his ongoing battle against sin. Yet in the midst of that struggle, he repeatedly affirmed his yearning to obey (vv. 15–16, 18, 21–22; see also footnote 13, page 190).

Paul did not see God's grace as a static attribute whereby he passively accepts sinners. Rather, he described it as a dynamic force that transforms thought and behavior: "For the grace of God has appeared, bringing salvation to all men, instructing us to deny ungodliness and worldly desires and to live sensibly, righteously and godly in the present age" (Titus 2:11–12).

If you think Paul's doctrine of justification by faith makes it possible for people to lay hold of Christ without letting go of sin, consider these passages:

> Do you not know that the unrighteous shall not inherit the kingdom of God? Do not be deceived; neither fornicators, nor idolaters, nor adulterers, nor effeminate, nor homosexuals, nor thieves, nor the

covetous, nor drunkards, nor revilers, nor swindlers, shall inherit the kingdom of God (1 Cor. 6:9–11).[2]

The deeds of the flesh are evident, which are: immorality, impurity, sensuality, idolatry, sorcery, enmities, strife, jealousy, outbursts of anger, disputes, dissensions, factions, envying, drunkenness, carousing, and things like these, of which I forewarn you just as I have forewarned you that those who practice such things shall not inherit the kingdom of God (Gal. 5:19–21).

This you know with certainty, that no immoral or impure person or covetous man, who is an idolater, has an inheritance in the kingdom of Christ and God (Eph. 5:5).

Brethren, join in following my example, and observe those who walk according to the pattern you have in us. For many walk, of whom I often told you, and now tell you even weeping, that they are enemies of the cross of Christ, whose end is destruction (Phil. 3:17–19).

God has not called us for the purpose of impurity, but in sanctification. Consequently, he who rejects this is not rejecting man but the God who gives His Holy Spirit to you (1 Thess. 4:8).

For Paul, perseverance in the faith is essential evidence that faith is real. If a person ultimately and finally falls away from the faith, it proves that that person never really was redeemed to begin with:

> He has now reconciled you in his fleshly body through death, in order to present you before Him holy and blameless and beyond reproach—*if indeed you continue in the faith* firmly established and steadfast, and not moved away from the hope of the gospel that you have heard, which was proclaimed in all creation under heaven, and of which I, Paul, was made a minister (Col. 1:22–23, emphasis added).

Paul regarded those who fell away—such as Hymenaeus, Alexander, and Philetus—as unbelievers (cf. 1 Tim. 1:20; 2 Tim. 2:16–19). This did not contradict his teaching on the eternal security of salvation. Those men were never saved to begin with. Their faith was a sham. They were false prophets whose motives from the beginning were suspect (cf. 1 Tim. 6:3–5). Although they had once professed to know the truth, they "did not receive the love of the truth so as to be saved" (2 Thess. 2:10).

Paul preached the gospel according to Jesus. In fact, his defense of

---

[2]I am aware of Zane Hodges' view that to "inherit the kingdom" is somehow different from entering the kingdom. But Revelation 21:7–8 makes the meaning of these verses indisputable: "He who overcomes shall inherit these things, and I will be his God, and he will be My son. But for the cowardly and unbelieving and abominable and murderers and immoral persons and sorcerers and idolaters and all liars, their part will be in the lake that burns with fire and brimstone, which is the second death."

his apostleship was based on the claim that he received his gospel directly from Jesus (Gal. 1:11–12). He summarized his entire ministry with these words: "I did not prove disobedient to the heavenly vision, but kept declaring both to those of Damascus first, and also at Jerusalem and then throughout all the region of Judea, and even to the Gentiles, that they should repent and turn to God, performing deeds appropriate to repentance" (Acts 26:19–20, cf. 20:20–27).

Jude

Jude likewise warned those who professed to know Christ but failed to live accordingly. Having set out to write his epistle on the subject of salvation, he was constrained instead to warn about the danger of apostasy (Jude 3–4). He portrayed apostates as those who claim to live under grace but live in immorality, rejecting Christ's lordship: "ungodly persons who turn the grace of our God into licentiousness and deny our only Master and Lord, Jesus Christ" (v. 4). Their end, Jude said, was destruction by eternal fire (v. 7). His point was that all who deny the lordship of Christ are damned.

Peter

Preaching the first sermon of the church age, the apostle Peter concluded, "Therefore let all the house of Israel know for certain that God has made Him *both Lord and Christ*—this Jesus whom you crucified" (Acts 2:36, emphasis added). The Christ Peter preached was not merely a Savior with open arms, but also a Lord who demanded obedience. "He is Lord of all" (Acts 10:36). "He is the one whom God exalted to His right hand as a Prince and a Savior, to grant repentance to Israel, and forgiveness of sins" (Acts 5:31).

Thus Peter called for repentance before he preached the good news of forgiveness; his invitations to the lost started with repentance (cf. Acts 2:38; 3:19). Yet he saw all of salvation—including repentance—as a work of God, not an effort of man (Acts 11:17–18). The new birth as he described it was a work of God (1 Peter 1:3), who sovereignly elects sinners to salvation (1 Peter 1:1–2; 2 Peter 1:10).

Here's how Peter described God's saving work: "His divine power has granted to us *everything pertaining to life and godliness,* through the true knowledge of Him who called us by His own glory and excellence" (2 Peter 1:3, emphasis added). Yet he taught that the proof of faith's reality is the virtue it produces in the life of the believer (vv. 5–9). He wrote, "Therefore, brethren, be all the more diligent to make certain about His calling and choosing you; for as long as you practice these things, you will never stumble; for in this way the entrance into the eternal kingdom of our Lord and Savior Jesus Christ will be abundantly supplied to you" (vv. 10–11).

The standard of righteousness Peter held up was the same he heard from Jesus: "Like the Holy One who called you, be holy yourselves also in all your behavior; because it is written, 'You shall be holy, for I am holy'" (1 Peter 1:14–15; cf. Matt. 5:48).

James

We have seen already that James denounced faith without works as dead and useless (James 2:17, 20). His entire epistle consists of tests of true faith, all of which are the practical fruits of righteousness in the believer's life: perseverance in trials (1:1–12); obedience to the Word (vv. 13–25); pure and undefiled religion (vv. 26–27); impartiality (2:1–13); righteous works (vv. 14–26); control of the tongue (3:1–12); true wisdom (vv. 13–18); hatred of pride and worldliness (4:1–6); humility and submission to God (vv. 7–17); and right behavior in the body of believers (5:1–20).

One of the most comprehensive invitations to salvation in all the Epistles comes in James 4:7–10. While James directs most of his epistle to genuine believers, it is also evident that he is concerned about those who are not genuine. He wants no one to be deceived regarding true salvation, so he calls for a real, living, saving faith that is distinct from the dead faith of chapter 2. He states his objective in 5:20. It is to see "the sinner converted from the error of his way and his soul saved from death."

The invitation in 4:7–10 is directed at those who are not saved— guilty, wicked hearers of the Word who are not doers (cf. 1:21–22), who are still captive to dead faith (cf. 2:14–20), who are bitter, selfish, arrogant liars whose "wisdom is not what comes from above but is earthy, natural, demonic" (3:15), who are loving the world and thus are the enemies of God (4:4), whose inner spirit is still dominated by lusts (cf. 4:5), and who are proud and self-sufficient (cf. 4:6). They are in desperate need of God's grace. But since God only "gives grace to the humble" (v. 6), James calls these "sinners" (a term used in Scripture only of the unregenerate) to turn from their pride and humble themselves. Ten imperatives delineate the commands in James' call to sinners: submit yourself to God (salvation); resist the devil (transferring allegiance); draw near to God (intimacy of relationship); cleanse your hands (repentance); purify your hearts (confession); be miserable, mourn, weep, and let your laughter and joy be turned to gloom (sorrow). The final imperative summarizes the mentality of those who are converted: "Humble yourselves in the presence of the Lord." All this is a work of God, who gives his more abundant grace (v. 6).

John

The apostle John also wrote an entire epistle about the marks of a true believer (cf. 1 John 5:13). His counsel to those struggling with assurance was not that they should pin their hopes on a past incident or a moment of faith. He gave instead a doctrinal test and a moral test, and reiterated them throughout his first epistle. The moral test requires obedience: "If we say that we have fellowship with Him and yet walk in darkness, we lie and do not practice the truth" (1:6) "By this we know that we have come to know Him, if we keep His commandments. The one who says, 'I have come to know him,' and does not keep His commandments, is a liar, and the truth is not in him" (2:15) "If you know that He is righteous, you know that everyone also who practices righteousness is born of Him" (2:29). "And everyone who has this hope fixed on Him purifies himself, just as He is pure" (3:3). Scores of other passages throughout the epistle confirm the same truth: the one who is truly saved cannot continue in a pattern of unbroken sin (3:6–10).

The doctrinal test that John gave relates to Jesus' deity and lordship: "Who is the liar but the one who denies that Jesus is the Christ? This is the antichrist, the one who denies the Father and the Son. Whoever denies the Son does not have the Father; the one who confesses the Son has the Father also" (1 John 2:22–23). "By this you know the Spirit of God; every spirit that confesses that Jesus Christ has come in the flesh is from God" (4:2). "Whoever believes that Jesus is the Christ is born of God" (5:1).

John was so confident of the ultimate triumph of faith over sin that he had a special name for the believer: "the one who overcomes" (5:5; cf. Rev. 2:7, 11, 26; 3:5, 12, 21; 21:7).[3] He wrote, "Who is the one who overcomes the world, but he who believes that Jesus is the Son of God?" (1 John 5:5). For John, a true believer could never ultimately fail to overcome.

---

[3]See James E. Rosscup, "The Overcomer of the Apocalypse," *Grace Theological Journal* 3 (Fall 1982), 261–86, for an excellent study on the meaning of the term *overcomer*. Rosscup shows conclusively that the term is equivalent to "believer."

The Writer of Hebrews

I have examined elsewhere[4] the warning passages in Hebrews that
were addressed to people who identified with and intellectually
accepted Christ but had not yet laid hold of him by faith. No matter
how one interprets the warning passages of the book, there is no
escaping the clear and obvious implications of Hebrews 12:10–14:
"He disciplines us for our good, that we may share His holiness. . . .
[Therefore pursue] the sanctification without which no one will see
the Lord."

When all is said and done, those who are utterly lacking in holiness
will be sent away from God's presence into everlasting destruction
(cf. Matt. 25:41). The context of Hebrews 12 confirms that this means
practical holiness. Thus the writer of Hebrews, like John, James,
Peter, Jude, and Paul, confirmed the necessity of righteous works to
validate genuine faith.

The few brief passages I have cited here only scratch the surface of
the rich truth of the way of salvation outlined in Acts and the
Epistles. I have dealt more thoroughly with the apostles' soteriology
in a separate book.[5]

One thing is clear: the gospel according to Jesus is the gospel
according to his apostles. It is a small gate and a narrow road. It is
free, but it costs everything. And though it is appropriated by faith
and repentance, it cannot fail to produce the fruit of true righteousness in the life and behavior of the believer.

[4]John F. MacArthur, *The MacArthur New Testament Commentary: Hebrews*
(Chicago: Moody Press, 1983).
[5]John F. MacArthur, *Faith Works: The Gospel According to the Apostles*
(Dallas: Word, 1993).

Appendix 2
The Gospel According to
Historic Christianity

Those who want to eliminate Jesus' lordship from the gospel message often insinuate that it is heresy equal to Galatian legalism to demand that sinners forsake their sins, commit themselves to Christ, obey his commands, and surrender to him.[1] It is a galling and reckless allegation, which indicts some of the true church's finest leaders over the span of nearly twenty centuries.

Some attempt to portray "lordship salvation" as a new doctrine. One example is Zane Hodges, who writes:

> In the same way [as first-century legalism], the most telling modern assaults on the integrity of the Gospel do not deny the cruciality of faith in Christ. On the contrary, they insist on it. But to faith are added other conditions, or provisos, by which the essential nature of the Gospel is radically transformed. Often, in fact, a distinction is drawn between the kind of faith which saves and the kind which does not. But the kind of faith which *does* save is always seen to be the kind that results in some form of overt obedience. By this means, the obedience itself becomes at least an implicit part of the transaction between man and God. "Saving" faith has thus been subtly redefined in terms of its fruits. In the process, the unconditional freeness of the Gospel offer is seriously, if not fatally, compromised.[2]

So in Hodges' estimation, the concept that faith necessarily produces obedience is a new invention and a serious threat to the integrity of the gospel. He equates it with the danger posed to the early church by the Judaizers.

That is a grave charge. Is it substantiated by church history? Not at

---

[1]Cf. Charles C. Ryrie, *Balancing the Christian Life* (Chicago: Moody Press, 1969), 170, where Ryrie writes, "The message of faith only and the message of faith plus commitment of life cannot both be the gospel; therefore, one of them is a false gospel and comes under the curse of perverting the gospel or preaching another gospel (Gal. 1:6–9)."

[2]Zane C. Hodges, *The Gospel Under Siege* (Dallas: Redención Viva, 1981), 4.

all. The truth is, what Hodges decries as a "modern assault" on the gospel is exactly what the true church has always believed. All the greatest saints throughout centuries of church history have repudiated the notion that salvation effects anything less than the complete transformation of a believer's character, behavior, and way of life.

For example, in the *Didache,* one of the earliest of all extrabiblical church writings, written perhaps as early as the end of the first century, we read: "Every prophet who teaches the truth but fails to practice what he preaches is a false prophet."[3]

From the words of Ignatius, the Bishop of Antioch, writing near the beginning of the second century, we read, "What matters is not a momentary act of professing, but being persistently motivated by faith."[4]

Another of the earliest church writings, known as the *Second Epistle of Clement to the Corinthians,* penned about A.D. 100, contains these words:

> Let us not merely call Him Lord, for that will not save us. For He says, "Not everyone who says to me, Lord, Lord, will be saved, but he who does what is right." Thus, brothers, let us acknowledge him by our actions. . . . This world and the world to come are two enemies. This one means adultery, corruption, avarice, and deceit, while the other gives them up. We cannot, then, be friends of both. To get the one, we must give the other up.[5]

Augustine, writing in A.D. 412, described works of righteousness as an inevitable proof of the operation of the Holy Spirit in one's life:

> We for our part assert that the human will is so divinely aided towards the doing of righteousness that, . . . besides the teaching which instructs him how he ought to live, he receives also the Holy Spirit, through which there arises in his heart a delight in and a love of that supreme and unchangeable Good which is God; and this arises now, while he walks by faith and not by sight. That by this earnest, as it were, of the free gift he may burn to cleave to his Maker, and be on fire to approach to a share in that true light. . . . But to the end that we may feel this affection "the love of God is shed abroad in our hearts" not "through the free choice which springs from ourselves," but "through the Holy Spirit which has been given to us" (Romans 4:5).[6]

[3]Cyril C. Richardson, ed., *Early Christian Fathers* (New York: Macmillan, 1970), 177.
[4]Ibid., 92.
[5]Ibid., 194–95.
[6]Henry Bettenson, ed., *Documents of the Christian Church* (New York: Oxford Univ. Press, 1963), 54.

In the years after Augustine's death, his doctrine gave way to semi-Pelagianism, the teaching that the sinner's own will and efforts are the ultimate determining factor in salvation. Catholicism began to place more and more emphasis on sacramental works. Then monasticism, sacerdotalism, and Romanism eventually eroded the organized church's understanding of salvation. The prevailing view of redemption came to be an unbiblical notion that people must perform meritorious works to earn favor with God. Celibacy, solitude, and self-flagellation were seen as some of the means to appease him. The Dark Ages descended on the world, all but obscuring the light of the true gospel.

When the Reformers rediscovered the truth of justification by faith, the darkness was finally dispelled. The Reformers began to teach again that divine sovereignty, not human will, is the determining factor in salvation. The heart of their doctrine was the truth that faith, not works, is the instrument through which sinners obtain salvation. That truth freed multitudes from the religious slavery that Romanism had imposed on Christendom.

But did Reformation theology allow for a brand of faith that does not produce practical righteousness? Certainly not. The clear conviction of all the leading Reformers was that true faith inevitably manifests itself in good works.

The incident that symbolically marked the beginning of the Reformation was Martin Luther's posting of his *Ninety-Five Theses* on the door of the Wittenberg Castle Church in 1517. The first four theses show clearly what Luther thought of the necessity of good works:

1. Our Lord and Master Jesus Christ, in saying "Repent ye, etc.," meant the whole life of the faithful to be an act of repentance.

2. This saying cannot be understood of the sacrament of penance (i.e., of confession and absolution), which is administered by the priesthood.

3. Yet he does not mean interior repentance only; nay, interior repentance is void if it does not externally produce different kinds of mortifications of the flesh.

4. And so penance remains while self-hate remains (i.e., true interior penitence); namely, right up to entrance into the kingdom of heaven.[7]

Luther also wrote:

[7]Ibid., 186.

When we have thus taught faith in Christ, then do we teach also good works. Because thou hast laid hold upon Christ by faith, through whom thou art made righteous, begin now to work well. Love God and thy neighbour, call upon God, give thanks unto him, praise him, confess him. Do good to thy neighbour and serve him: fulfill thine office. These are good works indeed, *which flow out of this faith*.[8]

"Luther believed that faith brought all religious activities along with it. . . . While he had condemned mere legal good works, intended to procure blessedness for the doer, he defended good works arising from faith. Good works are, according to him, the end and aim of faith."[9] "For Luther, good works are not determinative of one's relation to God; they follow from faith as day follows night, as good fruit comes from a good tree. Where there are no good works, there is no faith."[10] Luther wrote, "If (good) works and love do not blossom forth, it is not genuine faith, the gospel has not yet gained a foothold, and Christ is not yet rightly known."[11]

Although Luther fought intensely for the truth that we are saved by faith and not by good works, he never wavered from insisting that works are necessary to validate faith. In the preface to his famous commentary on Romans, he wrote:

Faith is not something dreamed, a human illusion, although this is what many people understand by the term. Whenever they see that it is not followed either by an improvement in morals or by good works, while much is still being said about faith, they fall into the error of declaring that faith is not enough, that we must do "works" if we are to become upright and attain salvation. The reason is that, when they hear the gospel, they miss the point; in their hearts, and out of their own resources, they conjure up an idea which they call "belief," which they treat as genuine faith. All the same, it is but a human fabrication, an idea without a corresponding experience in the depths of the heart. It is therefore ineffective and not followed by a better kind of life.

Faith, however, is something that God effects in us. It changes us and we are reborn from God, John 1. Faith puts the old Adam to death and makes us quite different men in heart, in mind, and in all our powers; and it is accompanied by the Holy Spirit. O, when it comes to faith, what a living, creative, active, powerful thing it is. It cannot do other than good at all times. It never waits to ask whether there is some good work to do, rather, before the question is raised, it has done the deed, and

[8]John Dillenberger, ed., *Martin Luther* (New York: Doubleday, 1961), 111–12 (emphasis added).
[9]Karl Theime, "Good Works,' *The New Schaff-Herzog Religious Encyclopedia* (Grand Rapids: Baker, 1977), 5:19–22.
[10]Dillenberger, *Martin Luther*, xxix.
[11]Ibid., 18.

keeps on doing it. A man not active in this way is a man without faith. He is groping about for faith and searching for good works, but knows neither what faith is nor what good works are. Nevertheless, he keeps on talking nonsense about faith and good works.

. . . It is impossible, indeed, to separate works from faith, just as it is impossible to separate heat and light from fire.[12]

Philip Melancthon, an associate of Luther and another leading Reformer, wrote:

It must be obvious that if conversion to God does not happen, and the heart continues in sin against conscience, that there is no true faith that desires or receives forgiveness of sins. The Holy Spirit is not in a heart in which there is no fear of God, but instead a continuing defiance. As clearly expressed, I Corinthians 6:9f., "Whores, adulterers, etc., will not inherit the kingdom of heaven."[13]

Virtually all the creeds that came out of the Reformation identified good works as the inevitable expression of saving faith. The Augsburg Confession of 1530 said:

Moreover, ours teach that it is necessary to do good works; not that we may trust that we deserve grace by them, but because it is the will of God that we should do them. By faith alone is apprehended remission of sins and grace. And because the Holy Spirit is received by faith, our hearts are now renewed, and so put on new affections, so that they are able to bring forth good works. For thus saith Ambrose:"Faith is the begetter of a good will and of good actions."[14]

The Belgic Confession of 1561 reads:

We believe that this true faith, being wrought in man by the hearing of the Word of God and the operation of the Holy Ghost, doth regenerate and make him a new man, causing him to live a new life, and freeing him from the bondage of sin. Therefore it is so far from being true, that this justifying faith makes men remiss in a pious and holy life, that on the contrary without it they would never do any thing out of love to God, but only out of self-love or fear of damnation. Therefore it is impossible that this holy faith can be unfruitful in man.[15]

The Heidelberg Catechism (1563) asks, "But does this doctrine [justification by faith] make men careless and profane?" and offers this answer: "No; for it is impossible that those who are implanted

[12]Ibid., 23–24.

[13]Clyde L. Manschreck, ed. and trans., *Melancthon on Christian Doctrine* (Grand Rapids: Baker, 1965), 182.

[14]Phillip Schaff, ed., *Creeds of Christendom*, 3 vols. (Grand Rapids: Baker, 1977), 3:24–25.

[15]Ibid., 3:410–13.

into Christ by true faith, should not bring forth fruits of thankfulness."[16]

The Canons of the Synod of Dort (1619) describe the work of the Holy Spirit in regeneration:

> He pervades the inmost recesses of the man; he opens the closed and softens the hardened heart, and circumcises that which was uncircumcised; infuses new qualities into the will, which, though heretofore dead, he quickens; from being evil, disobedient, and refractory, he renders it good, obedient, and pliable; actuates and strengthens it, that, like a good tree, it may bring forth the fruits of good actions.[17]

The Westminster Confession of Faith (1647) summarized the doctrine of sanctification:

> They who are effectually called and regenerated, having a new heart and a new spirit created in them, are further sanctified, really and personally, through the virtue of Christ's death and resurrection, by His Word and Spirit dwelling in them; the dominion of the whole body of sin is destroyed, and the several lusts thereof are more and more weakened and mortified, and they are more and more quickened and strengthened, in all saving graces, to the practice of true holiness, without which no man shall see the Lord. . . . Although the remaining corruption, for a time may much prevail, yet, through the continual supply of strength from the sanctifying Spirit of Christ, the regenerate part doth overcome; and so the saints grow in grace, perfecting holiness in the fear of God.[18]

Historic Protestant theology has seen and underscored the truth that practical righteousness is an essential and inevitable result of saving faith. Reformer Ulrich Zwingli viewed faith as an ongoing work of the Holy Spirit in the believer. Thus he believed true faith could never be slothful or inactive but would produce good works in every true Christian. Those works, Zwingli taught, were the proof of a believer's election and the necessary evidence of faith.[19]

John Calvin wrote:

> We dream not of a faith which is devoid of good works, nor of a justification which can exist without them. . . . Would ye then obtain justification in Christ? You must previously possess Christ. But you cannot possess him without being made a partaker of his sanctification:

[16]*Heidelberg Catechism* (Freeman, S.Dak.: Pine Hill, 1979), 75.
[17]Schaff, *Creeds of Christendom*, 3:590–91.
[18]Ibid., 629–30.
[19]Basil Hall, "Ulrich Zwingli," Hubert Cunliffe-Jones, ed., *A History of Christian Doctrine* (Philadelphia: Fortress, 1978), 362.

for Christ cannot be divided. . . . Thus it appears how true it is that we are justified not without, and yet not by works.[20]

In a published debate with a Catholic Cardinal, Jacopo Sadoleto, Calvin wrote:

We deny that good works have any share in justification, but we claim full authority for them in the lives of the righteous. . . . It is obvious that gratuitous [grace-wrought] righteousness is necessarily connected with regeneration. Therefore, if you would duly understand how inseparable faith and works are, look to Christ, who, as the Apostle teaches (1 Cor. i. 30) has been given to us for justification and for sanctification. Wherever, therefore, that righteousness of faith, which we maintain to be gratuitous, is, there too Christ is, and where Christ is, there too is the Spirit of holiness, who regenerates the soul to newness of life. On the contrary, where zeal for integrity and holiness is not vigor, there neither is the Spirit of Christ nor Christ himself; and wherever Christ is not, there is no righteousness, nay, there is no faith; for faith cannot apprehend Christ for righteousness without the Spirit of sanctification.[21]

The Puritans in particular wrote much about the nature of saving faith and the role of righteous works in the life of the believer. In 1658, William Guthrie wrote as clear a statement of "lordship salvation" as has ever been put to paper:

A godly man may argue thus, Whosoever receive Christ are justly reputed the children of God—"But as many as received Him, to them gave He power to become the sons of God" (John 1:12); but I have received Christ in all the ways which the word there can import: for I am pleased with the device of salvation by Christ, I agree to the terms, I welcome the offer of Christ in all His offices, as a King to rule over me, a Priest to offer sacrifice and intercede for me, a Prophet to teach me; I lay out my heart for Him and towards Him, resting on Him as I am able. What else can be meant by the word RECEIVING? . . .

   The *second* great mark of a gracious state, and true saving interest in Jesus Christ, is the new creature—"If any man be in Christ, he is a new creature." (2 Cor. 5:17). . . . In all who do warrantably pretend to Christ, this new creature must be; . . . This new creature is called the "new man" (Col. 3:10), which points out the extent of it. It is not simply a new tongue or new hand, but a new man. There is a principle of new life and motion put in the man, which is the new heart; which new principle of life sendest for the acts of life, or of "conformity to the

[20]John Calvin, *Institutes of the Christian Religion*, 2 vols. (Grand Rapids: Zondervan, 1972), 2:98–99.
[21]John C. Olin, ed., *A Reformation Debate* (Grand Rapids: Baker, 1966), 68.

image" of him who created it,so that the party is renewed in some measure of every way (Col. 3:10.)[22]

In 1672, a work by Joseph Alleine was published posthumously, in which he wrote:

Conversion then, lies in the thorough change both of the heart and life. . . . If ever you would be savingly converted, you must despair of doing it in your own strength. It is a resurrection from the dead (Eph ii 1), a new creation (Gal vi 15; Eph ii 10), a work of absolute omnipotence (Eph i 19). Are not these out of the reach of human power? If you have no more than you had by your first birth, a good nature, a meek and chaste temper etc., you are a stranger to true conversion. This is a supernatural work.[23].

Puritan Thomas Vincent's explanation of The Westminster Shorter Catechism (1674) contains these lessons, which read almost as if they were written specifically to refute the gospel that has become popular in our time:

Q. 7. How is Jesus Christ to be received by faith?

A. Jesus Christ is to be received by faith as he is offered to us in the gospel.

Q. 8. How is Jesus Christ offered to us in the gospel?

A. Jesus Christ is offered to us in the gospel, as priest, prophet, and king; and so we must receive him, if we would be saved by him.

Q. 9. When doth the soul rest upon him for salvation?

A. The soul doth rest upon Christ for salvation when, being convinced of its lost condition by reason of sin, and its own inability, together with all creatures' insufficiency, to recover it out of this estate, and having a discovery and persuasion of Christ's ability and willingness to save, it doth let go all hold on the creatures, and renounce its own righteousness, and so lay hold on Christ, rely upon him, and put confidence in him, and in him alone, for salvation.

Q. *What is repentance unto life?*

A. Repentance unto life is a saving grace, whereby a sinner, out of a true sense of his sin, and apprehension of the mercy of God in Christ, doth, with grief and hatred of his sin, turn from it unto God, with full purpose of, and endeavour after, new obedience.

Q. 3. *Wherein doth repentance unto life consist?*

[22]William Guthrie, *The Christian's Great Interest* (Edinburgh: Banner of Truth, 1982), 24–25, 76.

[23]Joseph Alleine, *An Alarm to the Unconverted* (Marshallton, Del.: National Foundation for Christian Education, n.d.), 26–27.

A. Repentance unto life doth chiefly consist in two things—1. In turning from sin, and forsaking it. "Repent, and turn yourselves from all your transgressions: so iniquity shall not be your ruin."—Ezek. xviii. 30. "He that covereth his sins shall not prosper: but whose confesseth and forsaketh them shall find mercy."—Prov. xxviii. 13. 2. In turning unto God. "Let the wicked forsake his way, and the unrighteous man his thoughts; and let him return to the Lord, and he will have mercy upon him, and to our God, for he will abundantly pardon."—Isa. lv. 7.

Q. 15. *What is that turning from sin which is part of true repentance?*

A. The turning from sin which is a part of true repentance, doth consist in two things—1. In a turning from all gross sins, in regard of our course and conversation. 2. In a turning from all other sins, in regard of our hearts and affections.

Q. 16. *Do such as truly repent of sin never return again unto the practice of the same sins which they have repented of?*

A. 1. Such as have truly repented of sin do never return unto the practice of it, so as to live in a course of sin, as they did before; and where any, after repentance, do return unto a course of sin, it is an evident sign that their repentance was not of the right kind. 2. Some have truly repented of their sins, although they may be overtaken and surprised by temptations, so as to fall into the commission of the same sins which they have repented of, yet they do not lie in them, but get up again, and with bitter grief bewail them, and return again unto the Lord.[24]

Thomas Watson wrote in 1692:

We must have conformity to Him in grace, before we can have communion with Him in glory. Grace and glory are linked and chained together. Grace precedes glory, as the morning star ushers in the sun. God will have us qualified and fitted for a state of blessedness. Drunkards and swearers are not fit to enjoy God in glory; the Lord will not lay such vipers in His bosom. Only the "pure in heart shall see God."[25]

Thomas Manton's commentary on James, first published in 1693, contains these words:

Works are an evidence of true faith. Graces are not dead, useless habits; they will have some effects and operations when they are weakest and in their infancy. . . . This is the evidence by which we must judge, and this is the evidence by which Christ will judge. . . . Works are not a

[24]Thomas Vincent, *The Shorter Catechism of the Westminster Assembly Explained and Proved from Scripture* (Edinburgh: Banner of Truth, 1980), 226–31.

[25]Thomas Watson, *A Body of Divinity* (Grand Rapids: Baker, 1979), 16.

ground of confidence, but an evidence; not the foundations of faith, but the encouragements of assurance. Comfort may be increased by the sight of good works, but it is not built upon them; they are seeds of hope, not props of confidence; sweet evidences of election, not causes; happy presages and beginnings of glory; in short, they can manifest an interest, but not merit it.[26]

"Manton held strongly to the perseverance of God's elect; but that did not hinder him from teaching that holiness is the grand distinguishing mark of God's people, and that he who talks of 'never perishing' while he continues in wilful sin, is a hypocrite and a self-deceiver."[27]

Another Puritan, Thomas Goodwin wrote:

Where mourning for offending God is wanting, there is no sign of any good will yet wrought in the heart to God, nor of love to him, without which God will never accept a man. . . .

Else there is no hope of amendment. God will not pardon till he sees hopes of amendment. Now, until a man confess his sin, and that with bitterness, it is a sign he loves it, Job xx. 12–14. Whilst he hides it, spares it, and forsakes it not, it is sweet in his mouth; and therefore till he confess it, and mourn for it, it is a sign it is not bitter to him, and so he will not forsake it. A man will never leave sin till he find bitterness in it; and, if so, then he will be in bitterness for it, Zech. xii. 10; and "godly sorrow works repentance," 2 Cor. vii. 10.[28]

Commentator Matthew Henry, writing at the beginning of the 1700s, said:

We are too apt to rest in a bare profession of faith, and to think that this will save us; it is a cheap and easy religion to say, "We believe the articles of the Christian faith;" but it is a great delusion to imagine that this is enough to bring us to heaven. Those who argue thus wrong God, and put a cheat upon their own souls; a mock-faith is as hateful as mock-charity, and both show a heart dead to all real godliness. You may as soon take pleasure in a dead body, void of soul, or sense, or action, as God take pleasure in a dead faith, where there are no works. . . . Those works which evidence true faith must be works of self-denial, and such as God himself commands. . . . The most plausible profession of faith, without works, is dead. . . . We must not think that either, without the

[26]Thomas Manton, *A Commentary on James* (Edinburgh: Banner of Truth, 1963), 239.

[27]J. C. Ryle, *Estimate of Manton*, cited in A. W. Pink, *Gleanings from the Scriptures: Man's Total Depravity* (Chicago: Moody Press, 1969), 289.

[28]Thomas Goodwin, *The Work of the Holy Spirit in Our Salvation* (Edinburgh: Banner of Truth, 1979), 129.

other, will justify and save us. This is the grace of God wherein we stand, and we should stand to it.[29]

Thomas Boston, Scottish church leader in the late seventeenth and early eighteenth centuries, wrote:

We are to receive Christ as our King, renouncing the dominion of sin, death, the devil, and the world, and wholly giving up ourselves to him, to be ruled by him as our head: Isa. xxvi. 13, "O Lord our God, other lords besides thee have had dominion over us: but by thee only will we make mention of thy name." Psalm ii. ult., "Kiss ye the Son, lest he be angry, and ye perish from the way, when his wrath is kindled but a little: blessed are all they that put their trust in him." We are to make use of him as our King, daily applying and trusting to him, for life, strength, and defence, and victory over our enemies: 2 Tim. ii. 1, "Thou therefore, my son, be strong in the grace that is in Christ Jesus." 2 Cor. i. 10, "God delivered us from so great a death, and doth deliver: in whom we trust that he will deliver us."[30]

George Whitefield, the great preacher and defender of the faith in Britain and colonial America, wrote in his journal of August 6, 1739,

Had a conference after sermon with one, who I fear with some others, maintained antinomian principles. From such, may all that know them turn away; for though, (to use the words of our Church Article) good works, which are the fruits of faith, cannot put away our sins, or endure the severity of God's judgment (that is, cannot justify us), yet they follow after justification, and do spring out necessarily of a true and lively faith, insomuch that by them a lively faith may be as evidently known as a tree discerned by the fruit.[31]

Jonathan Edwards, possibly the finest preacher and clearest theological thinker of the 1700s, wrote:

That religion which God requires, and will accept, does not consist in weak, dull, and lifeless wishes, raising us but a little above a state of indifference. God, in his word, greatly insists upon it, that we be in good earnest, fervent in spirit, and our hearts vigorously engaged in religion. . . .

Those who thus insist on persons' living by faith, when they have no experience, and are in very bad frames, are also very absurd in their notions of faith. What they mean by faith is, believing that they are in a

[29]Matthew Henry, *Commentary on the Whole Bible* (Old Tappan, N.J.: Revell, n.d.), 981–83.

[30]Thomas Boston, "A Brief Explication of the First Part of the Assembly's Shorter Catechism," in *The Complete Works of the Late Rev. Thomas Boston, Ettrick*, 12 vols. (Wheaton, Ill.: Roberts, 1980 reprint), 7:67–68.

[31]George Whitefield, *Journals* (Edinburgh: Banner of Truth, 1960), 323–24.

good estate. Hence they count it a dreadful sin for them to doubt of their state, whatever frames they are in, and whatever wicked things they do, because it is the great and heinous sin of unbelief; and he is the best man, and puts most honour upon God, that maintains his hope of his good estate the most confidently and immovably, when he has the least light or experience; that is to say, when he is in the worst frame and way; because forsooth, that it is a sign that he is strong in faith, giving glory to God, and against hope believes in hope. But from what Bible do they learn this notion of faith, that it is a man's confidently believing that he is in a good estate? If this be faith, the Pharisees had faith in an eminent degree; some of whom Christ teaches, committed the unpardonable sin against the Holy Ghost. . . .

. . . It may be from unbelief, or because they have so little faith, that they have so little evidence of their good estate. If they have more experience of the actings of faith, and so more experience of the exercise of grace, they would have clearer evidence that their state was good; and so their doubts would be removed. . . .

. . . It is not God's design that men should obtain assurance in any other way than by mortifying corruption, increasing in grace, and obtaining the lively exercises of it. And although self-examination be a duty of great use and importance, and by no means to be neglected; yet it is not the principal means, by which the saints do get satisfaction of their good estate. Assurance is not to be obtained so much by self-examination, as by action. The apostle Paul sought assurance chiefly this way, even by forgetting the things that were behind, and reaching forth unto those things that were before, pressing towards the mark for the prize of the high calling of God in Christ Jesus; if by any means he might attain unto the resurrection of the dead. And it was by this means chiefly that he obtained assurance, 1 Cor. ix. 26. "I therefore so run, as not uncertainly." He obtained assurance of winning the prize more by running than considering. . . . Giving all diligence to grow in grace, by adding to faith, virtue, etc., is the direction that the apostle Peter gives us, for making our calling and election sure, and having an entrance ministered to us abundantly into Christ's everlasting kingdom. Without this, our eyes will be dim, and we shall be as men in the dark; we cannot plainly see either the forgiveness of our sins past, our heavenly inheritance that is future, and far off, 2 Pet. i. 5–11.[32]

John Gill, a British Baptist minister, wrote in 1767:

The foundation of *sanctification* is laid in *regeneration*; as it is a holy principle, it is first formed in that; the new creature, or new man, is created in righteousness and true holiness; and it appears in *effectual vocation*, which is an *holy calling*; and is to be seen in conversion, which is a turning of men *from their iniquities*: and that holiness which

[32]Edward Hickman, ed., *The Works of Jonathan Edwards* (Edinburgh: Banner of Truth, 1979), 237, 259, 263.

is begun in regeneration, and is manifest in effectual calling and conversion, is carried on in sanctification, which is a gradual and progressive work, and issues and is finished in glorification.[33]

Describing genuine believers, Gill wrote:

In subjection to him, as King of saints; they not only receive him as their Prophet, to teach and instruct them, and embrace his doctrines; and as their Priest, by whose sacrifice their sins are expiated; but as their King, to whose laws and ordinances they cheerfully submit; esteeming his precepts, concerning all things, to be right, none of his commandments grievous; but from a principle of love to him, keep and observe them.[34]

Surely the best-known of all preachers of the 1800s was Charles Haddon Spurgeon. In a book on personal evangelism, he wrote:

Another proof of the conquest of a soul for Christ will be found in *a real change of life*. If the man does not live differently from what he did before, both at home and abroad, his repentance needs to be repented of, and his conversion is a fiction. Not only action and language, but spirit and temper must be changed. . . . Abiding under the power of any known sin is a mark of our being the servants of sin, for "his servants ye are to whom ye obey." Idle are the boasts of a man who harbors within himself the love of any transgression. He may feel what he likes, and believe what he likes, he is still in the gall of bitterness and the bonds of iniquity while a single sin rules his heart and life. True regeneration implants a hatred of all evil; and where one sin is delighted in, the evidence is fatal to a sound hope. . . .

There must be a harmony between the life and the profession. A Christian professes to renounce sin; and if he does not do so, his very name is an imposture.[35]

In his autobiography, Spurgeon recalled his battle against antinomianism:

In my first pastorate, I had often to battle with Antinomians—that is, people who held that, because they believed themselves to be elect, they might live as they liked. I hope that heresy has to a great extent died out, but it was sadly prevalent in my early ministerial days. I knew one man, who stood on the table of a public-house, and held a glass of gin in his hand, declaring all the while that he was one of the chosen people of God. They kicked him out of the public-house, and when I heard of it, I felt that it served him right. Even those ungodly men said that they did not want any such "elect" people there. There is no one

[33]John Gill, *A Body of Divinity* (Grand Rapids: Sovereign Grace, 1971), 552.
[34]Ibid., 555.
[35]Charles H. Spurgeon, *The Soul Winner* (Pasadena, Tex.: Pilgrim, 1978), 32–33.

who can live in sin—drinking, swearing, lying, and so on—who can truly declare that he is one of the Lord's chosen people. . . . From my very soul, I detest everything that in the least savours of the Antinomianism which leads people to prate about being secure in Christ while they are living in sin. We cannot be saved *by* or *for* our good works, neither can we be saved *without* good works. Christ never will save any of His people *in* their sins; he saves His people *from* their sins. If a man is not desiring to live a holy life in the sight of God, with the help of the Holy Spirit, he is still "in the gall of bitterness, and in the bond of iniquity." . . . The idea of "saving faith" apart from good works, is ridiculous. The saved man is not a perfect man, but his heart's desire is to become perfect, he is always panting after perfection, and the day will come when he will be perfected, after the image of his once crucified and now glorified Saviour, in knowledge and true holiness.

While I was minister at Waterbeach, I used to have a man sitting in front of the gallery, who would always nod his head when I was preaching what he considered sound doctrine, although he was about as bad an old hypocrite as ever lived. When I talked about justification, down went his head; when I preached about imputed righteousness, down it went again. I was a dear good man in his estimation, without doubt. So I thought I would cure him of nodding, or at least make his head keep still for once; so I remarked, "There is a great deal of difference between God electing you, and your electing yourself; a vast deal of difference between God justifying you by His Spirit, and your justifying yourself by a false belief, or presumption; this is the difference," said I—and the old man at once put me down as a rank Arminian—"you who have elected yourselves, and justified yourselves, have no marks of the Spirit of God; you have no evidence of genuine piety, you are not holy men and women, you can live in sin, you can walk as sinners walk, you have the image of the devil upon you, and yet you call yourselves the children of God. One of the first evidences that anyone is a child of God is that he hates sin with a perfect hatred, and seeks to live a holy, Christlike life." The old Antinomian did not approve of that doctrine, but I knew that I was preaching what was revealed in the Word of God.[36]

Bishop J. C. Ryle, an evangelical Anglican bishop, wrote these stinging words nearly a century ago:

I doubt, indeed, whether we have any warrant for saying that a man can possibly be *converted* without being consecrated to God! . . . If he was not consecrated to God in the very day that he was converted and born again, I do not know what conversion means. Are not men in danger of undervaluing and underrating the immense blessedness of conversion? Are they not, when they urge on believers the "higher life"

[36]Charles H. Spurgeon, *Autobiography: Volume 1: The Early Years, 1834–1859* (Edinburgh: Banner of Truth, 1962), 224–25.

as a second conversion, underrating the length, and breadth, and depth, and height, of that great first chapter which Scripture calls the new birth, the new creation, the spiritual resurrection? I may be mistaken. But I have sometimes thought, while reading the strong language used by many about "consecration," in the last few years, that those who use it must have had previously a singularly low and inadequate view of "conversion," if indeed they knew anything about conversion at all. In short, I have almost suspected that when they were *consecrated,* they were in reality *converted* for the first time![37]

Benjamin B. Warfield, professor of theology at Princeton, wrote this at the turn of the century in an essay on faith:

No true faith has arisen unless there has been a perception of the object to be believed or believed in, an assent to its worthiness to be believed or believed in, and a commitment of ourselves to it as true and trustworthy. . . . We cannot be said to believe that which we distrust too much to commit ourselves to it.[38]

R. A. Torrey, then president of Moody Bible Institute, in his textbook on personal evangelism, told students to make the lordship of Christ a focus of the gospel invitation to a sinner: "Lead him as directly as you can to accept Jesus Christ as a personal Saviour, and to surrender to Him as his Lord and Master."[39]

W. H. Griffith Thomas, an early dispensationalist and founder of Dallas Theological Seminary, acknowledged the inseparability of justification and sanctification,[40] as well as the necessity of good works as the certain outcome of faith.[41] He succinctly explained, "St. Paul uses Gen. xv to prove the necessity of faith; St. James uses Gen. xxii to prove the necessity of works. St. Paul teaches that works must spring from faith; St. James teaches that faith must be proved by works."[42] Commenting on Romans 14, he wrote:

Our relation to Christ is based on His death and resurrection and this means His Lordship. Indeed the Lordship of Christ over the lives of His people was the very purpose for which He died and rose again. We have to acknowledge Christ as our Lord. Sin is rebellion, and *it is only as we surrender to Him as Lord that we receive our pardon from Him as our Savior.* We have to admit Him to reign on the throne of the heart, and *it*

[37]John Charles Ryle, *Holiness* (Grand Rapids: Baker, 1979), 57.

[38]Benjamin B. Warfield, *Biblical and Theological Studies* (Grand Rapids: Baker, 1968), 402–3.

[39]R. A. Torrey, *How to Work for Christ* (Old Tappan, N.J.: Revell, n.d.), 32.

[40]W. H. Griffith Thomas, *The Principles of Theology* (Grand Rapids: Baker, 1979), 186–87.

[41]Ibid., 200–205.

[42]Ibid., 205.

is only when He is glorified in our hearts as King that the Holy Spirit enters and abides.[43]

About twenty-five years ago, Oswald T. Allis, writing on the two covenants, said:

> By the covenant of grace the Christian is not offered faith as an easy substitute for works of righteousness. It offers him an unmerited and unearned righteousness, the righteousness of Christ received by faith which challenges him and demands that he walk worthy of his high calling that he learn to say as Paul did, "the love of Christ constraineth us." The fact that he is not under the law as a basis of works-salvation does not set before the Christian a lower standard than that of the Mosaic law, but a far higher one.... When Jesus gave his disciples a new commandment, "As I have loved you that ye also love one another," He set them a standard of obedience that surpassed the commandment of the Law, "Thou shalt love thy neighbor as thyself." Little wonder then that Paul answers the question, "Do we then make void the law through faith?" with the emphatic words, "God forbid: yea, we establish the law."[44]

Under the heading "Antinomianism," Allis added:

> The whole teaching of the New Testament is that justification has as its objective sanctification, redemption from all iniquity. A faith which does not bring forth fruit unto righteousness is not a living faith. The bandit who comes secretly to the priest for confession and absolution only that he may with a quieted conscience return to his life of thievery and violence is like the Jews of old who made the Temple "a den of robbers," a refuge against the consequences of their evil deeds.[45]

Other recent writers have expressed shock at what they see plainly as spreading antinomianism in the twentieth-century church. A. W. Pink, for example, recognized the failure of modern evangelism as early as 1937. He wrote:

> The terms of Christ's salvation are erroneously stated by the present-day evangelist. With very rare exceptions he tells his hearers that salvation is by grace and is received as a free gift; that Christ has done everything for the sinner, and nothing remains except for him to "believe"—to trust in the infinite merits of his blood. And so widely does this conception now prevail in "orthodox" circles, so frequently has it been dinned in their ears, so deeply has it taken root in their minds, that for

[43]W. H. Griffith Thomas, *St. Paul's Epistle to the Romans* (Grand Rapids: Eerdmans, n.d.), 371, emphasis added.

[44]Oswald T. Allis, "The Covenant of Works," in Carl F. H. Henry, ed., *Basic Christian Doctrines* (Grand Rapids: Baker, 1962), 98.

[45]Ibid., 99.

one to now challenge it and denounce it as being so inadequate and one-sided as to be deceptive and erroneous, is for him to instantly court the stigma of being a heretic, and to be charged with dishonoring the finished work of Christ by inculcating salvation by works. . . . Salvation is by grace, by grace alone. . . . Nevertheless, Divine grace is not exercised at the expense of holiness, for it never compromises with sin. It is also true that salvation is a free gift, but an empty hand must receive it, and not a hand which still tightly grasps the world. . . . A heart that is steeled in rebellion cannot savingly believe; it must first be broken. . . . Those preachers who tell sinners they may be saved without forsaking their idols, without repenting, without surrendering to the Lordship of Christ, are as erroneous and dangerous as others who insist that salvation is by works and that heaven must be earned by our own efforts.[46]

Pink also wrote:

Divine grace is not bestowed with the object of freeing men from their obligations but rather with that of supplying them with a powerful motive for more readily and gratefully discharging those obligations. To make God's favor a ground of exemption from the performance of duty comes perilously near to turning His grace into lasciviousness.[47]

A. W. Tozer, like Pink, turned the charge of heresy on those who presented a message of easy-believism. Many of his sermons and writings challenge the popular gospel of our day. His messages on 1 Peter were posthumously edited and published in a book appropriately titled *I Call It Heresy!* Tozer stated:

[Years ago] no one would ever dare to rise in a meeting and say, "I am a Christian" if he had not surrendered his whole being to God and had taken Jesus Christ as his Lord as well as his Saviour, and had brought himself under obedience to the will of the Lord. It was only then that he could say, "I am saved!"

Today, we let them say they are saved no matter how imperfect and incomplete the transaction, with the proviso that the deeper Christian life can be tacked on at some time in the future.

Can it be that we really think that we do not owe Jesus Christ our obedience?

We have owed Him our obedience ever since the second we cried out to Him for salvation, and if we do not give Him that obedience, I have reason to wonder if we are really converted!

I see things and I hear of things that Christian people are doing, and as I watch them operate within the profession of Christianity I do raise the question of whether they have been truly converted.

[46]Arthur W. Pink, "Signs of the Times," *Studies in the Scriptures,* 16:373–75.
[47]Pink, *Gleanings,* 291.

Brethren, I believe it is the result of faulty teaching to begin with. They thought of the Lord as a hospital and Jesus as chief of staff to fix up poor sinners that had gotten into trouble!

"Fix me up, Lord," they have insisted, "so that I can go my own way!"

That is bad teaching, brethren.[48]

Any doctrine that makes surrender to Christ's lordship optional is bad teaching. Clearly it is a departure from what Christians have always affirmed.

Thus "lordship salvation" is neither modern nor heretical but is the very heart of historic Christian soteriology. To label it as false teaching is foolhardy and thoughtless at best. To teach anything else is to withdraw from the mainstream of church teaching through the ages.

[48]A. W. Tozer, *I Call It Heresy!* (Harrisburg, Pa.: Christian Publications, 1974), 18–19.

Appendix 3
Answers to Common Questions

Within days after this book's initial publication, I began to receive mail from readers. In the first few weeks alone I answered more letters about this book than I had ever received on any other subject.

Five years later the mail is still coming in. My staff and I continue to respond individually to all readers' comments and questions. Here are some responses that represent the issues most commonly raised:

If your view of salvation is correct, how can we lead people to Christ and offer them immediate assurance? You seem to be saying that people need to seek assurance in their works.

First of all, I do not believe it is the task of the evangelist to "offer assurance." That is the Holy Spirit's work: "The Spirit Himself bears witness with our spirit that we are children of God" (Rom. 8:16).

Having said that, however, I do believe there is an immediate aspect to assurance, grounded in the promises of the gospel. How did the thief on the cross know he was saved? He had the Lord's own promise. We find many promises in Scripture that assure believers of their eternal destiny (e.g., John 3:16; 1 John 5:1). Those promises offer objective assurance to genuine believers. Even a brand-new believer can look to such promises and find a measure of assurance.

Other Scripture passages speak of subjective means of assurance. For example, 1 John 2:3 says, "By this we know that we have come to know Him, if we keep His commandments." This aspect of assurance grows and deepens as one walks consistently with the Lord. And Christians who persist in sin for a time forfeit this aspect of assurance for as long as they are grieving the Holy Spirit.

Both the objective and subjective means of assurance are spoken of in Romans 15:4: "Whatever was written in earlier times was written for our instruction, that through perseverance [subjective] and the encouragement of the Scriptures [objective] we might have hope."

Also it is important to understand what Scripture is teaching about subjective assurance. It is not that we seek assurance in *our works*, but that we gain assurance from sensing the *Spirit's work in us*.

Again, it is the Holy Spirit who bears witness with our spirit that we are children of God.

We do not gain assurance by convincing our intellect that we are saved. True assurance is not an academic issue. There are no formulas that can bring it about. It is an important part of the lifelong growth process of the Christian life. For more detail, see my book *Saved Without a Doubt* (Wheaton, Ill.: Victor Books, 1992).

You acknowledge that believers can and do sin for extended periods of time. How can such people know whether their sin is a temporary failure or proof that they are unsaved?

Obviously even in Scripture we see that believers sometimes sinned grievously and over long periods of time. David is one example (2 Sam. 11–12; Ps. 51); Lot is another (2 Peter 2:7–9). Christians who sin in such a fashion should not expect to enjoy assurance, however. Of course, true believers do not lose their salvation when they sin (cf. Rom. 8:35–39), but even David testified that he had forfeited the joy of salvation (Ps. 51:12).

When believers sin, they dishonor Christ (1 Cor. 6:15–17), they grieve the Holy Spirit (Eph. 4:30), and they subject themselves to the discipline of a loving Father (Heb. 12:5–7). If they can continue in sin without experiencing divine discipline, something is terribly wrong: "If you are without discipline, of which all have become partakers, then you are illegitimate children and not sons" (v. 8).

Moreover, our Lord established a process for dealing with sin among believers:

> If your brother sins, go and reprove him in private; if he listens to you, you have won your brother. But if he does not listen to you, take one or two more with you, so that by the mouth of two or three witnesses every fact may be confirmed. And if he refuses to listen to them, tell it to the church; and if he refuses to listen even to the church, let him be to you as a Gentile and a tax-gatherer. Truly I say to you, whatever you shall bind on earth shall be bound in heaven; and whatever you loose on earth shall be loosed in heaven. Again I say to you, that if two of you agree on earth about anything that they may ask, it shall be done for them by My Father who is in heaven. For where two or three have gathered together in My name, there I am in their midst (Matt. 18:15–20).

Notice that the discipline process Jesus outlined is specifically intended to answer the question of whether a person in sin is a true brother or an outsider. "If he listens to you [if he repents], you have won your brother" (v. 15). But ultimately, "if he refuses to listen even to the church, let him be to you as a Gentile and a tax-gatherer"

(v. 17)—that is, regard him as an unbeliever and pursue him evangelistically. The Lord goes on to state that he personally mediates his rule on earth through this process (v. 20).

No one who persists in willful, deliberate sin and rebellion against the Lord should be encouraged with any promise of assurance. If you know someone like that who professes faith in Christ, follow the process of Matthew 18 and call that person to repentance. But do not encourage him or her with the promise of security. Such a person may be clinging to a false hope.

I love Christ, but I struggle constantly with sin in my life. Should I doubt my salvation?

No. The perpetual struggle with sin was even Paul's experience (Rom. 7:7–25). All of us struggle continually with sinful thoughts, sinful attitudes, sinful habits, and sinful desires. It is those who do not struggle—those who deliberately and eagerly revel in their sin— who need to have their false sense of security shaken.

If all Christians have already yielded to Christ's lordship, why did Paul write Romans 12:1–2, commanding believers to make a once-for-all surrender?

Here is what Paul wrote:

> I urge you therefore, brethren, by the mercies of God, to present your bodies a living and holy sacrifice, acceptable to God, which is your spiritual service of worship. And do not be conformed to this world, but be transformed by the renewing of your mind, that you may prove what the will of God is, that which is good and acceptable and perfect.

Those words in no way imply that the Romans had not yet submitted to Christ. The phrase "present your bodies" is an aorist-tense verb in the Greek text, and some have tried to argue that it speaks of a first-time, once-for-all surrender. That is an overly simplistic understanding of the aorist tense. It is more accurate to understand the sense of Paul's command as calling for decisive, deliberate, but continuous surrender. Romans 6:17–18 proves that Paul knew these believers had "obeyed from the heart that form of doctrine which was delivered [to them]. Being then made free from sin, [they] became the servants of righteousness" (KJV). Obviously he was not now calling them to yield to Christ for the first time.

No one would argue that the command in verse 2 to "be transformed" negates the truth that these people were already transformed—new creations in Christ (2 Cor. 5:17). Similarly, in Ephesians 3:17, Paul prayed for the Ephesians that Christ would dwell in their hearts by faith. He was not implying that Christ did not yet dwell in their hearts by faith.

The simple teaching of Scripture is that faith, surrender, and the transformed life are not one-time events that never occur again. Believers are exhorted to have faith, surrender, and obey continuously. That does not mean they have never done those things before. In this life we can never have too many encouraging reminders to apply God's Word more diligently. God himself uses such commands as means to assure our perseverance.

Why do you use language like "forsake everything," "death to self," and "unconditional surrender"? The absoluteness of those demands is intimidating. Aren't you afraid you'll turn people away from Christ?

Actually, it was Jesus himself who said, "Whosoever he be of you that forsaketh not all that he hath, he cannot be my disciple" (Luke 14:33 KJV). And he said, "If anyone wishes to come after Me, let him deny himself, and take up his cross daily, and follow Me" (Luke 9:23).

Jesus also preached, "If your hand causes you to stumble, cut it off . . . and if your foot causes you to stumble, cut it off . . . and if your eye causes you to stumble, cast it out; it is better for you to enter the kingdom of God with one eye, than having two eyes, to be cast into hell" (Mark 9:43–47). And, "I came to set a man against his father, and a daughter against her mother, and a daughter-in-law against her mother-in-law. . . . He who does not take his cross and follow after Me is not worthy of Me" (Matt. 10:35, 38). And, "If anyone comes to Me, and does not hate his own father and mother and wife and children and brothers and sisters, yes, and even his own life, he cannot be My disciple" (Luke 14:26).

It was Jesus, after all, who first stated, "No one, after putting his hand to the plow and looking back, is fit for the kingdom of God" (Luke 9:62).

We could go on and on quoting from Jesus' hard sayings, which he often preached to unbelieving multitudes but never offset with any qualification. Clearly he was insisting on wholehearted commitment. He did not soften his demands with words that would accommodate the halfhearted.

Our Lord was certainly not fearful that people would be turned away by such hard demands. He said, "All that the Father gives Me shall come to Me" (John 6:37). Likewise, I am confident that those being drawn by the Father and convicted by the Holy Spirit will not be turned away by the straightforward truth of his Word.

You acknowledge that no one can obey perfectly. Doesn't that dampen the force of the demand for absolute surrender?

No one in the Old Testament obeyed Moses' law perfectly, either, but that did not diminish the standard of perfection established by the law.

The whole point is that the gospel calls for a response to Christ that is humanly impossible. To reduce the demands of the gospel so that anyone can respond with a nod of the head or a raising of the hand is the essence of easy-believism.

"Then who can be saved?" (Matt. 19:25) is the right question to ask. "With men this is impossible, but with God all things are possible" (v. 26). Conversion to Christ is a supernatural, divinely wrought miracle. The response of faith is born in the believer's heart through the gracious quickening work of God. That does not occur until we acknowledge (1) that he has a right to demand whatever he wishes from us, and (2) that our inability to respond with absolute obedience is only because of our own sinful wretchedness.

Where in the Bible is it taught that all believers will be spiritually fruitful? Does this mean there is no room for failure in the Christian life?

Of course we all experience some degree of failure, but *ultimate* failure—returning permanently to unbelief and wanton sin—is not possible for true Christians. Romans 8:29–30 guarantees that every believer will be ultimately conformed to the image of Christ. The Spirit of God indwells each believer (Rom. 8:9). We have been made completely new (2 Cor. 5:17). And we are being transformed into the image of Christ (2 Cor. 3:18). Each of those truths guarantees that we cannot experience ultimate failure.

The inevitability of fruit-bearing is repeatedly emphasized in Scripture. The basic principle of creation, stated in Genesis 1:11, is that everything bears fruit of its own kind. Here are just a few verses that expressly underscore this truth:

Proverbs 12:12—"The wicked desires the booty of evil men, but *the root of the righteous yields fruit.*"

Jeremiah 17:7–8—"Blessed is the man who trusts in the LORD and whose trust is the LORD. For he will be like a tree planted by the water, that extends its roots by a stream and will not fear when the heat comes; but its leaves will be green, and it will not be anxious in a year of drought *nor cease to yield fruit.*"

Matthew 3:10—"Every tree therefore that does not bear good fruit is cut down and thrown into the fire."

Matthew 7:17–19—"Even so, *every good tree bears good fruit;* but the bad tree bears bad fruit. A good tree cannot produce bad fruit, nor can a bad tree produce good fruit. Every tree that does not bear good fruit is cut down and thrown into the fire."

Matthew 12:33—"Either make the tree good, and its fruit good; or make the tree bad, and its fruit bad; for the tree is known by its fruit."

Matthew 13:23—"And the one on whom seed was sown on the good soil, this is the man who hears the word and understands it; who *indeed bears fruit,* and brings forth, some a hundredfold, some sixty, and some thirty."

Luke 6:43–44—"For there is no good tree which produces bad fruit; nor, on the other hand, a bad tree which produces good fruit. For each tree is known by its own fruit. For men do not gather figs from thorns, nor do they pick grapes from a briar bush."

John 15:5—"I am the vine, you are the branches; *he who abides in Me, and I in him, he bears much fruit;* for apart from Me you can do nothing."

Romans 7:4—"Therefore, my brethren, you also were made to die to the Law through the body of Christ, that you might be joined to another, to Him who was raised from the dead, *that we might bear fruit for God."*

One reader cited the thief on the cross as an exception to this rule. But that thief bore more fruit in a few minutes than many churchgoers bear in an entire lifetime. His repentance was manifested by a striking change in behavior. He did count the cost; he acknowledged that his cross was just and deserved. And he did bow to Christ's lordship; "Lord" is how he addressed the Savior. That dying thief was no example of inactive, fruitless faith.

You seem to blame dispensationalism for the deficiencies of modern evangelicalism. Are you abandoning dispensationalism?

No. Dispensationalism itself is not to blame for easy-believism or antinomianism. Dispensationalism, reduced to its barest form, is simply the belief that God still has a future program for national Israel, and the promises of the Old Testament covenants are yet to be fulfilled literally.

Many fine dispensationalists of the past, including H. A. Ironside; Donald G. Barnhouse; and my mentor, Dr. Charles Feinberg, opposed trends of easy-believism in the movement. Unfortunately fewer dispensationalists today are willing to speak out on these issues.

Legitimate dispensationalist distinctives have nothing to do with easy-believism. Nothing necessary to dispensationalism logically mandates the cheap-grace approach to the gospel; these teachings are a misapplication of dispensationalist teaching. I have tried to affirm what is right with dispensationalism while identifying some problems that the dispensationalist movement has unfortunately opened its doors to. But I have no intention of abandoning the dispensationalist distinctives that I am convinced are biblical.

How can I explain the gospel to my children without toning down the hard demands of Christ? Must a child understand Jesus' lordship to be saved?

Certainly children are limited in their ability to understand spiritual truth, but so are adults. Very few people intellectually understand all the gospel truth at the moment of salvation. Fortunately, the essential truths are basic enough that even a child can understand. Jesus himself characterized saving faith as childlikeness (Mark 10:15). True belief is not a function of advanced intellect, sophisticated theological understanding, or complex doctrinal knowledge.

Children old enough to be saved ought to be able to grasp the concept of coming to Christ with an obedient heart, and they need to be willing to let Christ be boss in their lives. That concept is not above the comprehension of children old enough to believe.

When teaching children spiritual truth, remember that repetition and restatement are especially helpful. Give the gospel simply and briefly, but do not assume that the first positive response means that they have received all the truth they need to know. Continue explaining and expanding your explanations. Too many ministries to children equate every uplifted hand with a real conversion.

Use Scripture and explain it clearly. Even with children, God's Word is the seed that produces life (1 Peter 1:23). I do not like approaches that give gospel outlines with no Scripture. Only the Bible can speak with authority to the human heart—including a child's heart.

Another inherent danger in outlines and prefabricated presentations is that they tend to follow a predetermined agenda that may bypass the child's real needs or fail to answer his or her most important questions.

Finally, remember that the issues in salvation are the same for a child as for an adult. The gospel is the same message for every age group. D. Martyn Lloyd-Jones wrote:

> We must be careful that we do not modify the gospel to suit various age groups. There is no such thing as a special gospel for the young, a special gospel for the middle-aged, and a special gospel for the aged. There is only one gospel, and we must always be careful not to tamper and tinker with the gospel as a result of recognizing these age distinctions. At the same time, there is a difference in applying this one and only gospel to the different age groups; but it is a difference which has reference only to method and procedure.[1]

Children must be able to understand that sin is an offense to God's holiness and that they are personally guilty (though because of their limited experiences, obviously most children will not have as deep a sense of personal guilt as adults). There is nothing wrong with telling children about hell and God's wrath. In my experience, children do not have a difficult time grasping such concepts. They understand punishment for wrongdoing and are capable of understanding that Jesus died to take the punishment for others' sin. They need to be told that Jesus expects to be obeyed, and they will understand even better than some adults that trusting Jesus means obeying him. Those are all truths that need to be emphasized repeatedly, even after the child makes a profession of faith.

How can you deny the existence of carnal Christians when Paul himself uses that expression in 1 Corinthians 3 (KJV)?

Christians can be carnal. That is, they can behave in carnal ways. But "carnal Christian" is not a plane of spiritual existence where one can remain indefinitely. Carnality is never spoken of by Scripture as a perpetual state for believers. In other words, while Christians can be carnal in their behavior, they are never carnal by nature. That is the distinction I have tried to make.

What about those who come to Christ after hearing a message of easy-believism? Do you regard their salvation as questionable?

The implanted Word of God is able to save our souls, often even when the message accompanying it is flawed or confused. Jesus said, "All that the Father gives Me shall come to Me" (John 6:37). The glorious truth of God's sovereign election guarantees that those he has chosen will respond to his Word with true faith and repentance. So we can be assured that God can work in the hearts of those we

[1]D. Martyn Lloyd-Jones, *Knowing the Times* (Edinburgh: Banner of Truth, 1989), 2.

love in response to our prayers, even if the gospel they hear from some Christians is not complete.

But that great truth does not mean that the kind of gospel we preach is of no consequence. The problem with easy-believism is not that it will keep God's elect from getting saved, but that it allows people who are not genuine Christians to live comfortably with a false assurance—which leads to the tragedy described in Matthew 7:21–23.

Can a person be saved who does not *consciously* count the cost of following Christ at the time of conversion?

A person might be truly born again without explicitly considering the cost of following Christ, but no one can be saved who counts the cost and is unwilling to pay it. Again, I am certain that no one understands the full implications of Christ's lordship at the moment of conversion; in fact, none of us ever reaches full knowledge of such spiritual realities in this life. But the work of the Holy Spirit in the heart of a true believer prompts some degree of surrender to Christ's authority even at the inception of the new birth.

Can a true Christian "backslide"?

Certainly true Christians can "backslide," if by that you mean they can regress into a period of spiritual dullness or disobedience. Those who do incur God's discipline (Heb. 12:6–11). Those who are not disciplined are not true sons (v. 8).

But if you are thinking of backsliding as a perpetual state of willful rebellion or ungodly indifference on the part of one who professes faith in Christ but does not love him, that is a sign of false profession (Matt. 7:21–23; 1 John 3:4–10). Sometimes the term *backslider* is used to describe one who has forsaken Christ and abandoned the faith. In that case it describes a person who was never truly saved (John 8:31; 1 Tim. 2:12; 1 John 2:19). The word *backsliding* is used two ways in Scripture. It is found only in Old Testament references to the nation of Israel (Jer. 3:22; 31:22; 49:4; Hos. 4:16; 11:7; 14:4 KJV). Sometimes it speaks of backsliding as the action of unregenerate people who turn stubbornly away from God (cf. Jer. 8:5). In that sense the Word cannot be used to describe true Christians.

Other times true believers are said to backslide (Jer. 14:7). All believers go through times when they do not grow or are set back in their growth by sin—they seem to be sliding backwards like a calf on a muddy slope (cf. Hos. 4:16 KJV). In that sense the word could apply to true believers. But it cannot be used to support the notion that true Christians might abandon the faith completely.

Does 1 Corinthians 3:11–15 prove that a true Christian might live a wholly fruitless life?

Those verses say this:

No man can lay a foundation other than the one which is laid, which is Jesus Christ. Now if any man builds upon the foundation with gold, silver, precious stones, wood, hay, straw, each man's work will become evident; for the day will show it, because it is to be revealed with fire; and the fire itself will test the quality of each man's work. If any man's work which he has built upon it remains, he shall receive a reward. If any man's work is burned up, he shall suffer loss; but he himself shall be saved, yet so as through fire.

Those verses in no way imply that a Christian can be devoid of fruit or works. In fact, they teach the opposite—that every Christian will have works of some sort (ministry, service, evangelism, etc.), but that the works may vary as to their quality. Some people's good works are cluttered with wrong motives or unbiblical methods, so our rewards will differ. But no true Christian will be utterly lacking in good works.

How should we act toward those who profess to be Christians but seem indifferent to spiritual things?

This is a common question posed by those who realize how truly narrow the way is (Matt. 7:13–14). It can be frightening to think that many people in the church (including many whom we love) may not be true Christians. I often wonder if those who espouse easy-believism have simply adapted their theology in order to try to get a sinning loved one into the kingdom.

There are two extremes to be avoided in assessing the spiritual status of others. On the one hand, we must realize that we are not ultimately the judge of anyone's salvation, because we cannot see anyone's heart. Only God can do that (1 Sam. 16:7). And people express their love for God and faith in Christ in different ways.

But on the other hand, we must hold firmly to the truth of God's Word concerning salvation and not offer false assurance to people who may not be truly saved.

If you have a friend or loved one whose lifestyle seriously discredits his or her profession of faith, I suggest you speak frankly to that person about your concerns. Certainly we have the Lord's own warrant for that in Matthew 18:15–20. If you carefully and lovingly follow the steps Jesus outlined in that passage you will soon know whether to treat the person as a brother or sister in Christ, or as "a

Gentile and a tax-gatherer" (v. 17). Either way, your attitude toward the person is not to be judgmental, but loving and compassionate.

What caused you to change your views on the gospel? Your book seems like a total departure from what I thought you believed.

My views on the gospel have not changed. My first sermon as a pastor, nearly twenty-five years ago, was a message on the two gates and the two ways (Matt. 7:13–27). One of my earliest books was published by Zondervan in 1973, titled *The Church: The Body of Christ*. It includes a chapter on salvation that said essentially the same thing as this book. My book *Kingdom Living: Here and Now*, published in 1980 by Moody Press, specifically deals with the lordship issue. These are not views I developed recently or expressed for the first time in this book.

So why did a major controversy erupt with the publication of this book? I cannot say with certainty, but it seems to be because in this book for the first time I named those with whom I disagreed. People who otherwise were content for me to state my views suddenly were offended that I would name someone whom I believe is in error.

Don't you believe it is better to ignore divisive issues like the lordship controversy and keep harmony in the body of Christ?

I do not enjoy controversy. I realize I am sometimes cast in the role of a controversialist, but the only times I have willingly entered into public controversy have been when I have perceived some teaching as a threat to biblical authority or the purity of the gospel.

Although I have strong opinions about such matters as modes of baptism, church polity, prophecy, and many other biblical matters, I would not engage in public debate about them. But the lordship controversy deals with the gospel itself. It is not a minor difference that can be glossed over and ignored. It is precisely the kind of issue the church needs to think through carefully, discuss, debate, and come to consensus on.

Sadly, the issue of "lordship salvation" has proved divisive. But that is true of every crucial doctrine that has ever been examined by any church council. Unfortunately, doctrinal controversies often cause division and strife among the brethren. But where such discord exists, it is not because of books that attempt to deal with the doctrinal issues. The blame lies with those who are unwilling to confront doctrinal differences biblically and forthrightly without seeing every disagreement or critique as tantamount to a personal attack. Let's not allow the discussion of this most important doctrinal issue to be poisoned with bitter emotion or harsh personal invective.

We certainly need to be fair, gracious, and Christlike in what we say. But we cannot and must not pretend that so crucial a matter really makes no difference. Even in the early church, that was never the approach to controversies and differences of opinion (e.g., Gal. 2:11–14).

Bibliography

Alleine, Joseph. *An Alarm to the Unconverted*. Marshallton, Del.: National Foundation for Christian Education, n. d.

Allis, Oswald T. "The Covenant of Works." *Basic Christian Doctrines*. Carl F. H. Henry, ed. Grand Rapids: Baker, 1962.

Barclay, William. *The Gospel of Matthew*, vol. 2. Philadelphia: Westminster, 1958.

Behm, J. "*Metanoia*." Gerhard Kittel, ed. *Theological Dictionary of the New Testament*. Grand Rapids: Eerdmans, 1967.

Berkhof, Louis. *Systematic Theology*. Grand Rapids: Eerdmans, 1939.

Bettenson, Henry, ed. *Documents of the Christian Church*. New York: Oxford University Press, 1963.

Blauvelt, Livingston, Jr. "Does the Bible Teach Lordship Salvation?" *Bibliotheca Sacra* (January–March 1986): 37–45.

Bock, Darrell L. "Jesus as Lord in Acts and in the Gospel Message," *Bibliotheca Sacra* 143 (April–June 1986): 146–54.

Boice, James M. *Christ's Call to Discipleship*. Chicago: Moody Press, 1986.

Boston, Thomas. *The Complete Works of the Late Rev. Thomas Boston, Ettrick*, 12 vols. Wheaton, Ill.: Roberts, 1980 reprint.

Calvin, John. *Institutes of the Christian Religion*, 2 vols. Grand Rapids: Zondervan, 1972.

Chafer, Lewis Sperry. *Grace*. Grand Rapids: Zondervan, 1922.

———. *He That Is Spiritual*, rev. ed. Grand Rapids: Zondervan, 1967.

———. *Systematic Theology*. Dallas: Dallas Seminary Press, 1948.

Cocoris, G. Michael. *Lordship Salvation—Is It Biblical?* Dallas: Redención Viva, 1983.

Constable, Thomas L. "The Gospel Message." *Walvoord: A Tribute*. Chicago: Moody Press, 1982.

Dillenberger, John, ed. *Martin Luther*. New York: Doubleday, 1961.

English, E. Schuyler, et al., eds. *The New Scofield Reference Bible*. New York: Oxford University Press, 1967.

Flavel, John. *The Works of John Flavel*. London: Banner of Truth, reprint.

Gallup, George, Jr., and David Poling. *The Search for America's Faith*. Nashville: Abingdon, 1980.

Gentry, Kenneth L. "The Great Option: A Study of the Lordship Controversy." *Baptist Reformation Review* 5 (Spring 1976): 63–69.

Gill, John. *A Body of Divinity*. Grand Rapids: Sovereign Grace, 1971.

Goetzman, J. "Conversion." Colin Brown, gen. ed. *New International Dictionary of New Testament Theology*, vol. 1. Grand Rapids: Zondervan, 1975. 357–59.

Goodwin, Thomas. *The Work of the Holy Spirit in Our Salvation*. Edinburgh: Banner of Truth, 1979.

Guthrie, William. *The Christian's Great Interest*. Edinburgh: Banner of Truth, 1982.

Hall, Basil. "Ulrich Zwingli." Hubert Cunliffe-Jones, ed. *A History of Christian Doctrine*. Philadelphia: Fortress, 1978.

Henry, Matthew. *Commentary on the Whole Bible*. Old Tappan, N.J.: Revell, n.d.

Hickman, Edward, ed. *The Works of Jonathan Edwards*. Edinburgh: Banner of Truth, 1979.

Hodges, Zane C. *The Gospel Under Siege*. Dallas: Redención Viva, 1981.

———. *The Hungry Inherit*. Portland: Multnomah, 1980.

———. "Untrustworthy Believers—John 2:23–25." *Bibliotheca Sacra* (April–June 1978): 139–52.

Hogan, William LeGrange. "The Relationship of the Lordship of Christ to Salvation." Th.M. thesis, Dallas Theological Seminary, 1959.

Ironside, H. A. *Except Ye Repent*. Grand Rapids:Zondervan, 1937.

Larkin, Clarence. *Dispensational Truth*. Philadelphia: Larkin, 1918.

———. *Rightly Dividing the Word*. Philadelphia: Larkin, 1918.

Lenski, R. C. H. *The Interpretation of Matthew's Gospel*. Columbus, Ohio: Wartburg, 1943.

Lightfoot, J. B. *The Epistle of St. Paul to the Galatians*. Grand Rapids: Zondervan, n.d.

Lloyd-Jones, D. Martyn. *Studies in the Sermon on the Mount*. Grand Rapids: Eerdmans, 1959.

———. *Knowing the Times*. Edinburgh: Banner of Truth, 1989.

———. *Romans: The New Man*. Grand Rapids: Zondervan, 1974.

Luther, Martin. *Table Talk*. Vol. 54. Theodore G. Tappert, ed. Helmut T. Lehmann, gen. ed. *Luther's Works*. 55 vols. Philadelphia: Fortress, 1967.

MacArthur, John F. *Faith Works: The Gospel According to the Apostles.* Dallas: Word, 1993.

_____. *Kingdom Living Here and Now.* Chicago: Moody Press, 1980.

_____. *The MacArthur New Testament Commentary: Matthew 1–7.* Chicago: Moody Press, 1985.

_____. *The MacArthur New Testament Commentary: Romans 1–8.* Chicago: Moody Press, 1991.

_____. *The MacArthur New Testament Commentary: Hebrews.* Chicago: Moody Press, 1983.

_____. *The Ultimate Priority.* Chicago: Moody Press, 1983.

Macaulay, J. C. *Behold Your King.* Chicago: Moody Press, 1982.

Machen, J. Gresham. *The Christian View of Man.* Edinburgh: Banner of Truth, 1937.

Manschreck, Clyde L., ed. and trans. *Melancthon on Christian Doctrine.* Grand Rapids: Baker, 1965.

Manton, Thomas. *A Commentary on James.* Edinburgh: Banner of Truth, 1963.

Miller, Johnny V. Review of *The Gospel Under Siege. Trinity Journal* 4 (Spring 1983): 93–94.

Morgan, G. Campbell. *The Gospel According to John.* Old Tappan, N.J.: Revell, 1931.

Mueller, Marc. "Jesus Is Lord." *Grace Today* (August 1981): 6.

Murray, John. *Collected Writings.* 4 vols. Edinburgh: Banner of Truth, 1977.

Olin, John C., ed. *A Reformation Debate.* Grand Rapids: Baker, 1966.

Packer, J. I. *Evangelism and the Sovereignty of God.* Downers Grove, Ill.: InterVarsity, 1961.

Pink, Arthur W. *Eternal Security.* Grand Rapids: Guardian, 1974.

_____. *An Exposition of the Sermon on the Mount.* Grand Rapids: Baker, 1953.

_____. *Gleanings from the Scriptures: Man's Total Depravity.* Chicago: Moody Press, 1969.

_____. "Signs of the Times." *Studies in the Scriptures* 16:373–75. N.p.: n.d.

Richardson, Cyril C., ed. *Early Christian Fathers.* New York: Macmillan, 1970.

Robertson, A. T. *Word Pictures in the New Testament.* Nashville: Broadman, 1933.

Rosscup, James E. "The Overcomer of the Apocalypse." *Grace Theological Journal* 3 (Fall 1982): 261–86.

Ryle, John Charles. *Holiness.* Grand Rapids: Baker, 1979.

Ryrie, Charles C. *Balancing the Christian Life*. Chicago: Moody Press, 1969.

————. *Dispensationalism Today*. Chicago: Moody Press, 1965.

————. Foreword to Zane C. Hodges, *The Hungry Inherit*. Portland: Multnomah, 1980.

————. *The Ryrie Study Bible*. Chicago: Moody Press, 1976.

Schaff, Phillip, ed. *Creeds of Christendom*, 3 vols. Grand Rapids: Baker, 1977 reprint.

Scofield, C. I., ed. *The Scofield Reference Bible*. New York: Oxford University Press, 1909.

Spurgeon, Charles H. *Autobiography: Volume 1: The Early Years, 1834–1859*. Edinburgh: Banner of Truth, 1962.

————. *Expository Encyclopedia*, vol. 4. Grand Rapids: Baker, 1977.

————. *The New Park Street Pulpit*. Grand Rapids: Zondervan, 1962 reprint of 1858 volume.

————. *The Soul Winner*. Pasadena, Tex.: Pilgrim, 1978.

Stanford, A. Ray. *Handbook of Personal Evangelism*. Hollywood, Fla.: Florida Bible College, n.d.

Stott, John R. W. *Basic Christianity*. London: Inter-Varsity, 1958.

————. *Christian Counter-Culture*. Downers Grove, Ill.: InterVarsity, 1978.

Strong, Augustus. *Systematic Theology*. Philadelphia: Judson, 1907.

Thayer, Joseph Henry, trans. *Greek-English Lexicon of the New Testament*. Grand Rapids: Zondervan, 1962.

Theime, Karl "Good Works." *The New Schaff-Herzog Religious Encyclopedia*. Grand Rapids: Baker, 1977.

Thieme, R. B. *Apes and Peacocks or the Pursuit of Happiness*. Houston: Thieme, 1973.

Thomas, W. H. Griffith. *The Principles of Theology*. Grand Rapids: Baker, 1979.

————. *St. Paul's Epistle to the Romans*. Grand Rapids: Eerdmans, n.d.

Torrey, R. A. *How to Work for Christ*. Old Tappan, N.J.: Revell, n.d.

Tozer, A. W. *I Call It Heresy!* Harrisburg, Pa.: Christian Publications, 1974.

Vincent, Thomas. *The Shorter Catechism of the Westminster Assembly Explained and Proved from Scripture*. Edinburgh: Banner of Truth, 1980.

Vine, W. E. *Vine's Expository Dictionary of Old and New Testament Words*. Old Tappan, N.J.: Revell, 1981.

Vos, Geerhardus. *The Kingdom of God and the Church*. Nutley, N.J.: Presbyterian and Reformed, 1972.

Wager, Rich. "This So-Called 'Lordship Salvation.'" *Confident Living* (July–August 1987): 54–55.

Warfield, Benjamin B. *Biblical and Theological Studies.* Grand Rapids: Baker, 1968.

_____. Review of Lewis Sperry Chafer's *He That Is Spiritual. Princeton Theological Review* (April 1919): 322–27.

Watson, Thomas. *A Body of Divinity.* Grand Rapids: Baker, 1979.

Westcott, B. F. *St. Paul's Epistle to the Ephesians.* Minneapolis: Klock and Klock, n.d., reprint of 1906 volume.

Whitefield, George. *Journals.* Edinburgh: Banner of Truth, 1960.

Wiersbe, Warren W. *Meet Yourself in the Parables.* Wheaton: Victor, 1979.

Witmer, J. A. Review of Zane Hodges' *The Gospel Under Siege. Bibliotheca Sacra* 140 (January–March 1983): 81–82.

Scripture Index

292   *The Gospel According to Jesus*

Subject Index